Stories in the Stars

by

Annie Dieu-Le-Veut

ABOUT THE AUTHOR
Annie Dieu-Le-Veut is a shaman, author and former newspaper journalist. Previous books include *Reclaiming Sovereignty, The Bright World of the Gods* and *The Grail Mysteries*. She can be found on her own blog, ***Annie Dieu-Le-Veut***.

COVER
Image from Shutterstock. Design by Sam Richardson.

ILLUSTRATIONS
Sam Richardson and Yuri Leitch.

PUBLISHER
John Board for The Holistic Works.

COPYRIGHT
All content in this book, *Stories in the Stars,* is copyright **The Holistic Works**. Copyright © August 2018. All rights reserved. This book or any portion thereof may not be reproduced or used in any manner whatsoever without the express written permission of the publisher, except for the use of brief quotations in a book review.

ISBN-13:978-1723284373
ISBN-10:1723284378

Illustration by Glastonbury artist and author Yuri Leitch showing the cosmological mindset of Alexandrian astrologers and alchemists around the first century BCE, with the Three Realms of the World Tree as a process of the Vesica Piscis set within the constellations of inner space.

We locked up our wisdom into our bones
And swallowed the keys.
They sank in our Rivers of Blood,
And we forgot the maps
Because we had to forget the Mysteries
To keep them safe.
We wove our hair into brooms
And swept over our paths,
And then burned the earth with our rage.
We didn't teach our children;
It was the only way to protect them,
we thought.
But in them we planted seeds, seeds and keys
And told them stories and riddles and songs
With no roots, just tangled threads
That would take years to unwind,
Just enough time
For the rains to fall again
and put out the fires,
For the dams to break,
For the rivers to flood,
For the paths
to be walked again,
For the soil to breathe.
And as the old bones crumble
Deep beneath the rubble
We find we've always had the keys.
Our stories and our maps,
Our paths are revealed to some,
And the seeds grow again
The threads are unspun
And woven again.

Amara Bronwyn MacEachern, Hollow Bones

Dedication

This book is dedicated to Gwyn ap Nudd, Lord of the Wildwoods, King of the Fae Peoples, Leader of the Wild Hunt.

Acknowledgements

I am most grateful to Sam Richardson and Yuri Leitch for allowing me to use their artwork for the cover and the illustrations, to Alan Royce for his biro scribbles on paper napkins in the Lazy Gecko cafe, to Rosemary Taylor for teaching me about the Norse *Eddas*, and to Patrick Lyons for all his highly perceptive archaeological input over more than a decade.

I'm also indebted to Sam Richardson for his meticulous attention to detail in proof-reading this book, not to mention his sweet wife, Holly Hazeltree, for loving it all.

Last but by no means least, I must thank John Board of The Holistic Works for continuing to have faith in me and support my work.

Table of Contents

Dedication 9
Acknowledgements 11
Table of Contents 13
Table of Figures 15
Foreword 17
Introduction 23

Part 1 29
INTO THE DELUGE 29
1. The Dark Side of the Moon 31
2. Weather Shamans at Sea 43
3. The Holographic Universe of Music 51
4. The Fall of Atlantis 61
5. The Serpent and the World Tree 73
6. Camelot of the Polar Stars 87
7. Ladders and Cauldrons 109

Part 2 135
THE LANGUAGE OF THE INITIATES 135
8. The Quickening 137
9. The Vesica Piscis 147
10. When You Wish Upon a Star … 153
11. The Double Goddess of the Secret Fire 171
12. The Saturn Return 181
13. The Anunnaki and the Star Peoples 187
14. Interpreting Numbers in Myths 199

Part 3 211
INTO THE ZODIAC 211
15. The Zodiac Hero 213
16. The Trials of Pinocchio 227
17. The Epic of Gilgamesh 243
18. The Mills of the Gods 265
Appendix A – Flood Myths 275
Appendix B – The Ecstasy of the Heart 287
Bibliography 291
FURTHER READING 293

Table of Figures

Figure 1: Camelot in the Stars of the Northern Hemisphere 106
Figure 2: "True South" in the Southern Hemisphere 107
Figure 3: The Alchemical Ladder of the Wise 110
Figure 4: Positions of Planets on the Ladder of the Wise 111
Figure 5: Timings for Alchemical Operations 112
Figure 6: Symbols Occurring in Altered States 124
Figure 7: Traditional Taoist Three Cauldrons 126
Figure 8: The Three Cauldrons of Inspiration by Yuri Leitch 127
Figure 9: Comparing the Celtic, Norse and Taoist systems 128
Figure 10: The Vesica Piscis 148
Figure 11: The Three Cauldrons as found in the Dream of Macsen 149
Figure 12: The Planetary Rulers and their Influences 156
Figure 13: The Zodiac of the Alexandrian system 157
Figure 14: The Ciphers of the Planets 158
Figure 15: The Mithraic Rock Birth and the Mirrored Planets 158
Figure 16: The Inner Cosmology of the Babylonians 195
Figure 17: The Alexandrian system (repeated) 219
Figure 18: The Trials of Pinocchio 229
Figure 19: The Evolution of the Tarot 239
Figure 20: Cosmology found in the Epic of Gilgamesh 247

Foreword

"The only difference between mythology and history is that myths are true." Anon

IT IS often said that history is written by the victors; that after a military campaign has been won, the information war begins when the court scribes and hagiographers of a mytho-industrial complex are appointed to provide written content designed to provide a narrative with the aim of winning the hearts and minds of the people who have just been conquered.

Humanity has been ruled in this way for thousands of years, the only difference nowadays being that what our descendants will come to call "history" is currently being written in live time by digital propagandists who broadcast their narrative throughout the internet, mainstream media and the silver screen.

So much of received history could be described as a tissue of lies or, at least, propaganda and spin, as the myths of the indigenous peoples are often plundered and twisted to provide the storylines when a new historical "backstory" is required for a nation. For instance, after the Norman conquest of Britain in the 11th century, Geoffrey de Monmouth wrote *Historia regum Britanniae* (*The History of the Kings of Britain*), which he based on ancient myths. However, his book was no history, because those Arthurian legends were not about characters that had actually lived or events that really happened; they were metaphors for alchemico-cosmological truths that are, in themselves, eternal and *in that way* have veracity as guides and blueprints to help us thrive and evolve today.

Hence, the only difference between mythology and history is that myths are true, so long as they are excavated properly and – just as importantly – interpreted correctly, by those who have the eyes to see, because they were composed by people who thought very differently to how we do today. And so this is where I come in with this book.

I'm a shaman and also a sort of story archaeologist. I have a mental image of myself, digging and digging and digging underneath all the rotting story mats of the wandering troubadors and tale-tellers of old in an attempt to find the original story. Some of those story mats have become quite ragged by now; others have gone decidedly mouldy.

However, the deeper I dig, the closer to the primary story I get.

Most of the ancient myths that have survived and are available to us today were translated either by Christian monks or by PhD scholars. As far as I know, none of them were transcribed by shamans, which is crucial because our forebears, who composed these stories, had a much more shamanic mindset than we may realise. So I view these old sagas from antiquity through a more multi-dimensional lens and thus find the themes running through them are based upon a cosmologically-based wisdom that has almost vanished from awareness today. I then weave these myths into my own stories in a way that I think better reflects their true, original nature, so that they can be of help to us today in the same way that they acted as psychological Sat Navs for aiding the ancients to make sense of their lives.

So I keep on digging and, sometimes, I hit gold.

For instance, in my books *The Bright World of the Gods* and *The Grail Mysteries*, I excavate and clear up the modern-day misunderstanding about what the ancients meant when they used the word "virgin".

The misinterpretation of that one word by monks and scholars with very little understanding compared with the shamanic sapience of those sages of old has actually changed history over thousands of years. It has transformed – and not in a good way – how we think about fertility, sex, abundance and fecundity, and its connection to spiritual wisdom has been all but completely lost.

More importantly, if this mistaken idea is taken to its furthest extreme along the trajectory it is currently flowing in the sea of consensual consciousness, its ultimate terminus could be the end of our species on Earth. It will lead the human vessel into storm-tossed waters and on to jagged rocks - unless there is a sea change.

It is not too late. We can recover the mytho-poetic vision that was key to how our ancestors saw themselves as an integral part of the forces that generate and regenerate life on Earth, which they experienced and honoured in sacred rites and shamanic journeying. So this book is organised to provide a smooth and simple, stepped upward journey in laying out this philosophy in which each teaching is based upon the one behind it.

We begin at the end of the last major Ice Age, and the stories told by our nomadic ancestors around their camp fires that were, so to speak, written in the stars. In other words, they would draw out their characters, dot-to-dot, in sparkling lines across the pitch-black skies and then compose and recount stories about them. But you may not know who they really were and why they actually did this. You may still believe that they were grunting, monosyllabic, club-dragging caveman incapable of intelligent thought – and with a standard Western education, you could hardly be blamed for that.

So in **Part 1: Into the Deluge,** I make the case for their advanced astronomical-astrological wisdom and technology that was holographically connected to their spiritual wisdom and profound understanding about the value and purpose of human life before going on to their earliest star stories – the deluge myths – that follow the challenges and travails of the courageous hero who erects each of the new pole stars as they precess from age to age.

In **Part 2: The Language of the Initates,** we stop to examine some of the common symbols and metaphors used in these ancient myths to uncover their hidden astrological and alchemical significance, and then we learn how to apply them to our spiritual progress today, before going on to…

Part 3: Into the Zodiac, in which we will analyse slightly later myths, through the lens of our new understanding about their meaning, that developed from the agricultural revolution onwards and that featured the zodiac hero of the 12 Sun signs.

A note for women

You may wonder why the hero in so many ancient stories is a male and not a female, and you might find it annoying that I continually use the pronoun "he" rather than "he or she" throughout this book. So I will explain.

Largely speaking, I didn't want to use "he or she" because it smacks too much to me of political correctness in this present time, with the women's movement purporting to fight "the tyranny of the patriarchy".

I don't subscribe to that view. In fact, to me, the idea that the male of the species unfairly dominates the female is a complete canard, although these particular ladies are quite correct in that we do not have equality with men. The way I see it, women for millennia have dominated and controlled men in the most subtle of ways and it is to those feminine arts, passed on from mother to daughter, that I attribute the success of the human race as a species. Otherwise, how could it be that a gender which is innately polygamous when going through its late adolescence and early adulthood evolves so quickly into settling down quietly with one woman, to help her raise a family?

In ancient times, the grandmothers were the shamanic storytellers and the singers over the cradle who developed myths featuring a male hero who journeyed through the stars as vehicles or "arks" in which to convey, to their charges, the secret keys that seed the wisdom needed to climb the alchemical ladder of life in order to develop successfully into full manhood. Those sagas (so named after the keeper of the ancestral memory Sága of the Norse *Eddas*, meaning "great grandmother") eventually became part of a series of what were known as Mystery teachings, and young men would learn them during rites of passage retreats, away from the village.

These same "arks" have now come down to us, floating on our Rivers of Blood (our DNA or "race memory") and thus they still create the narrative that has underpinned our mores and laws for countless thousands of years that are responsible for the success and good fortune of the human race. Conversely, when this narrative is turned on its head, it leads to a reversal of fortune.

This stellar-based blueprint is based upon the notion of hierarchy; the original Greek meaning of the word being "spiritual rule". So these most ancient of tales are designed to impregnate the cosmological understanding in the subconscious about the universal governance to which the individual must submit in order for their heriditary line to thrive and survive.

But what does that mean for us today?

For the male, spiritual initiations have always had to be more formally structured through rites-of-passage retreats and ceremonies. This is because, unlike the women, men do not naturally receive their initiations as a matter of course from the Moon at the first period, and then again at the time of giving birth and finally, at the menopause. This is one of the allegorical meanings behind the symbol of three-faced goddess of the maiden, the mother and the crone.

Having said all that, women also benefit from the story of the mythological hero, partly because it helps them develop their male side and partly because literature that is designed to help the man to better understand himself also informs women in that it helps them improve their relationships with the male of the species. Finally, women need to fully comprehend ancient myths in order to be able to educate their own children properly.

And so in learning about the wisdom buried in these stories in the stars about the archetypal champion, both men and women will end up discovering a deeply-rooted alchemical map for their own lives and thus will develop a more metaphorical, cosmological view and a growing feel for eternal truths that helps to make sense of our own existence.

A note for Christians

If you are Christian, please have no fear. This book is not anti-Christian – quite the contrary, in fact. My intention in teaching you about the astrological and alchemical roots of your religion is to help you become a better Christian – to understand the original meaning of what it is to be a pilgrim, like the 17th century author John Bunyan's hero, Christian, who undertook a pilgrimage to the Celestial City.

According to my research, the original Christians were Gnostics who based their inner spiritual experiences on a metaphorical, metaphysical narrative that was popular across the whole of Mesopotamia and beyond, the literary scaffolding for which was constructed by our earlier ancestors in order to encourage real inner spiritual growth and thus give the tribe its deeper values from which to draw strength.

It is my understanding that it was those Gnostic-types who were the Christians thrown to the lions in the Roman Coliseum. Certainly, they were following a narrative that quickly became inconvenient in the early centuries.

But in delving down into the roots of Christianity and learning how to put these teachings into practice, I hope that you will become whole and at peace again.

Introduction

Western civilisation over the last few centuries has been oddly schizoid. We often claim that we value freedom and creativity above everything else, and yet we trace our cultural pedigree back to the hierarchic despotisms and state-mandated religions of the ancient Near East. Today, with the contest between freedom and repression once again coming to a head, it seems more important than ever to locate our historical roots not in despotism, but in the most radically innovative and imaginative cultures of the past. *Cory Panshin*

THERE was a time – a long, long time ago – when mile-high slabs of blue-white ice covered great swathes of the northern hemisphere. Our nomadic ancestors were confined to the more temperate climes of the lower mountain steppes as they followed their herds and the stars along well-worn pathways across vast plains of waving "seas of grass" their grandfathers and forefathers had traversed for untold thousands of years before them.

In those dim and distant days, there was a young man named Kroy-khasis. His name meant "ice-shining" and "white with snow" - just like his birthplace, the shining white region that towered over them on the horizon, the home of the mountain gods known as the Acheru, which we now call the Caucasus.

During the day, Kroy would walk with the others as they followed the trods of the reindeer and then, in the evening, he would help to pitch a new camp of felt tents. But he would most look forward to the darkest hours, when he would listen in awe to Tabiti as she told her stories around the blazing campfires.

These sagas often featured a hero of similar age to him, who would wander through the constellations and use enchanted stones, swords and spears in battles over beautiful goddesses and achieve victories which won him a great magical chalice.

To Kroy, Tabiti seemed like a goddess herself, in her tall wooden head-dress embossed with carved cats painted in gold leaf, and her red and yellow silk-and-wool garments that flowed over thigh-high white felt leggings – indications of her high status within the tribe as a teller of sacred stories.

From her heavily braided corded belt around her slender waist hung a mirror – a magical mirror, she told them – that was engraved on the back with the image of a reindeer. And whether it was the effects of the flickering fire or the heady aromas emitting from the smouldering pine branches he never knew, but strange soot-black beasts with long wavy antlers tipped with red ochre flowers would dance along her snow-white arms as she waved them towards the glittering vault above to draw out the images of the fantastic creatures the hero would meet in the stars.

There were giants, dragons and faeries - some of whom were kind and helpful but others that attacked the hero so that he had to find all his courage to fight back and conquer them. But as he overcame these challenges, so Kroy also found himself surmounting his own difficulties in understanding who he was and discovering his place, not only in the tribe but within the whole universe. In this way, he learned much about the rituals, traditions and natural cycles of the world he lived in and, through that vital rite of passage, he grew into a strong adult who was capable of leadership.

Although we might call Kroy's people wandering nomads, there was nothing haphazard or accidental about their journeys across the pale green, grassy steppes year after year after year. And so as Tabiti's stories about the animal spirits in the ice-glittering blackness above unfolded, Kroy started to become aware of their symbolic presences lining the tribe's circular passage through the waving grasslands. It was as if the undulating plains, forests, rivers and embankments had formed themselves below into outlines of the same creatures that featured in those night-time stories above and they towered majestically over them in great earthworks.

So in those days, the wise men followed the stars above and stars below, and thus were able to correctly navigate to the right place, at the right time of year, where they could most benefit from the Earth's seasonal largesse. In this way, they were able to stay in tune with Mother Nature's cycles through the changing planetary influences and thus to live their lives in harmony with Her.

For instance, they always knew when and where the salmon would be running, because it was under the stars of what we call today Pisces. There would be handfastings when they reached Taurus and bull rites there too, in celebration of the sacred marriage. The tribes would gather once a year, on the Summer Solstice, to trade with each other and for their young people like Kroy to meet, so that arrangements could be made for the following year's handfastings. In this way, the gene pools were kept healthy.

Their kings would be crowned under the great lion at a summer festival we now call Lammas and, further on in the year, at Samhain they would remember and give thanks to their ancestors.

When it came to the Winter Solstice, they would be hauled through the snows on reindeer-driven sleighs that were festively decked out in red-berried holly and tinkling bells, with lanterns to light up the dark, until they reached the effigy of the great horned white stag, where they would celebrate under the pulsating peacock-blues of the aurora borealis.

Their reindeer would eat red-and-white mushrooms which the shamans, like Tabiti, would imbibe through the reindeers' urine because it contained *Amanita muscaria*, a powerful hallucinogenic that fired up their pineal glands and gave them deep and profound dreams which further inspired their storytelling.

To Kroy, it must have seemed like living in a gigantic life-sized picture book in which a new page was only turned at the bidding of the rotating wheel of the seasons. The people thrived under a life aligned with the hands of this giant sky clock that told them where they were, and where they needed to head to next, just as well as any GPS does today.

Kroy eventually felt highly honoured when he was chosen to help in carrying out sacred work to maintain the forms of these creatures when they had eroded. He would join in with widening a river, or redirecting it slightly, to make an effigy clearer. Or sometimes an earthwork might need reinforcing or widening. This practice went on for very long periods of time with each generation improving upon the efforts of the last one.

It could have gone on for ever that way but for one inescapable act of Nature – one day, the stars moved.

Thus the wise Elders gathered Kroy and the tribe together, to be addressed by their principal shaman, Maya Daitya.

Maya was so old there was no-one still alive who could remember his birth. But despite his body now being wrinkled and bent, his mind was as sharp as ever and he remembered all the lore he'd been taught by the teachers who had gone through the Veil before him. Not only that but, as a shaman, he was in contact with the celestial gods of the Upper World and the Nature spirits and ancestors of the Underworld, and gained much wisdom from those supernatural sources.

So he told all those assembled that huge gushing rivers and waterfalls would soon come crashing down across their "seas of grass" in a great silvery deluge, which would create enormous inland lakes that would overflow and wash away the great earthworks of their sacred landscape zodiac temples.

He said that it was the end of life as they knew it because the stars had moved. It was perhaps simpler to explain it that way. The Elders, though, whose brilliant brains were repositories of records going back thousands of years, knew that it was just a matter of perspective and that, in reality, the orb of the Earth that had tilted slightly as part of a natural cycle known today as the precession of the equinoxes. However, Maya went on to explain, whichever way you look at it, the upshot was that the Sun was now streaming down for longer each day on the mile-high ice crust on the roof of the world. Thus, the aged wisdom keepers knew that the tribes would have to move – and move quickly, before the glaciers retreated and the brooks and streams that had been trapped underneath them began to flow again and flood across the steppes.

There was no time to waste.

Luckily, they were highly skilled horseman. So there was soon a thundering of hooves across the plains as thickly muscled and tattooed warriors and shamans led teams of horses, jingling with gold and brass plaques embossed with mythical beasts, which were dragging their felt tent-covered wagons behind them in a huge and colourful migration – a patchwork quilt of tribes that shared a common gene pool, a kindred dialect and a culture whose values were derived from similar stories in the stars.

They moved south-westwards, racing ahead of the fast-thawing ice, which quickly created a huge inland sea to the north-east and what was soon to become the longest river in the world, full of freezing meltwater, running through the Black Sea and into the Mediterranean.

This eventually had the knock-on effect of making the Atlantic Ocean's conveyor current become much colder and thus it was not long before another ice age began.

Eventually, though, the roof the world started to warm again and Kroy's descendants decamped again to travel further southwards, ahead of the floods, until they reached the lands around Persia (now Iran) and northern India, where they continued to recount the stories that are still told today – and one of them is about their great navigator shaman, Maya Daitya.

There, they settled for several thousand years before some of them joined up with later waves of Caucasian migrants and, in their tribes of various assorted Scythians, Sarmatians and Alans, they began to fan out. Some went west, across the land bridge at Constantinople into Eastern Europe and then south into Mediterranean countries, while others rode into Northern Europe.

And as you would expect, over time, a fair few of them found their way to the south-west of Britain, where they waited, high up in lofty cliff caves, for the floods on the plains below to recede... and waited.

Most of us in Britain today are descended from those who migrated from the steppes later on, about 6,000 years ago, and these are known to archaeologists as the Bell Beaker people because of their distinctive pottery and ceramic ware.

In the next part of the book, I'm going to tell you something about them – how they lived and their spiritual, shamanic practices – so that you can start to better comprehend this cultural mindset and gain a firm cognitive foundation for when I go on to explain what their star stories were all about, and how they can help us to find our true spiritual roots today.

Part 1
INTO THE DELUGE

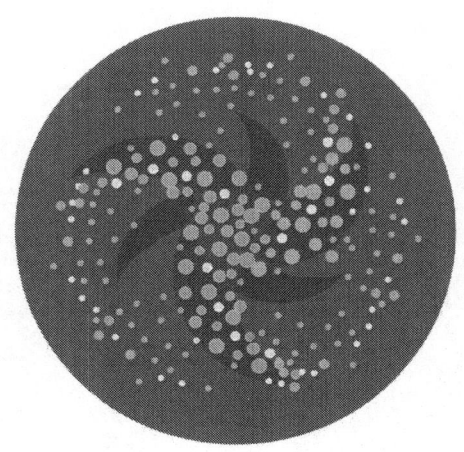

1. The Dark Side of the Moon

I DON'T know if you were anything like me at school but I used to find history lessons extremely boring. I would spend them gazing out of the window or doodling in my rough book, just waiting for the bell to ring to signal the next lesson.

It didn't help that the teachings were so fragmented; first we learned about the Romans; the next year, it was the Tudors and Henry VIII; the year after that it was the ancient Egyptians. It was all over the place and so with no continuity it was difficult to perceive "the bigger picture".

On top of that, I came to see that what I had been taught was not really history, as such, but political history with its long lists of kings and endless battles fought and re-fought over wives and territory. It was a history seen through the eyes of the rulers with very little about us ordinary folk and how we thought and lived our lives. And there was next to nothing about our earliest ancestors. On the few occasions the subject did arise, they were dismissed as monosyllabic, grunting, knuckle-dragging cavemen who were so stupid they had no idea about how to build a multi-storey shopping mall or invent a television, and therefore there were relegated to the pile of "nothing to see here".

Thus the whole huge subject about who we really are, and where we come from, has been pushed out of our consciousness, like the dark side of the Moon.

What do I mean by that? Well, we know that there is another side to the Moon as well as the one facing us, but we never get to see it. Because of a phenomenon called "tidal locking" in the Moon's orbit, it rotates at the same speed as the Earth, and so we are always presented with the same lunar face.

This is probably why when Pink Floyd brought out their album *The Dark Side of the Moon*, it struck a chord in the deepest archetypal levels of our minds, which is what musicians always hope to do if they're at all commercially-minded. Indeed, it went on to sell 45 million copies, making it Pink Floyd's best-selling album of all time. So how did they manage to trigger our imaginations so successfully? Which golden seam of moonbeams, long buried in the dark, tangled roots of our unplumbed, unfathomed subconscious memories, were they tapping into?

The dark side of the Moon could be regarded as a metaphor for everything we do not know, which is hidden from us – like the advanced intelligence of our earliest ancestors. Another word for "hidden" is "occluded" and so in this chapter, I'll be revealing some previously occluded, or occult, knowledge. I'm going to take you to the dark side of the Moon – because in astrological and alchemical practices, it is that silvery heavenly orb that reflects our memories, or the voices of our ancestors that are buried deep in our Rivers of Blood, which was what the ancient Celts called our DNA, and shines them into our dreams at night to remind us of our destiny in a human body.

So set your controls:

You will probably know that the Moon changes its size every single day of a month (or 28 days). But before it becomes the crescent new Moon, it is invisible for about three days and this is referred to, in magical circles, as "the dark period". After that, it slowly grows and grows until, after about two weeks, it becomes the full moon. Then gradually, gradually, over the next fortnight, it shrinks and shrinks until it goes into its dark phase again. This whole 28-day period is called a synodic cycle.

Now, many thousands of years ago, shamans like Maya and Tabiti were much more intrigued by all things lunar than we are today, despite our rush to get a man on the Moon. But they were not so much interested in mining the Moon's minerals to make Teflon pans; they were much more concerned with the impact of the Moon's cycles on all life forms. They needed to know when it was going to be "dark", for example, and for how long, because they realised that the face presented by the Moon at any one time held the key to fertility.

Dozens of ancient lunar calendars, engraved on stone, bone and horn, have been found across Europe, and further evidence of our ancestors' knowledge of astronomy is evident in the cave paintings of France and Spain, most of which are dated to the Upper Palaeolithic period, which ended about 10,000 years ago.

Of course, there are some who believe that what appears to be the earliest star maps were just the meaningless doodles of ignorant, bored cavemen. But is that because to admit that our earliest ancestors were practising a form of astronomy would also mean facing some awkward questions? Of course, any good farmer who follows traditional methods and almanacs knows sowing seeds according to Moon cycles produces bumper crops. So if there were evidence –

which there is – of our ancestors recording the movement of the stars before the agricultural revolution, what reason would they have for doing so? It's not as if they needed to know when to plant their crops because they were roaming hunter-gatherers.

However, it is my understanding that ancient lunar calendars dated to before the agricultural revolution are pointing to a more shamanic or alchemistic approach to fertility - which is a much bigger subject than just knowing when to sow your seeds.

So am I saying that our early ancestors knew more about natural cosmic cycles and how to apply them than we do today? Well, they knew at least as much as us, in my experience, and from a much more holistic, multi-layered perspective. But why would that be? And how do I know? We need to go back a bit.

For the past couple of centuries, we've been led to believe that our earliest ancestors were ignoramuses who shivered in draughty caves because they did not have the know-how to build a house with a nice tiled fireplace. This erroneous viewpoint seems to be the direct result of the promotion of the ideas of the Victorian biologist Charles Darwin who believed, with no evidence to support such a belief, in the continual upgrading or upward evolution of man's intelligence and literacy over time, from when he was a grunting ape to today as the so-called "crown of the creation". However, his theories – beyond a handful of experiments with fruit flies - were never proven and at the same time artefacts have been discovered that indicate our prehistoric forefathers benefited from advanced and most probably shamanic cognition.

What do I mean by "shamanic cognition"? I touched on this in the Introduction when describing how Maya achieved such great wisdom – by being in contact with the spirits of the Other Worlds. Shamans use altered consciousness techniques to "fly" into these parallel but timeless dimensions where they gain guidance and information from the entities and beings they meet there, and then they return, bringing back that wisdom to their tribes or communities.

The shaman lives in two simultaneous realities: the inner dream space in which spiritual encounters transform perception of the external world, and the external world which becomes the stage on which the shaman acts out his divine purpose as healer. Each time the shaman enters trance for the good of patients and community and confronts the agents of affliction, there is psychological integration for the shaman. The shaman brings together heaven and earth, spirit and humankind.

Shamanism appears in every culture. Amongst Tibetan people, it predates (and is woven into) Buddhist philosophy and practice, and is a vital and living

wisdom tradition practiced from ancient times into present day.

From *The Ghe-Wa (Tibetan Death Rite) for Pau Karma Wang Chuk Namgyal*, by Larry Peters (for Shaman's Drum)

Shamans were known as such in Siberia. But they had many different names, and still do, when they are found all over the world. For instance, a Scandinavian female shaman is called a Volva, a Nigerian shaman is a Babalawoo, an Indian Vedic shaman is a Rishi and Inuit shamans are known as Angakoks.

Thousands of years ago, no culture could function without these shamans. Their roles were multitudinous and ranged, in service to the individual members of the tribe, from the cradle to the grave as they presided over the hatching, matching and despatching (births, marriages and deaths) of each member of their communities. They were the midwives, the handfasters and the psychopomps who carried the spirit of the Deceased to join the ancestors in the Realms of the Dead in the Other Worlds. They were the healers who would carry out soul retrievals and entity extractions. They were the storytellers, skilled in imprinting the metaphorical narrative gleaned from the totem spirits on young men who would then go on to become strong male leaders. They were navigators who led their people by the stars to their next encampment. And running throughout all their roles, and inspiring their actions, was a golden seam of wisdom they gained through their interaction with those in the Other Worlds.

Nowadays, scientists are beginning to realise about the advanced intelligence of our earliest ancestors – such as the Neanderthals, the Denisovans and the Natufians - while archaeologists and anthropologists are specialising in uncovering evidence of ritual activities and shamanism. However, as I write, little of it is reaching mainstream thought and so, generally speaking, it remains occluded.

There seems also to be an unspoken, almost racist prejudice against the idea of considering people intelligent when there's no evidence of their using marks that we recognise as writing as a means of communication. But this ignores the fact that they conversed and interacted much more through metaphor and images rather than in the written word, as we see from their cave paintings dating to about 40,000 years ago.

It's also evident, when we study the Indian *Vedas*, that they must have had prodigious memories because the lore – by which I mean the multi-layered myths that contained the coded wisdom teachings - was passed down through a multitude of generations while hardly suffering any erosion from a kind of Chinese Whispers effect. Of course, it helped that it was usually in rhyme and so if there were a "missing beat" or an "off note" in the poem or song, it would be more obvious. At the same time, modern scientists have discovered that relying on the written word leads to memory erosion – in other words, we don't bother to store data in our memory banks when we know we can refer to them on our computer. This makes our brains "lazy".

We can trace the earliest form of writing to about 10,000 years ago, from runes found carved on rocks in Russia – although the official dating for the first runes of the Elder Futhark is the first century CE. In a way, runes are a form of pictograph, as were the hieroglyphs of the ancient Egyptians. It wasn't until the 12th and 13th centuries BCE that the sort of writing with which we are more familiar became the norm. Before that, there were only images – images either scratched, etched or painted with haematite on cave walls and rocks because, we are discovering, early man was more in touch with the right-side hemisphere of his brain and thus his thinking was more holistic and shamanic.

The right side of the brain deals with metaphors, pictures and feelings and has no consciousness of time because it is the part of us that exists in the ever-present eternity. The left side of the brain, where we spend most of our waking lives these days, thinks more linearly and is constantly making calculations about how we should move into the future based on its vast databanks of past experiences.

Shamanism is much more right-brained in its approach to scientific investigations. Modern Western science is almost entirely left-brained and so I sometimes wonder whether rock art scientists are the best people to try to interpret shamanically-produced art. In fact, when viewing the ancient cave paintings in France and Spain through the cold, objective lens of scientific research — whether cognitive epistemology, palaeoart studies, general and replicative archaeology, soil science, speleology, semiotics and geomorphology, to name but a few — I think we may be using the wrong tools for the job. Perhaps it would be better to lie down in the darkness of the cave and commune shamanically with the symbols and effigies depicted in those paintings, to gain the wisdom teachings that have been imprinted there by our ancestors?

It is a completely different approach. While the scientist is crawling all over, say, the famous cave painting of the Birdman in the Shaft of the Lascaux cave, armed only with a microscope and a BA Hons in Art History, the shaman is silently and empathically communing with the Birdman himself.

From my own Otherwordly communions, I have come to believe that the image of the Birdman and bird goddesses are so prevalent in the art of the ancients worldwide because our forebears knew something it's taken us a while to catch up with. Scientists have only recently discovered that levels of IQ correlate with the number of neural fibres that are in a brain and not with the size of the cranium, and they also now know that many species of birds have trillions more of those fibres packed into their tiny skulls than humans.

But what else can we learn from the Birdman?

The bird god or goddess goes back into the deepest recesses of antiquity. However, the Birdman in the Lascaux caves, in the Dordogne region of south-west France, is probably one of the oldest yet found and one can only reach it by going into the "underworld" – through a long and deep shaft into a dark and secret space that is several metres below the cave's surface. Down there, we also find a painting of a large bison bull that has been speared through its anus and sexual organs. It stands before a prostrate man wearing a bird mask; his phallus is erect and pointing towards the speared bull; his splayed hands are more like bird claws and beside him there is a staff topped with the image of a bird. Behind this Birdman, there is a large rhinoceros that is defecating as it walks away.

So with the erect phallus of the Birdman, the speared genitals of the bull and the poo of the rhino, it is obviously – to me, anyway - depicting a shaman in trance during a fertility ritual. But what does that mean? Archaeologists like to talk about "hunting magic" but as these scenes often feature animals these ancients did not hunt for food, like bears and lions – not to mention rhinoceroses - then surely fertility is about much more than merely tracking down the evening meal? As a shaman myself, I can confirm that it is about more – much more. It is about Sovereignty and birthing new worlds.

But is it scientific? As I understand it, the transmission of wisdom from the parallel, timeless realms of the spirits to the shaman in trance is just a different way of receiving information, as rock art scientist David Lewis Williams found out.

When Lewis Williams published his seminal book, *The Mind In the Cave: Consciousness and the Origins of Art*, it marked the first time, metaphorically-speaking, that a rock art scientist crossed the corpus callosum – that thick wedge of neural fibres separating the hemispheres of the brain - to make the case that these vividly colourful Upper Palaeolithic paintings were the equivalent of stained glass windows into the other worlds of the soul, which were reached by those who went before us lying in trance within their dark, cold and cavernous Ice Age cathedrals.

Back in the 1970s, Lewis Williams gained his PhD through his epigraphic work with the San Bushmen of southern Africa, one of the few remaining indigenous tribes with a tradition of shamanic practices going back for thousands of years.

In training with their shamans, Lewis Williams discovered that they use different tools to the rock art scientist, such as clairaudience, clairvoyance, clairsentience - cognitive tools he then went on to develop himself over many years of training.

In *The Mind in the Cave*, Lewis-Williams wrote that the patterns of images leading from the cave entrances in Lascaux and Chauvet in France to the dark, almost inaccessible recesses, provide an almost mirror image of the shaman's journey into trance:

"...the entry into Upper Palaeolithic caves was probably seen as virtually indistinguishable from entry into the mental vortex that leads to the experiences and hallucinations of deep [shamanic] trance... The embellishing images blazed (possibly in a fairly literal sense) a path into the unknown."

So from this perspective we can understand that early humans regarded the universe as alive, conscious and multidimensional, and from the wisdom gleaned from spirit guides they came to understand their lives were no random accident. On the contrary, they were as intrinsic and vital to the Creation as the brightest star in the sky. And so, just like the tribe of Kroy-Khasis, Tabiti and Maya, they organised their spiritual and ritual activities around a circular calendar that correlated with the spiralling cycles of the Sun, the Moon and the constellations above them.

For instance, Maya would have needed the stars to tell him when to hold the rituals that would ensure the tribe reproducing and thriving into the future. The Autumn Equinox, signalled by the setting of the Pleiades, would have alerted him that the ritual fertility dance of the clashing antlers of the elks was about to begin. He would have also watched for the "rutting Moon", which came seven days after the second full Moon during October and November, so that he would know when the white-tailed deer were coming into season.

Maya would have carried his lunar calendar on a small piece of stone, bone or antler – in other words, these were all materials that held great mythic value to our earliest ancestors, given their fundamental nature. It also meant the calendars were light and portable, an important advantage to nomads. It has also turned out to be handy for modern archaeologists who are continually digging them up, such as the late Upper Palaeolithic bone knife discovered in the French Pyrenees. On one side is depicted a bellowing rutting bison under leafless autumn trees with branches bearing nuts, seeds and cones. Turn over the knife and you find a doe and an ibex among spring flowers and serpentine lines that trace out the cycles of the Moon.

An ivory plaque dated to the late Upper Palaeolithic was also found in the French Pyrenees and it is engraved with a moulting bison under carved Moons in a serpentine pattern that indicates the moult of spring and early summer.

Spring is often shown on these ancient artefacts as a snake shedding its skin, which is probably the oldest mythological symbol of regeneration and rebirth.

The cycles of the Moon are very much connected to the cycles of the female's menstrual cycles, to the tides and to other seasonal wheels as well, including those experienced by plants and animals. And so some believe such an advanced understanding about how women's, plants' and animals' cycles are in tune with the Moon could possibly have led to the population explosion of modern man which took place after the last Ice Age.

Anyway, the advanced astronomical knowledge of Maya and his peoples is now receiving attention from a whole new breed of cosmologists called palaeoastronomers and among the foremost in that field are Alexander Marshank and Michael A Rappengluck.

Towards the end of the 20th century, Marshank published his interpretation of Upper Palaeolithic cave art in which he showed evidence for the deep mathematical and astronomical knowledge of those who lived up to 65,000 years ago – before the Neanderthals became extinct.

It was already known that the sets of crescents and lines carved into animal bones and on cave walls, which we have already discussed, were likely to be records of the cycles of the Moon.

However, what Marshank concluded from his discoveries was even more remarkable in throwing light on the advanced cognition of our early ancestors. He realised that the sets of serpentine-arranged crescents and lines were not completely accurate in reflecting the phases of the Moon, because this kind of accuracy would have been impossible to achieve by the naked eye; not all nights are clear and cloudless. But the arithmetical counting skills, shown in these stone and bone calendars, were obvious to him. So too was the fact that even their acknowledgement that they needed to record these cycles indicated the profundity of their thought processes.

As Bennett Blumenberg writes in *The Origins of Mythology in the Upper Palaeolithic Cultures of Eurasia*:

All animal activities are time factored, simply because time passes, the future is forever arriving. The reality of time factoring is objective physics and does not depend upon human awareness or consciousness. Until Marshack's work, many archeologists believed the sets of marks he chose to study were nothing but the aimless doodles of bored toolmakers. What Marshack uncovered is the intuitive discovery of mathematical sets and the application of those sets to the construction of a calendar.

Another palaeoastronomer, Michael A Rappenglück, has identified evidence for the ancients' knowledge of astronomy in some of the paintings in the caves of Lascaux, which were painted at least 16,000 years ago – and some believe even earlier.

For instance, he believes the serpentine line of 29 marks below the painting of a dappled brown horse represents the synodic cycle. He has also found there what he believes to be marks showing the Pleiades and the stars of Taurus the Bull. And as he went down the shaft to the aforementioned Birdman, he came upon an illustration symbolising the Summer Triangle of Vega, Deneb and Altair

– a part of the night sky that would have been prominent during the Spring Equinox 17,000 years ago.

He said: "It's a map of the prehistoric cosmos. It was their sky, full of animals and spirit guides."

Rappenglück also discovered what he interprets as a 14,000-year-old star map in the mountains of Pico del Castillo, Spain. The Ceuva del Castillo cave contains a section that is dubbed the Frieze of Hands, so named because its walls are decorated with the red ochre imprints of the palms of many human hands – as if our ancestors are waving to us from across the oceans of Time.

On that wall, he found a curved pattern of dots.

He said: "Nobody had paid much attention to it, but it's obviously a drawing of the constellation we call the Northern Crown. It's remarkable."

Many of the animals found in cave art – such as bears, lions, and rhinos - were valued as what shamans today call "power animals" or "totem animals". These creatures were considered to be sacred. Each tribe had its own totem spirit animals that would have often appeared as Otherworldly guides to Maya and his like, just as they do to shamans today.

And so I hope that's given you something of a perspective on how our earliest ancestors thought. It's a million miles from how most of us were taught history and also from how many in academia are approaching the subject today.

As William Irwin Thompson said in his highly acclaimed *The Time Falling Bodies Take to Light*:

Because we have separated humanity from nature, subject from object, values from analysis, knowledge from myth, and universities from the universe, it is enormously difficult for anyone but a poet or a mystic to understand what is going on in the holistic and mythopoetic thought of Ice Age humanity. The very language we use to discuss the past speaks of tools, hunters and men, when every statue and painting we discover cries out to us that this Ice Age humanity was a culture of art, the love of animals, and women.

He might have added..."and of the stars."

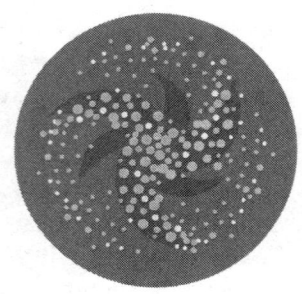

Practical exercise

Getting in touch with your ancestors

As you go through this book, you will learn a new way to map your life more successfully, much as Kroy-Khasis learned how to chart his. You will understand better the potential of the extraordinary vessel of the human body and how the gods above guide the voyage of your "ship" in harmony with the spirits and the ancestors below. And once you learn how to take hold of the wheel at your helm, through an ages-old method I'll explain to you in a simple, stepped progression, with each step building upon the last, you'll be able to take better control of your life and, if you want to, quicken the rate at which your evolution progresses.

Some call the whole process magic. But please don't be concerned because there is no base trickery about it. It's only called "the occult" because it has been hidden, until recently. It is just about getting your life into holistic alignment with its true purpose by plugging into the natural alchemical and astrological processes and forces that guide and govern the progress of the human being. These natural drives will clear away any highwaymen and roadblocks along the way. Then, once you have successfully traversed the way of the hero, you can be a way-shower for future generations.

In my view, the method that you will learn from this book is the only way to find a contented and fulfilling life. Otherwise, we are continually drifting off course with a broken rudder, or suddenly having to turn on a sixpence in order to avoid an iceberg.

The best place to start with this work is in engaging with your ancestors because they will quickly become your guides, along with a host of other overlighting spirits – some of whom, when they appear, may seem familiar to you because they have been guiding your family for countless generations.

There are many different ways you can approach your forebears and you do not have to be a shaman, although if you are, you will probably already be journeying to meet them. I remember the first time I met mine. It was a wonderful experience. They were all standing along a winding riverbank and looking up and waving and cheering at me as I flew past. I remember thinking, as I reached nearer to the source of the ancestral Rivers of Blood, that some of their facial features looked quite archaic.

But if you are not yet able to go into shamanic trance, then you can start to contact your forebears by tracing your family tree. You may already have one or know of a relative who has begun to put one together. Sometimes, family trees are handed down, in written form, in the front of the family Bible.

You can use online applications that find your ancestors for you and it's a good place to start, although they base their findings on certificates of births, marriages and deaths, so they can only get back so far, and certainly no earlier than the Reformation of the 16th century, when many of the churches that used to contain those sorts of records were destroyed.

There are also places where you can send a drop of your blood and they will provide you with a DNA reading. The results will show where your progenitors originally came from. Typically, most Western white people have a mix that reflects, to varying degrees, the widespread fanning out across Europe and Scandinavia of Kroy-Khakis's tribes from the Eurasian steppes.

However, there is a more spiritual aspect to the exercise of searching out those who came before you. You may find this difficult to believe right now but in my experience, once I started looking for my ancestors, they began looking for me. In fact, they may have always been looking for me and perhaps it was more the case that I didn't notice until I began to search for them.

So participating in Naming of the Dead ceremonies that take place on Samhain is usually an effective way of opening this portal. Samhain is the Christian All Hallows Eve or Halloween, at the end of October. Even if there are no such rituals taking place near you, you can still light a candle in your own front room and remember, out loud, the names of any recently deceased relatives. In my experience, that moves mountains.

In building a connection with our ancestors, we become much more rooted and stable in our existence and thus feel more guided and empowered. We also start to get more context on our own individual life's path by feeling a part of something that is much greater.

2. Weather Shamans at Sea

IN this chapter, we will continue to get ourselves into the minds and thoughts of our earliest ancestors by learning more about their perceptions regarding their lives and place in the cosmos.

We will discover how different their cognitive reality was from how we think today and we will learn too how to tune into these differences through their mytho-poetic stories. In that way, we will soon realise that viewing our ancestors as if they were just a more primitive version of us could not be more wrong. Not only is that far from the truth but, in fact, the reverse is the case. They had a much greater vision of the universe and their holographic and holistic place in it, and because of this more effective engagement with reality, they were more skilled in traversing the paths and pitfalls of life with greater competency.

One of those differences is found in how they viewed their domiciles. Today, we lead more fixed lives, going every day to the same job from the same home, while their day-to-day actions and interactions were much more fluid. For instance, very few people, these days, make their lives on the seas. Of course, we do occasionally cross the "great blue" to get from one place to another, or we may enjoy swimming and surfing off the coast in our leisure time. But afterwards, we usually return to our landlubbers' bricks-and-mortar abodes, firmly constructed on dry land.

The sea is ever-changeable and humans now avoid too much change. Even highly proficient sailors tell us we should be wary of the sea, that it sometimes seems to have a mind of its own and a storm can suddenly come out of nowhere. So we prefer to make our home in one place, and stay there as much as possible. We mostly only up-sticks and transfer ourselves and our belongings to another place across the waters if and when circumstances render it unavoidable.

Another difference is that our logical reasoning is conditioned, it now turns out wrongly, by a Darwinian mindset. According to that rationale, the open sea must have been a terrifying environment for the ignorant, grunting *Homo erectus* – only a few steps up from an ape - who may have just about had the nous to throw together a flimsy raft. But then, we ask, how would that frail contraption have made it through weeks of voyaging, out of sight of land, as its crew tried to cope with unpredictable currents, storms and tempests?

The earliest attested boat is only 7,000 years old. None have been found that can be dated earlier. However, given how quickly wood rots and dissolves back into the forest floor from whence it came, it is hardly surprising. All the materials that those who went before us used for building their homes and transport were what we call today "biodegradable". Therefore, lack of material evidence for a so-called civilised culture does not mean one did not exist. It could even be argued our ancestors were more civilised than we are in being able to bequeath to us a planet fit to sustain life for millions of years, unlike those of us today who seem to be hell-bent on turning the oceans into dumps for chemicals and plastic.

However, there are other ways to find evidence for early transoceanic voyaging.

Research carried out by anthropologists John L Sorenson and Carl L Johannessen concluded that man must have had nautical skills around at least 9,000 years ago.

They undertook a study of more than 100 plants, which have come to light through a combination of archaeological research, ancient art and historical and linguistic sources, and they found that from their spread between continents, it was clear that our ancestors were happily navigating the waves across great distances during the 7th millennium BCE.

In their book *Scientific Evidence for Pre-Columbian Transoceanic Voyages To and From the Americas*, they write:

Well over half the plant transfers [examined] consisted of flora of American origin that spread to Eurasia or Oceania, some at surprisingly early dates. The only plausible explanation for these findings is that a considerable number of transoceanic voyages in both directions across both major oceans were completed between the 7th millennium BCE and the European age of discovery.

Our growing knowledge of early maritime technology and its accomplishments gives us confidence that vessels and nautical skills capable of these long-distance travels were developed by the times indicated.

But there is much older evidence now increasingly being found.

Human-carved tools found on the island of Crete were discovered to be about 130,000 years old.

There is also now evidence that Australia was colonised by people with advanced cognitive skills who came from the seas 50,000 years ago. In a study published in *Quaternary Science Reviews*, researchers used environmental reconstructions, voyage simulations and genetic population estimates to show for the first time this nautical migration was achieved by a globally significant phase of purposeful and coordinated marine voyaging. There are very strong currents to the north of Australia that could only have been crossed by expert seamen and which would have required knowledge of watercraft construction along with sailing and navigation technology, planning ability, information sharing and enough provisions to sustain an open ocean voyage over at least four to seven days.

More recently, even older traces of human activities – butchered rhino bones – were discovered in the Philippines and dated to about 700,000 years ago. In other words, this was at a time and a place in which there were no land bridges, meaning man could only have got there by boat.

So our earliest ancestors were not all landlubbers and that they were travelling long distances means they would not have considered it an impossible feat to be at sea for long periods. From that, we can deduce that they did not rule out the water as an inhospitable terrain in which to make their homes. We know that they built wooden settlements on sticks in marshlands, which gave them access to a plentitude of wildfowl and fish, while estuaries on coastlands provided salt and seaweed.

But I'd like to invite you to consider a further reason for their proficiency on the open oceans – one that orthodox science has yet to catch up with. We have weather shamans today that make rain and control the winds. So surely our ancestors, then, would have had shaman navigators who not only used the stars to guide them but could control and redirect the elements to prevent the boat from capsizing in a squall?

We see remnants of these early navigator shaman types in ancient myths, with characters like Maya Danava of the Vedics, Noah and his Ark, Moses who parted the Red Sea and Jesus Christ who calmed the troubled waters for his fisherman disciples.

Of course, these are mythological characters that did not actually exist as real people. But the fact that they appear in the oldest myths as representing a certain recognisable archetype - navigators, explorers and leaders of migrations who have the ability to calm or part the seas, or protect their people from deluges - tells us something about ancient thinking.

So I think we can be fairly confident that during the time of the migration from the steppes, Maya would have helped in leading his tribe to safer and drier lands by following marine pathways and shamanic practices that had been passed down orally from generation to generation. He would have been aware of those who had gone before, at the beginning of that great Ice Age, and who crossed a much shallower Mediterreanean Sea to find refuge in certain spots that benefitted from the warmth of the Gulf Stream.

At that time, there were about half a dozen isolated milder havens that his forebears would have headed to and this dispersal eventually gave rise to the Celtic, Germanic, Italic, Balkan, Balto-Slavic and Indo-Iranian language families of Indo-European. One of those refuges for the steppes' tribes was the Basque country of northern Spain and legends tell us that the Sons of Mil eventually left there to travel by sea to found the land we now call Ireland.

Others settled in Gibraltar, while some went to Sicily, which was then connected to the Italian mainland. In addition, with sea levels being about 425 feet lower than they are today, it was only a 30-mile voyage from Italy to Africa – a trip they could easily have made and did, according to recent archaeological evidence.

The oceans were such a natural habitat for these nomadic wanderers who followed the stars that we can probably safely assume it's why so many of our ancient myths feature heroes whose mothers came from the sea, such as Achilles. The French Merovingian kings copied this popular backstory to give themselves more legitimacy. They claimed to be descended from Melusine, a beautiful woman who was a fish from the waist down. The word "mer" is French for sea, and the word "mere" is French for mother, giving us the maternal common ancestors of a mermaid. On top of that, there would have been sea faeries and water nymphs envisioned in trance by the ship's shamans, and relied upon for guidance.

Most Native American tribal groups had a rainmaker in days gone by and some still do, while it remains in practice in a few other places in Africa, Australia, New Zealand and wherever there is still some knowledge of the old ways.

A shaman may become a rainmaker after showing an inherited predilection for this specialised work and then undertaking a long apprenticeship. While the means and the methods of weather shamanism vary from culture to culture, they all stress the paramount importance of the relationship that is developed between the practitioner and the elemental forces that move and change the atmospheric conditions.

Currently, there are shamans who bring the rains that are based in the Coso Mountains of California, which has been the location of a ritual centre for weather shamans for more than 10,000 years. From the rock art in the caves there, we can see that rainmakers of the Coso Shoshone and the Kawaiisu, in ancient times, wore the typical quail topknot headdress of the weather shaman. They will describe to anyone who asks that they make the "rains come" by using the power of intention, prayers and medicine objects within rituals and ceremonies in which they express unconditional love to the ancestors, which is just one of many tools that help the shaman connect with an unseen force of nature that produces clouds, rain, thunder and lightning, winds and other weather phenomena.

There used to be a Native American weather shaman called Sun Bear who people said was a rainmaker of the first degree. Apparently, the weather seemed to follow him wherever he went. He brought the rains to drought-stricken areas and could also command the winds.

Sun Bear always said he worked with "the Grandfathers" through the holographic heart current of unconditional love. In other words, these were the ancestors he met through the shamanic trance. He said these ancestral spirits were specialised in weather-making and had been helping shamans for untold millennia in the timeless, ever-present realms.

In certain Native American traditions, such as the Hopi, the whole tribe participates in rainmaking ceremonies led by their shamans. In fact, in all the tribal and cultural lands where rainmakers have been found, the people have acknowledged the craft, the necessity, and the value of it in their lives.

The Celtic Druids were so proficient in weather shamanism that they attributed names and qualities to the winds that arose at certain times of year. For instance, a wind rising from the north in winter months would be called Red Sworded and bring wars, while a Yellow Wind during Maytime would herald good fruit and a White Wind around the Summer Solstice would predict a good harvest.

So let's imagine a prehistoric community undertaking a long sea voyage. How would they eat? How would they survive?

Getting enough food should not have been a problem, so long as they carried their own fruit on board, as the diet most recommended by nutritionists, even today, is one based on fish, seaweed and spirulina, a marine food largely made up of the same cyanobacteria or algae that fish eat. The health benefits of spirulina are too many to list here but we know that the Aztecs and other Meso-Americans were keen spirulina eaters until at least the 16th century. A soldier of the Spanish conqueror Cortes reported that the Aztecs called spirulina *tecuitlatl*, meaning "stone's excrement", and they harvested it from Lake Texcoco, and then made it into flat pancakes.

These most ancient of mariners may have been challenged in getting fresh water supplies when spending weeks and months at sea. But even then, just as we have desalination techniques today, it would not have been beyond the ken of these old sea dogs to know about which herbs to use to separate the salt from the seawater. Indians in the fifth century were able to turn salt water into the more potable kind, according to the astrologer and ayurvedic scientist Varahamihira, who lived at that time. In his treatise entitled *Brihatsamhita*, he suggested the use of five ayurvedic herbs for desalination of brackish water.

Laboratory tests since then that followed his recommendations have proved successful.

However, one of the best academic papers on the challenges faced by our nautical ancestors is found in *Ancient Transpacific Voyaging* by Steve Wyatt.

Wyatt writes:

> Undoubtedly, protacted ocean journeys in unsophisticated watercraft were possible. They have been accomplished on several occasions historically by accident and also by design for the specific purpose of 'proving' that high-tech boats and equipment were not a prerequisite (Finney, 1999, 2000). Kon Tiki's ill-founded 1947 voyage from Peru to the Tuamotu Islands is one well-known example; the 1976 voyage of the Hokule'a from Maui to Tahiti is another (Finney, 1999). But these successes notwithstanding, the most pertinent question still remains unanswered: Was transoceanic voyaging a feasible method for first initiating and then maintaining a New World Colony in antiquity?
>
> Attempting to answer this question pragmatically involves a slew of cross-discipline considerations. Outside of psychological factors, the success or failure of most human endeavours is governed by the interaction of elements falling into four broad classifications: technology, biology, culture and environment (Wyatt, 2002).
>
> Regarding the first, for this study it was assumed a priori that marine-oriented groups possessing somewhat more than basic rafting technology existed in the South Pacific during the late Pleistocene [c. 126,000 to 11,700 years ago]. As outlined already, this supposition is supported by circumstantial evidence and, to some degree, by experimentation.
>
> "An assessment of biological and cultural factors (e.g. the logistics of obtaining food and fresh water at sea, and the difficulties of an isolated founding population in maintaining reproductive viability) revealed that they would not have necessarily had a negative impact on oceanic exploration (Wyatt, 2002). From a feasibility standpoint, that is, there were no definitive reasons among biological or cultural factors alone to unequivocally declare impossible or even inconceivable successful settlement enterprises via the ocean. Technology, biology and culture aside then, left only environmental issues to cast the deciding vote. (Wyatt, 2002).

Wyatt then goes on to conclude that trans-Pacific voyaging would have been possible mainly because many tiny islands that are now underwater would have existed along the way, where the seafarers could have put in to take on fresh springwater, carry out repairs and even add to their gene pool - as sailors have been wont to do since time immemorial!

Then add into the mix of that hypothesis the shaman navigators and their knowledge of weather systems and currents and I think you could very easily have had a sophisticated sea world culture more than 100,000 years ago.

The only barrier to that possibility is in our own thinking.

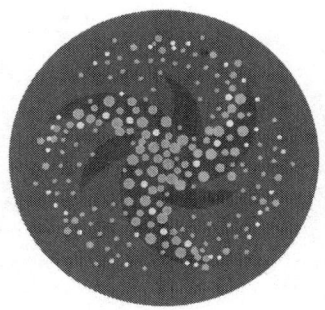

Practical exercise

If you already work shamanically, then here's what I hope you'll find to be an enjoyable and interesting exercise which will get you on the road to weather shamanism. It's one of the earliest journeys I did after my training and I have benefitted from it ever since.

Next time you see great, jagged lightening forks piercing the night skies and hear loud claps of thunder slowly rolling along in their wake, go into a shamanic journey with the intention of visiting the storm god.

He is known by many different names in many different languages and all of them work. If you favour the Old Norse way then he is Thor, and in the Celtic tradition he is Taranis.

If you don't yet know how to go into shamanic trance, you can still benefit from this exercise by doing it in meditation as a visualisation.

3. The Holographic Universe of Music

SO now we understand a little more about the intelligence and technological know-how of our earliest ancestors, we might be asking the question: where did it all come from? It is important to properly understand the fountainhead of this wisdom because otherwise we fall foul of all sorts of misunderstandings about space aliens building the Pyramids and such like. No, our earliest ancestors were more than capable of great engineering feats because they had an inner wisdom that grew out of their perception of their holographic interconnectedness with the universe – a perception that has been lost to most of us today.

As the Fire-Worshippers of the Southern Bu-Kongo tell us:

Man's environment is the world as a whole, and the latter's environment is our solar system. Man is part of the stars — and the stars, Sun and Moon are all part of man.

This understanding of the holographic interconnectedness of the human being was once widespread upon the Earth because it was taught about in the orally passed-on stories that we now call myths. This interconnectedness was given great value by our ancestors because they knew that the brain likes to think in stories and therefore, the right narrative, told correctly, moulds the individual's thought processes into helping him find his way and place in the cosmos. In losing that understanding, man quickly finds himself on the road to ruin and his journey to hell is summed up beautifully in these few paragraphs from the introduction to *Hamlet's Mill* by Giorgio de Santillana and Hertha von Dechen:

When man discovers remote galaxies by the million, and then those quasi-stellar sources billions of light-years away which confound his speculation, he is happy he can reach out to those depths. But he pays a terrible price for his achievement. The science of astrophysics reaches out on a grander and grander scale without losing its footing. Man as man cannot do this. In the depths of space, he loses himself and all notion of his significance. He is unable to fit himself into the concepts of today's astrophysics short of schizophrenia. Modern man is facing the inconceivable.

Archaic man, however, kept a firm grip on the conceivable by framing within his cosmos an order of time and an eschatology that made sense to him and reserved a fate for his soul. Yet it was a prodigiously vast theory, with no concessions to merely human sentiments. It too dilated the mind beyond the bearable although without destroying man's role in the cosmos. It was ruthless metaphysics.

Not a forgiving universe, not a world of mercy. That surely not. Inexorable as the stars in their courses - *miserationis parcissimae*, the Romans used to say. Yet it was a world somehow not unmindful of man, one in which there was an accepted place for everything, rightfully and not only statistically, where no sparrow could fall unnoted, and where even that which was rejected through its own error would not go down to eternal perdition; for the order of Number and Time was a total order preserving all, of which all were members; gods and men and animals, trees and crystals and even absurd errant stars, all subject to law and measure.

This is the philosophy of existence I am aiming to help re-establish with this book and it shouldn't be too difficult a task because these stories are seeded in the race memories we carry in our DNA, known in faery lore as the Rivers of Blood. At the same time, this ancient golden seam of advanced cognitive understanding has been left to us in coded myths by our ancestors and hidden in their underlayers are magical keys that unlock the doors of perception within the human mind.

Even modern stories that provide the plots for screenplays use the same devices and morphologies that storytellers like Tabiti would have employed to entrance and engage the young Kroy-Khasis's emotional intelligence. The only difference for us is we may leave the cinema after watching a science fiction movie, say, Star Wars with a smile on our faces, but the good mood doesn't last for long because we've not learned how to benefit from these great heroic comedies and tragedies. We have not been taught holographic interconnectedness; we have not been schooled in how to find our own heroic centre and face our own dragons. We are just encouraged to hero-worship Luke

Skywalker.

And so, we never get to learn that the meaning of life is the pursuit of virtue and wisdom. Further, in the vacuum left by the absence of such positive direction, we come to believe instead that the purpose of life must be the pursuit of fun and happiness.

David Bowie once sang: "We can be heroes, just for one day." One day is just about as long as the inspirational mood lasts when it's produced by a feelgood ending such as Luke Skywalker blowing up the Death Star, whereas true storytelling makes a hero for a whole Day of Brahma – and the Indian Vedics' Day of Brahma lasts for a universal cycle of trillions of years.

As you go through these teachings, you will learn how you can become a hero for a whole Day of Brahma.

But first, let's discuss what being holographically interconnected really means because once you get that, you will also understand much more about why certain symbols and numbers crop up in so many ancient myths.

First of all, the word holographic comes from hologram. So what is a hologram? A hologram is, technically-speaking, layered light – in other words, light photons that have been formed into layers by lasers. Thus, if you break off a piece of a holographic picture or photo, the whole of that image is found in that fragment. Every fragment of the hologram carries the entire picture. Another way of saying it is that the macrocosm of the photo is held within the microcosm of every piece. In the same way, the human being may just be a tiny fragment of the creation but he carries the whole universe within him.

This cosmological perception of our ancestors is found in their temple art and architecture, particularly in what we call "sacred geometry". Have you ever wondered why "sacred geometry" is thus named? It's because it reflects, in its dimensions, the holiness or holographic and holistic understanding of the true nature of the human being, which, at its most basic, is music.

We find this in the Bible's *Book of Wisdom*, addressed to God. "But you have disposed all things by measure and number and weight."

Ancient temples were planned and constructed according to this "measure, number and weight" of primordial vibrations and frequencies and for this reason they are sometimes dubbed "symphonies in stone". It is clear that the Vedics practised these same arts because we can see those mathematical principles at work in their fire altars, constructed thousands of years before Christianity was born. Later, many Norman churches and cathedrals were built on designs based on these sacred proportions and it makes them cosmic transponders.

What is a transponder? Let me explain: a satellite transponder receives coded signals from a ground station on Earth in the form of sound frequencies. It then amplifies and retransmits that code along a different set of frequencies to another ground station on Earth.

Now imagine that same principle but with the coded sound frequencies we voice in our songs of praise and prayers winging their way up like carrier pigeons. I expect that's why so many people enjoy visiting old churches and cathedrals, even when they are not Christians. They can instinctively sense they are benefitting from the holy holographic make-up of their surroundings.

It's a favourite pastime of mine to sit in the wooden pews of Wells Cathedral, in Somerset, England, when it's "off-season", with few tourists around to disturb me from drifting into a light shamanic trance. Once, the arch above the altar metamorphosed into the Milky Way. Another time, at a carol service, the angels joined in our chorus to Hark the Herald Angels Sing.

Even the crumbling ruins of Glastonbury Abbey, just a stone's throw from my house, still resonate with the symphonies of the celestial gods. I expect you know of similar religious buildings near you and so you will know that you don't have to become a Christian to talk to the gods, or God; it is just that whether the church knows it or not, they have the best transponders! Perhaps it makes more sense to us now that our technologists have engineered voice recognition technology that we can use instead of written passwords. In the same way, and for the same reason, there is no chance that our prayer will be muddled up with someone else's. The gods have been using Unique Voice Recognition software for untold aeons – and there are no mix-ups over regional accents!

In Part 2, you will come across a key to some of the numbers often used in ancient myths that make up the codes of the frequencies generated by the sacred geometry of these cosmic transponders.

But for now, we are going to examine the number eight because in just that one example we can see evidence for man's vision of how the individual has a musical holographic interconnectedness to the rest of the creation, as it appears in the earliest myths available to us.

Eight seems to have been a very important number to the ancients and maybe that is why it is found in the earliest deluge myths from the Old Testament in the Bible, as well as the earlier Egyptian and Sumerian versions.

I am sure most readers will know the story of Noah's Ark from the Book of Genesis, but for those who don't, here's a very quick summary:

God was displeased with humanity and wanted to wipe them off the face of the Earth with a Great Flood. He decided, though, to save the 600-year-old Noah and his family, and so he instructed the great patriarch to build a great ark of 300 cubits in length, 50 cubits in width and 30 cubits in height.

He also told Noah to bring onboard two of every species of animal and plant, to save them from the waters.

It rained and rained over 40 days and nights, until the waters measured 15 cubits in depth, and the mountains and trees disappeared under the floods,

but Noah and his family were safe on the Ark. Then eventually, the floods subsided, and on the 17th day of the seventh month, Noah steered the Ark to safety on the top of Mount Ararat.

God then promised that Noah and his descendants would be safe from his wrath in future, and he sent a rainbow as a sign of that covenant with man.

Many of the numbers found in dozens of myths from all over the world are used in this story, and many feature a great flood and a handful of survivors. You can read them all in Appendix A: Flood Myths from Around the World. But for now, I want to concentrate on the ==number eight.==

Noah's family on the Ark consisted of himself and his wife, with their three sons, Ham, Japeth and Shem, and their wives. That makes eight people. There were also eight people on board in the original myth from which the Hebrew one was derived. The Egyptian Nnu's barque contained himself and his wife with his three sons Shu, Taht and Seb of the Serpents, along with their wives.

So the number eight must have been important. Once you get further along in this book and have understood the teachings in **Part 2: The Language of the Initiates**, you will be able to make the alchemical connections and you will then realise that it is no coincidence that eight is also the number of notes in a musical octave.

==The number eight is regarded as the holiest number that represents the foundation stone of the creation.== The four men and four women (4 + 4 = 8) on the ark or barque were being required by God, once the floods had abated, to generate the human race anew from a regenerated foundation, or a new world.

The number eight is often expressed as 888, or in numerology 8:64 = 864. The late geomancer John Michell described it as the number of the foundation stone in the building of Jerusalem.

The number 864 is prominent in the temple measures, most of all in the 864-cubit distance between the two sacred rocks, the Rock of Foundation and Golgotha, or Place of the Skull.

In the language of symbolic number, 864 pertains to a centre of radiant energy, the Sun in the solar system.....the inner sanctuary of the temple, the altar and the corner stone on which the whole sacred edifice is founded.

... 864 is called the 'foundation number' ... and in the gematria of New Testament Greek, 864 corresponds to words or phrases such as 'altar', 'corner stone', 'sanctuary of the gods', 'holy of holies' ...

To the ancients, the number eight could not have been more holy in terms of expressing the holographic nature of man in his interconnectedness with the universe. Human DNA consists of 64 (8 x 8) codons and even our hearts beat in time with the macrocosmic heartbeat of Time and Space.

Our average heart rate is 60 beats per minute; multiply that by 60 minutes and it gives us 3,600 beats per hour, which comes to 86,400 beats every 24 hours – in other words, it is the time that the Earth takes to travel each day around the Sun, which is 864,000 miles across.

We should also note that the planetary orbit of Mercury is 88 days and there are 88 officially recognised celestial constellations.

This numerical way of expressing interconnectedness between the microcosmic human and the macrocosm also found its way into the plays, dances, artworks and even the board games and divinatory tools of those who went before us. There are 64 (8 x 8) hexagrams in the i-Ching, 64 sections to the Eye of the Horus and 64 squares on a chess board. The Hindu Lord Shiva has 64 manifestations and there are 64 dakinis (female nature deities) in the Vedas.

The Mayans used an eight-by-eight square of a total of 64 units and the same eight-by-eight square was known in ancient Indian temple design as the Vastu Parusha Mandala with eight ruling gods.

Sixty-four is also the atomic weight of copper, which is the metal associated with Venus, previously known in Babylonian times as Ishtar. Her city, the city of Babylon, meaning "gate of the gods", was similarly built on these principles. The eighth of the eight gates of Babylon was known as Ishtar's Gate, dedicated, as it was, to the goddess of the eight-pointed star.

So in just that one number, the so-called Doors of Perception are blown off their hinges. It is mathematics combined with poetry. For this reason, a storyteller has to be much more skilled, or at least differently skilled, than a teacher of mathematics. That is why a storyteller as experienced and cunning as Tabiti would have held high status in her tribe. Nowadays, the word "cunning" has connotations of a sly sort of evil. Not so in the past. In ancient Britain, the "cunning folk" were esteemed for their prowess in storytelling and poetry. Cunning then referred to a special and instinctive sort of intelligence that is required to correctly intuit which words, by their sound resonance or song, would be best to use in order to entrance the young along a path of inner transformation that would shape their ideals, ambitions and values forevermore.

These shamanic women would have to tell their stories well because the survival of the tribe depended upon it.

Their tales were sung or recited rhythmically like poems. Even today, shamans like myself communicate with our spirits more through rhyme than through reason and logic. The songs are sung to us in the voices of our ancestors from the Rivers of Blood and, like Jacob in the New Testament, we climb the ladders of the 64 DNA codons in trance to meet them, to receive their guidance and wisdom, and then bring it back to our tribes or communities.

Once a person reaches the shamanic, more right-brained perspective they enter into the consciousness experienced by our ancestors, which at its most ultimate expression is perceived as the whole of the creation singing. It is singing all the time: singing itself into existence with a joyful melody; singing to maintain itself with a lyrical choral symphony and then singing a slow and solemn dirge along the inevitable funeral march to its eventual destruction, death and rebirth.

The ancient Greeks referred to this continual cosmological concert as the Harmony of the Spheres, although these spheres are not to be confused with the planets. They are extra-dimensional bodies arranged in such a way as to create matter.

However, the planets sing too.

Around 530 BCE, the Ionian philosopher Pythagoras proposed that the Sun, Moon and the other planets emit their own vibrational sounds, which are not perceivable by the human ear.

Fast forward to the 21st century and it is clear to us now that planets do create their own "noise", although scientists are doubtful those noises are actually harmonic and only quantum physicists are in any way able to perceive the holographic part of the concept. However, that the music of the spheres is not harmonic is a purely subjective and anthropocentric viewpoint, added to which it is all a matter of subjective perception when the ears of the shaman hears so much more.

Some very good work has been carried out by more enlightened scientists with various plants, who found it possible to record their songs. I wonder if you have heard them? They are excruciatingly awful to the human ear, far worst than nails screeching down a blackboard. But does that mean that we wish the flowers should stop singing themselves into creation? Absolutely not.

Anyway, I think the best way to begin to learn to experience the universal song of creation resonating within and without you, as the shaman does, is to wake up in the morning with the dawn chorus.

The birdsong at dawn is particularly powerful and poignant because it constitutes the holographic rainbow of sound that contains the seed of the promise or the covenant of the New Day.

When we first listen to the dawn chorus, we can only hear the birds chirping away because their sound is on a frequency our ears are able to tune into. But when we learn how to meditate shamanically through a dawn chorus, we hear the whole of creation joining in and realise that even the quartz crystals in the stones of Stonehenge are bursting into a symphony of praise as the new Sun alights on them.

The children's author Kenneth Grahame evoked the magic of the sunrise in his book, *The Wind in the Willows*. I think it's quite the most magical chapter in the book when Toad and Mole discover the Piper at the Gates of Dawn at daybreak.

The same cunning imagery is conjured up by CS Lewis's serpent ship in *The Voyage of the Dawn Treader*, part of his Chronicles of Narnia series. It is a typical hero's sea journey in which he encounters many challenges and adventures that are, in effect, an integral part of a rite of passage that turns him from a child into an adult.

But for our brains to grasp the en-chanted magic of dawn, we have to appreciate the sacred geometry of light that is creating the chanting. Just as in a thunderstorm we see the lightning first, so the sound of the light, in the form of peals of thunder, reaches us several seconds later. In other words, light travels faster than sound but it is part and parcel of the same phenomenon.

In ancient myths, we find a god of thunder – known to the Celts as Taranis and to the Norse as Thor - and that's probably because while, to my experience anyway, in a shamanic state of consciousness thunder can sound like the voice of a god who is loudly instructing his servants to rearrange the elements.

Dawn is no exception; she has a similar, palpable presence to the shaman who experiences her holographically, deep in his inner space, with her long, flowing robes of rose madder, salmon pink, amber and golden yellow that also have a numbered sound frequency, which sing their own tune.

The ancient Greeks knew her as Aurora, while to the Celts she was Andraste. It is said that the female Iceni warrior queen Boudica released a hare to Andraste at daybreak, just before she went into battle against the Romans, in the hope of gaining her promise of victory.

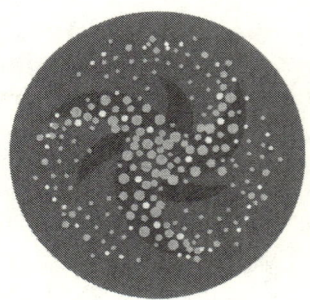

Practical exercise

Attune to the sunrise

So how can we benefit from the promise of the dawn? It has to be experienced subjectively because it is very difficult to find the words to convey her gentle, divine sweetness as she comes tiptoeing through the window at sunrise. Perhaps Dawn is best described as radiating invisible healing vibrations that are only present when her aurora penetrates the land and interacts with the green mantle at sunrise. Once the Sun has fully risen, her vibratory resonances vanish. You have to be up and awake when the night cracks open to reveal that "morning has broken, like the first morning" and "blackbird has spoken, like the first bird", because only the early bird catches the worm!

So next time you wake around sunrise, why not take advantage of this very special time when Dawn is impregnating the land with her innate healing frequencies and vibrations? Throw open your window, then snuggle back under your sheets and just relax, let your mind drift towards the sound resonance of the birdsong that holds all the promise of this new day.

By meditating on the dawn chorus, you will be gradually swept up into a much larger, holographic choir of creation that is being conducted by the Piper at the Gates of Dawn, otherwise known as the Lord of the Animals and the Wildwood. Then you'll realise that it's not just the birds singing; the trees will also be toning their harmonic greetings and even the shy-silken petals of the flowers will be opening in wide-eyed wonder to join in the joyful Hallelujah Chorus that heralds the dayspring.

It is only when I fly into this enchanted, ecstatic symphony that I realise the new day is exactly that – a new day. Whatever the suffering of all previous yesterdays, this day really is a newborn opportunity. It is a time of unique vibratory resonances that have never been birthed before and with it a whole new rainbow of promise, just like the rainbow that God sent to Noah.

Every single day is different because the cantata at sunrise sets the tone and the rhythm for the day with new songs made up of new vibrations, new frequencies and new notes from a composer who is conducting from an infinite musical score and libretto. When you realise, holographically, that you are made of this same pure music too – with your sinews and nerves vibrating, like strings, at different frequencies – then it will feel natural to just relax and allow any out-of-tune parts of yourself to be brought back into harmony by merging yourself in the universal choir.

4. The Fall of Atlantis

THE story of Plato's Atlantis is what's known as a "deluge myth" but before going into its interpretation we need to first understand more about the ancients' use of the word "deluge". For them, it was akin to the word "fall" – to "drop", "tumble down" and "descend" – or as we would use the words "rainfall" or "nightfall". And so by looking at it through that nuanced interpretation, we will come to comprehend much about the multi-layered depth and wisdom underlying our ancestors' thinking.

Modern-day thought tries to persuade us that human life is following a linear line of mounting progression that is shooting ever-upwards. However, there is nothing in Nature that reflects this trajectory; even trees have rings. The concept has no foothold in reality and so to follow it as a guide in devising a map for our lives leads us into no end of trouble and misery. Matter is governed energetically by cycles that spiral vortically. What goes around comes around and that which rises must one day fall.

The much wiser ancients knew that a "fall" always had to come at the end of a natural cycle, whether it's the microcosmic life of a cell that eventually dies if we are not to contract cancer, or the macrocosmic death of a star that one day explodes into trillions of points of light.

Every single part of the natural world, of which we are a part, follows the cycle of rising, maintaining and then falling. Take the Sun, for example. At daybreak, this flaming orb rises against an apricot sky and then climbs higher and higher into the cobalt blue until late afternoon when it begins to set against deep purples and pinks and then eventually falls, like a red ball, behind the black shadowy gloaming, which signals the end of our day and us falling asleep.

However, we do not always fall asleep so easily. Sometimes, we lie taut with tension; we toss and turn because we are torn with conflict. We will not allow ourselves to fall and, yes, maybe to fail, which is another poetically related word – as is fallow. We are like the plate-spinning stage performer. We feel that we have to keep all the plates of our lives spinning and never allow even one of them to crash to the floor. At these times, the ancestors in our Rivers of Blood are singing us a lullaby we cannot hear because we are spiritually deaf to our inner universe that is needing to fall, to drop into the abyss of the night, to lay fallow until daybreak.

We are a holographic part of what needs to descend to complete its cycle and so we can get utterly bent out of shape trying to stop the inevitable from happening - to fall, to fail, just like brown autumn leaves tumble down on to muddy ground during what the Americans call Fall and then, slowly and gradually, throughout the winter months, get trodden underfoot, turning eventually into leaf mould, which fertilises new soil for fresh life to spring forth.

For the purposes of fertility and renewal, falling is such an important part of our human experience and yet we are not taught how to fall – or rest content in being fallow – any more.

Falling in love is another expression we use. I once heard someone ask: "Why do we say 'fall in love' and not 'rise in love'?" Well, it is a fall in the way that the ancients perceived the meaning of that word. Falling in love signifies the end of a cycle because once the magical enchantment of deep love descends upon two people, what usually follows is the end of their lives as they had previously known them. They decide to create a new life, a new world, together, and promise to do so "till death do us part". And when it does part them the tears fall like a deluge because "the day thou gavest, Lord, has ended".

This is the cycle of life and in ancient myths this natural cyclical fall is often represented by a cataclysmic event like a deluge or a flood, which is why there are many references to deluges and falls in dozens of ancient myths from different and diverse civilisations worldwide.

On the macrocosmic level, they are about the cataclysmic falling of an age before the new one rises with the new pole star established on the mound or mountain by the hero who braves the floods of the firmamental waters to separate the land from the sea.

Each new age is marked by a new pole star which changes on a regular cycle known as the precession of the equinoxes, a phenomenon caused by the Earth's axis being tilted. This means that at the beginning of Egypt's Early Dynastic Period about 5,000 years ago, the pole star was alpha Draconis; at the time of the Plato, it was Ursa Minor; today it is Polaris.

The ancient Egyptians, from whom Plato took his story of Atlantis, used the metaphor of the deluge for all sorts of natural cycles. There were deluges of blood, deluges of beer – even a deluge of light that fell at daybreak and a deluge of dark that fell at night.

So when encountering deluge myths, what we're really looking at is a fall of some kind and I believe this is one of the reasons why shamans used lunar calendars, to show them the times of the moult – another kind of fall that is experienced by humans and animals alike. However, the seasonal dropping of hair is soon followed by new growth. In other words, a fall denotes the final stage before rebirth - it is the last part of the creation-maintenance-destruction cycle.

For those who Maya led, it would have been natural to use the idea of a cataclysmic flood as a metaphor for the end of an age. Over hundreds of thousands of years at least, they continually had to decamp and start a new life somewhere else in response to cycles of warming and cooling, and ride ahead of the floods when the glaciers melted.

But did they regard such deluges as some kind of divine retribution and therefore leave us those stories as warnings not to sin? I find that unlikely because until the creation of religions, man didn't know what sin was. It was Christianity that invented the Devil. In any case, the value judgement about what is sinful and what is not changes with the winds. Even during my own lifetime, the "love that dare not whisper its name" is now bellowing it all over town.

The deluge myths that were told around the Elders' campfires were not just simple and straightforward weather warnings. They were much longer tales and more complex, and threaded through with an intricate numerical code. In other words, they were metaphorical stories and used symbolic poetic language designed to help us better understand our lives as human beings here on Earth in a way that I'll explain as we go on.

So let's first go back to the original story about Atlantis, from which all others took their cue. People refer to the Greek Plato as a philosopher but he was primarily a playwright. It's just that all drama back then, around 360 BCE, was no light or frivolous entertainment. It was sacred drama that contained deep philosophical truths. And so the golden skeins of this wisdom was threaded into a play about a mythical empire, known as Atlantis, which was recounted to the audience in a dialogue between two of his characters, Timaeus and Critias.

We learn about Atlantis fourth-hand from his character Critias, who reports what his grandfather had been told by the Greek diplomat Solon, who in turn, apparently, had heard the story of Atlantis from Egyptian priests.

Here's the gist of it:

Solon had said to Critias's grandfather that the priests told him there had been a mighty empire a long time ago that ruled over many lands from an island in the Atlantic Ocean called Atlantis.

Atlantis, he said, had been engineered into concentric rings of alternating water and land, and it had become exceedingly rich through benefitting from its advanced technology. Thus the island boasted an extravagant architecture of bath houses, harbours and barracks. There were also canals on the central plain outside the city that irrigated the land, so there were always plenty to eat.

The island had been built by the god of the sea, Poseidon, for his lover, Cleito, and they had sired 10 sons, who went on to become kings of Atlantis. Under the kings, there was a government that was augmented by a huge and powerful organised military force that was unbeatable.

However, the audience is told, one day Atlantis over-reached itself by waging an unprovoked and imperialistic war on some lands it had not yet conquered, including those of ancient Greece. The Athenians fought back and, amazingly, triumphed over the much bigger and better equipped Atlantean forces, pushing them back. After the battle, the Atlanteans received vengeance from God in the form of earthquakes and floods, and eventually Atlantis disappeared in a great explosion under the waves.

So that's the original story of Atlantis in a nutshell - from which, to me, it's clear Plato was nothing if not a populist playwright. Just like any cunning storyteller, he knew how to engage an audience. His story mirrored back to those seated in the auditorium that they were descended from great heroes – a small but plucky band of Athenian foot soldiers who conquered the whole of the great, evil Atlantean empire, notwithstanding being outnumbered and at the mercy of advanced technological warfare.

On top of that, the Greeks in Plato's audience would have readily identified with such a power-hungry foe; they would still remember the imperial conquests of Persia and Carthage. Plus they would have been only too aware that islands could just explode and then disappear under the sea because there had been a huge volcanic eruption in the second millennium BCE that destroyed the island of Santorini, barely 200 kilometres south-east of Athens. It created a thick, choking black pall of ash and smoke over such a huge distance which lingered for a long time, making it almost an extinction event in that part of the world. It is thought to have destroyed the Minoan civilisation and caused turmoil in Egypt. So many people died and they took with them the knowledge of the Mysteries, which, at that time, had not been recorded in writing – and this gave rise, eventually, to the ignorance of the Dark Ages.

In other words, Plato gave his audience a thrilling and inspiring plotline that they could relate to and would ensure plenty of bums of seats – which is not a bad thing in itself so long as there is a Mystery teaching story buried in it somewhere. But was Plato just seducing the Athenians to watch his play so that it could become a money-spinning blockbuster? Or was he more intent on entrancing them into his tale so that they would subconsciously receive the hidden messages contained in the metaphors? As is so often the case in life, it was probably a mixture of both although he may not even have been aware of the deeper understory of the deluge myth long after even the Egyptians had forgotten it themselves. But with Atlantis perceived to be under the ocean, along with its advanced technology, it was the perfect candidate for the location of a Mystery plot.

However, all of that need not deter us from looking for the hidden clues in this play, because they are not buried under the Aegean Sea of the outer world but in the firmamental deeps of our own inner consciousness. In fact, in trying to understand the sacred geometrical subtext in deluge myths, I think that Atlantis, just like all Egyptian myths, is a good place to start because it offers a most comprehensive vault of data on this whole subject.

So let's begin by going through a portal into the Other Worlds.

Plato's audience had been told that the moats and canals of Atlantis were surrounding and protecting a mountain that had been carved into a palace by the god of the sea, Poseidon, for his lover Cleito. Their lovers' trysts on Atlantis had led to the births of five sets of twin boys, all of whom became gods in their own right. One of them, Atlas, went on to become king of Atlantis and in other myths he is the god condemned by Zeus to hold up the whole universe on his shoulders. When you learn more about the heroes of the deluge, as you will throughout this chapter, you will hopefully, like me, realise that Atlas was in fact another version of the pole star hero.

Anyway, the Egyptian priests had apparently told Solon that seafarers in those long-ago days would find Atlantis by navigating through the two Pillars of Hercules.

So where are they?

We see these two Pillars of Hercules again and again in religious iconography, for instance in the Temple of Sol-Ammon as Boaz and Jachim, and at Tyre, Byblus, Paphos, and Telloh. In shrines dedicated to Astarte, the two pillars are represented by two ash trees standing guard either side of the doorway. But perhaps the oldest version is found in the Sumerian two-pillared gateway to heaven, in the tale of the hero-initiate Adapa, which is guarded by the two serpents Tammuz and Gishzida.

In my experience, when we meet the dual pillars in ancient sagas, we are being invited to cross through some sort of portal – in other words, to leave the everyday world behind. It's the same dramatic or literary device used by today's storytellers when they start with: "Once upon a time, long, long, long ago, deep in the mists of the time." In other words, it is a coded signal to the listener that they should suspend their left-side brain and its logical judgment because they will now be entering another world with different rules. At the beginning of most films, these days, we're presented with a night sky of twinkling stars or the Moon reflecting on rippling water… it is another version of the same device.

In Renaissance literature, the two pillars were said to bear the legend NEC PLUS ULTRA (also NON PLUS ULTRA, meaning "nothing further beyond"), which was the equivalent of "Enter at your peril" for sailors and navigators.

In the 14th-century divine comedy of Dante Alighieri, the hero Odysseus justifies risking his crew's lives by going through into NEC PLUS ULTRA or the Pillars of Hercules, insisting that it is only the true explorer who dares to venture where others fear to tread in their quest for knowledge. After passing through the Pillars of Hercules and after a further five months at sea – the same time Noah's Ark was afloat - Odysseus sights the mountain of Purgatory or the Underworld.

In another Greek myth, Jason's ship the Argos has to pass safely through the two pillars of clashing rocks known as the Symplegades in his quest for the Golden Fleece, which is a sort of Holy Grail. The same device is used by Lewis Carroll when he has Alice fall down a rabbit hole into Wonderland and then, in his next book, step through a mirror into another world.

So now we have understood the doorway through the gates of perception, let's look at the word Atlantis itself.

The ancient Egyptians had no use for the letter L but in an oral tradition, where stories are passed on from mouth to ear, words have a habit of morphing to suit the teller's dialect. And so it is likely that the L was probably transliterated into Atlantis later on, by the Greeks, and it would have started off something like Atrantus.

Atrantus is a compound word that comes from the Egyptian for "water" and "water boundary" – "atr" meant "flood of water and "antu" meant "boundary", "limit", "division of land". In other words, "atr-antu" or Atrantus referred to an island of engineered waterways like canals and moats, just as Plato had described Atlantis.

The bricks of Atlantis were red, white and black; these colours will mean more as metaphors once we get into the chapters about alchemy.

The Egyptians, long before Plato had lived, had marked out the heavens above in "nomes", or departments, that were mirrored in the divisions of their town planning below. Poetically speaking, it was how they brought the stars down to Earth. The priests who studied the nomes in the astral space above were called astronomers. There were seven nomes and each of these was represented above by one of the seven pole stars atop a mound or mountain. The astronomers knew that, because of the precession of the equinoxes, the pole star changes roughly every 3,714 years. So the "sinking" of the pole star under the firmamental waters was an integral part of the story of the hero in the ark/barque who braves the floods of the Milky Way in order to separate the land from the water in the form of a mound or mountain, and then raise up the new pole like a flag of victory, signalling a new age.

The symbol of the mound or mountain in the story of Noah's ark is Mount Ararat, where the ark finally comes to rest. In the Vedic flood myth, the ark comes to rest on Mount Meru; in Babylonian myths, it is Mount Nizir and in the Egyptian, it is Mount Hetep. (You can find more flood myths from around the world in **Appendix A: Flood Myths from Around the World**, at the end).

So in other words, most cultures had the same or very similar story but whether it is coming from the Hebrew *Genesis*, the Sumerian *Enuma Elish*, the Norse *Edda*, the first cantos of the *Indian Srimad Bhagavatham*, the Mayan calendar or the Egyptian Ark of Nnu, all creation myths are set across Three Worlds and they usually start and end with a flood in the Heavens, otherwise known as the Upper World, as a metaphor for the End of Times and the Beginning of Times, and marked by the old pole star drowning under the deluge or fall, then being raised by a great hero who separates the land from the waters by engineering "atr-antu" around the mound or mountain to make way for a new age or new life, just as Poseidon does for Cleito and, later, their son Atlas.

But the whole of this story takes place not just in this one world, or one dimension; it is spread across the Three Worlds.

The Upper World of the ancient Egyptians was known as Aarru, this world of the Earth was called Seb and the Underworld or Lower World was known as Amenta.

To the Celts, the Upper World was Gwynvyd, this Earth of the Middle World was Abred and the Underworld was Annwn.

To the Norse peoples, these dimensions were known respectively as Asgard, Midgard and Hel. And I think you'll be pleased to know that there is nothing hellish about Hel – that was the product of a later Christian gloss.

The Three Worlds come from shamanism, which is not a New Age belief system but a holographic experience that is in fact Old Age - older than the hills. Within shamanic consciousness, the Three Worlds are ever present and exist parallel to this one, the only difference being that in the other worlds, time does not exist. They are the realms of eternity and infinity. They are parallel universes. And it was within those vast and timeless extra-dimensional landscapes and starscapes that our storytelling ancestors, like Tabiti, used the stars above to stage their sacred dramas.

Shamans then would have entered into the Three Worlds just as a shaman does today, through the imagination or the Nation of Images. The Imagi-Nation is the nation or realm of images that is accessed through the right-hand hemisphere of the brain, where thoughts manifest as images and symbols. As the saying goes, a picture is worth a thousand words. This means that these images and symbols are highly effective conduits for transmitting dense terabytes of data from the spirits.

I would also venture to suggest that so-called creation myths should really be called creation-maintenance-destruction myths, as reflected in triumvirate Indian gods such as Brahma the creator god, Vishnu the maintainer god and Shiva, the god of destruction. This is because the ancients had a holographic view of cosmological processes. Thus, they showed in their stories how the microcosm within the macrocosm was continually birthing, dying and then being reborn again, from the smallest atom to the largest galaxy. When a pole star fell under the flood, it fell within their deeper consciousness too.

Even in the most mundane sense, the waters are a key feature of any nativity. For instance, when a new human is about to arrive, the first sign that the birth is imminent is when the mother's waters "break". The amniotic sac splits, causing its milky fluids to flood out. Or, at the beginning of a new menstrual cycle, the woman's womb sheds its lining, like a snake sheds its skin. In the same way, a flood in mythology signifies a new creation or new life. However, because creation comes at the end of a previous and dying cosmological cycle, these mythological floods are associated with the death at the Fall, as well as the subsequent rebirth.

Our forebears based their cosmological stories and teachings on the alchemically-observed principle that everything in Nature processes around some sort of pole or nucleus, beginning with the smallest building block of matter, the atom, with its electrons circling the nucleus, and then progressing right up to the planets which circle the Sun, and even beyond that. Viewed holographically, this is known as the microcosm within the macrocosm.

The ancient Egyptians wanted to reflect these principles in their engineering feats. So they mapped out the River Nile to follow the course of the Milky Way, which, in their perception, was the white, lactic course of the amniotic fluid of the creation. Just like the deluge of the pole star hero, the Nile below flooded with periodic regularity to produce the black, fertile soil these people depended on for growing crops. Thus their storytellers told tales about the Milky Way being ruled by a cobra-headed fertility and "food-giving" goddess named Renenet.

So in the story of Atlantis we come across the familiar mythological themes of a mountain island carved out of the female fertility goddess's birth waters by a god – in other words, the lovers, Poseidon and Cleito - to conceive five sets of twins, one of which was the great pole star hero, Atlas.

In the system of alchemy and astrology that came out of Alexandria towards the end of the Age of Aries – which would have influenced Plato - the Milky Way was crossed, as a circle, with the circle of the zodiac and thus many of the sacred dramas mirrored this fluid, ever-changing relationship.

This is why, to my way of seeing things, Atlantis is continually being drowned and rising again in our lives, in continual life-death-rebirth cycles of the microcosm within the macrocosm.

Every night, Atlantis goes under and then rises up again, in the fertile river of the Milky Way, which seems to move around the Heavens throughout the year, appearing to undulate like a serpent because of the tilt of the Earth. And those with the eyes to see can look up at the celestial Nile and witness a continual fertility dance of the god and goddess of the waters – Poseidon and Cleito – in their never-ending celebration of life, death and rebirth.

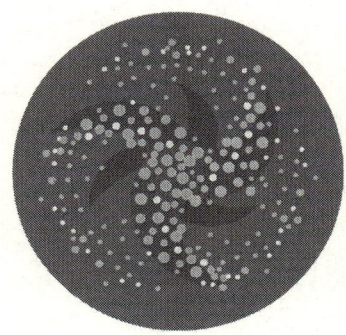

Practical exercise
Fall into the Well of Tears

My spirits have had to teach me how to fall and fail. When I first started in shamanism, I was so much a product of the modern world that my consciousness was ingrained with the need for "positive thinking" and "keeping a stiff upper lip" no matter how bad things got! But the trouble with positive thinking is that sometimes, equally, you need a negative mood to fall, just as much as night falls after day and yin needs to be balanced with yang.

So nowadays, I find it useful to practice "falling", from time to time, and I achieve this by getting in contact with my inner Well of Tears.

We all have this well – and the longer we've lived, the deeper it is, as we've given the span of human existence plenty of opportunities to fail us, or at least to not meet our expectations. But I'm also using the word "well" poetically, in this case, because water is associated with emotion, and releasing a flood or deluge of tears out of love and compassion for ourselves can do wonders for our progress.

I once had a guru who said there are as many different kinds of tears as there are stars in the sky. Well, that might have been an exaggeration, for effect. But anyway, what I think he he meant was there is a multitude of different catalysts for tears. There is a whole gamut of feelings that run from ecstasy to agony, from joy to grief and from laughter to compassion, and each of those feelings gives the tears their own specific spiritual "flavour". He said tears which fall on to the

Earth that come from genuine love and compassion move mountains.

I feel those mountains move inside of me when I practise this technique and I sense the Underworld smith god, who lives deep within their dark caves forging my magical sword of higher intellect and greater wisdom.

So I want to share that technique with you:

1. Just find a comfortable position where you can be alone for a space of time and then breathe softly and regularly until the ripples of your mind become more still.

2. Then imagine the last time you were disappointed by life. It might be just a small let-down – being passed over for a job or promotion, for instance, or not being asked out by the one you'd hoped liked you as much as you liked them. You might think that compared to great cosmological realisations, these are petty-fogging concerns. They may be, or they may not be. It doesn't matter. Superficial dashed hopes are useful tools for starting to dig the well because they're the simplest to get hold of. You have to go for the "digger" that's on top, however big or small it is.

3. Once you've found your digger, plunge down deep into your well of memories and then relive what happened and how it made you feel. Be realistic. Don't tell yourself glossy magazine stories to try to make it all alright. If you experience a kind of sinking feeling within your stomach or belly, that's a good sign it's working. We don't want any positive thinking in this work because it would just get in the way. Please do feel as miserable as you like. Go ahead – fill your boots! No-one here is going to judge you.

4. If your chest starts to become more concave, that may be because you're no longer feeling the need to thrust it out in a show of false bravado, which fools no-one but ourselves anyway.

5. If it hurts, don't stop. It merely means your sword of wisdom is being forged from your pain by the Underworld smith god. If you follow the Celtic tradition, it will be Gofannon. In the Norse tradition, he is Thor. To the ancient Greeks, he was Hephaestus. In Saxon myths, he was Wayland the Smith.

6. Sometimes, I hit a layer of anger that is covering the pain of the disappointment itself. If it burns, don't worry. That's just the smith putting your metal into the fire to melt so that he can work it into a sword.

7. If you start to shake or tremble, it might be because he is now pounding the metal flat with a hammer.

8. Let the tears fall free. That's just the smith whetting or sharpening your inner sword on his whetstone. Don't hold back.

9. If your tears are salty, that's your inner celestial ocean of the Milky Way flooding and overflowing down your cheeks with love and gratitude for its release.

10. Stay in this experience for as long as you want to and play with it in your own imagination, allowing symbols to come to you with judgement. Above all, let feelings of love and compassion for yourself to flow forth in that situation. As my guru said, tears that come from love and compassion are the most powerful.

11. When you are ready, slowly bring yourself out, back into the outer world. Sit and enjoy the feeling of "fallowness" for as long as you like. You should soon feel better and your mind and intellect will be a lot clearer.

12. Don't forget to give thanks to the Underworld smith god for all his help and next time you look up at the Milky Way above, express your gratitude there too. As Above, So Below.

Please use your own discretion with how much pain you "dig up" at one sitting and how often you do this exercise. You will probably find, as I do, that unprocessed bad memories tend to pile up on top of each other, each bit clinging on the last. So it can be like – sorry to mix metaphors! – when you're clearing thorns out of the garden. You tug on one and it brings up half-a-dozen others with it. Only you know your limits.

5. The Serpent and the World Tree

I SOMETIMES think of myself as a dowser of song lines and story lines because, just like those whose sixth senses tell them whenever an energetic dragon is snaking beneath their feet under the land, so I have to use my instincts to sense when and where it's worth getting out my spade in the mytho-poetic landscape through sensing that buried treasure lies below.

In that way, I'm a sort of story archaeologist, digging underneath the rotting story mats of the wandering troubadours and tale-tellers of old and searching for the original myths from which present-day stories and belief structures derive. And I have found that once you get down deep enough, what finally emerges is not just another muddy, tattered rug but a richly woven carpet depicting remarkably similar tales and sagas, with just small local differences, that must have been spread, many ages ago, all over the northern hemisphere.

The slight changes in the design of the weave and the patterning of the carpet depend upon where you are. Some are more in the style of a classical Persian rug, or a tightly woven Balkan *kilim* or an Indian jute *dhurri*; other parts of the carpet are of spun Chinese silk, or Irish linen, or Indonesian *ikat* tie-dye, or embroidered like a Bayeux tapestry, and so on.

However, whatever their stylistic variations, they all seem to be part of one worldwide carpet that is designed to depict remarkably similar stories. This is hardly surprising when you understand that ancient myths are stories that contain allegories and metaphors for cosmological truths our ancestors drew out in glittering celestial vault and that everyone looked up at the stars.

I call this deepest underlayer the "primordial carpet".

I'm hoping, now that you are this far into the book, that you're realising this form of storytelling was not just an idle pastime of the wandering nomadic tribes of Kroy's and Tabiti's times. They composed their sagas in the eternal stars because in the geometries they beheld there they found an eternal message that

73

had, at its core, the human being as a holographic part of a multi-dimensional universe and all that that entails.

I am going to explain to you, as this book unfolds, how you can begin to understand that cosmological concept and, even more importantly, learn how you can use it to deepen and enrich your own life. But first of all, in Parts 1 and 2, I am establishing the building blocks that will give you a firm cognitive foundation from which to proceed. And in this chapter, I'm going to be talking about the esoteric meaning of a very important character: the wily serpent.

The ubiquitous ophidian, in various forms, seems to turn up and slither through almost every heroic saga of antiquity. The flood, deluge or fall myths usually feature a huge and monstrous multi-headed water serpent the hero must battle and overcome in order to separate the water from the land and then engineer the *atr-antu*, the water border, by building a mound or mountain to support the newly erected pole.

What actually floods is the Milky Way; not the one we look up at but the one we sink down into when we enter the Underworld. You may have heard the expression as above, so below. Its most esoteric meaning is how the outer world mirrors the inner world. And so in old deluge myths, when it is time for the old pole star to die, it goes under the firmamental flood. The flood is being caused by the serpent that had swallowed or in some way dammed up the waters and is now releasing them. It is the role of the stellar hero, then, to bring order out of that watery chaos. That is why most deluge myths worldwide feature gods and heroes battling terrifying water serpents, such as the Greek Zeus versus Typhon, the Vedic Indra versus Vritra, the Egyptian Ra versus Apep, the Indian Ram versus Ravana, the Babylonian Marduk versus Tiammat, the Norse Thor versus the Midgard Serpent or Jörmungandr and Hercules versus Ladon.

The serpent theme can be traced back to the times of Kroi, Tabitia and Maya, to the days when the mile-high blue-white ice covered much of the northern hemisphere, causing many tribes of the Caucasus region to migrate into Europe over several waves, which began at least 33,000 years ago. Some of these tribes were the Serpent Peoples, otherwise known as the Sarmatians. They were known to the Greek "father of history" Herodotus as the Sauromatae, or the Lizard People, for their banners and flags emblazoned with their tribe's totem animal, the coiled serpent.

W. Winwood Reade writes in *The Veil of Isis*:

There is scarcely a spot in the world in which the serpent has not received the prayers and praises of men...the winged serpent was a symbol of the gods of Egypt, Phoenicia, China, Persia, and Hindustan. The Tartar princes still carry the image of a serpent upon a spear as their military standard.

Almost all the runic inscriptions found upon tombs are engraved upon the sculptured forms of serpents. In the Roman temple of the B*ona Dea*, serpents were tamed and consecrated. In the Mysteries of Bacchus, women used to carry serpents in their hands and twined around their brows, and with horrible screams cry, *eva! eva!*

In the great temple of Mexico, the captives taken in war and sacrificed to the Sun had wooden collars in the shape of a serpent put round their necks. and water-snakes are to this day held sacred by the natives of the Friendly Isles. It was not only worshipped as a symbol of light, of wisdom and of health, personified under the name of a god, but also as an organ of divination.

The snake shedding its skin was also used as a symbol of the completion of a cosmological cycle, or death-and-rebirth and thus fertility.

However, the serpent is conspicuous by its absence in the Hebrew deluge myth about Noah's Ark. It might be because it comes from a much older story that has become fragmented. So to find out where the Old Testament flood saga comes from, we need to go back to the Garden of Eden.

There is a small stone cylinder seal in the British Museum that is Babylonian in origin and dated to between 2200 and 2100 BCE. It is known as the Adam and Eve cylinder seal because it is engraved with two seated humans of indeterminate gender either side of a palm tree, and a serpent. One of the human figures is horned, which was the symbolic headdress for a god or goddess in those days.

Experts tell us that the god/goddess-human-tree-serpent imagery appears to have bee very popular at the time, as many have been discovered in Mesopotamian region.

So I believe this cylinder seal gives us a big clue to the meaning of a original Adam and Eve story before it was bastardised and broken up for propaganda purposes by the rabbinic scribes. It seems that the narrative of Genesis served well to promote the concept of Original Sin and then to divide the "sons of Cain" from the "sons of Abel" (Sunnis and Shi'ites) until Mark II Abrahamism was invented in the form of Christianity as a means to bind the Roman empire with a fresh story that relied upon the literal murder on a cross of a mythological Sun god to create Original Sin Redux.

However, what is often not often understood about evil is that it is rarely spiritual and it is almost always political. Our manipulators use scriptural texts to win us over to their viewpoint because these stories are most effective carriers, with their primal morphologies and devices containing secret messages that only our subconscious minds recognise, thus making us more amenable to their political narratives, while the "devils" in these stories are no more real than Voldemort or Sauron.

False prophets, phoney priests, specious *saddhus* and mendacious magicians have long been employed by kings and presidents alike to stoke up revolutions and wars by claiming that the "other side" are following demons while "we", on the other hand, "have God on our side". Every army that ever goes into battle believes it will win by Divine Right because it receives that psychological conditioning back in the barracks. Maybe if soldiers were not able to hold to that faith they would not fight and there would be no more wars. Most people would never dream of killing one another unless they were stoked up by these false ideas and fantasies. Wars are not commonly the fault of the common people, even though the common people can often be easily persuaded to form the "cannon fodder", mainly because we are no longer taught how to read myths. In other words, we are not trained in how to discern the multi-layered metaphors, symbols and allegories of the wise serpent teachers of the past.

So how can we untangle the threads, and separate and smooth out the skeins of the original star story from the artfully twisted Gordian Knots of various political imperatives over thousands of years? We have to study the primordial carpet through a shamanic, multi-dimensional lens.

Anyway, before we go back in time to discover the real identity of the "evil serpent", let's just remind ourselves of the story of Adam and Eve from the book of Genesis.

Here's a quick synopsis:

At the beginning of time, God plants a garden in the east, in Eden, and he fashions a man, Adam, to tend the garden. He tells him: "You are free to eat from any tree in the garden, but you must not eat from the Tree of the Knowledge of Good and Evil, for when you eat from it you will certainly die."

Then God decides to give Adam a woman helper, which he fashioned from one of Adam's ribs while he slept. Adam names her Eve and, from then on, the couple happily tend the garden together, naked.

However, one day Eve meet the serpent in the garden, who, we are told, is more wily than any other animal "in the field". He persuades Eve that she will not die from eating the fruit from the Tree of the Knowledge of Good and Evil, "for God knows that when you eat from it, your eyes will be opened and you will be like God, knowing good and evil".

Thus persuaded, Eve picks a fruit and eats it. After that, she takes some to give to her husband, Adam, who also eats it. Then, Genesis tells us "the eyes of both of them were opened, and they realised they were naked. So they sewed fig leaves together and made coverings for themselves".

Later on, though, God finds them and when he sees they are garbed in fig leaves, he is not pleased. "Who told you that you were naked?" he asks. "Have you eaten from the tree that I commanded you not to eat from?"

Eve admits that was the case, saying: "The serpent deceived me, and I ate."

Upon hearing this, God flies into a fury and he curses Adam and Eve and their descendents to lives upon lives of painful toil, and then banishes them for ever from the Garden of Eden.

So first of all, where does that *Genesis* story come from?

It is believed that the first book of the *Old Testament* was compiled from a body of myths collated and edited by scribes who lived from about the time of King Hezekiah to that of Ezra the Scribe – 715 to 440 BCE - and they were based on the much older stories of the Egyptians and Babylonians, which, in turn, were bastardised by Alexander the Great's men.

So let's go on a magical mystery tour of the primordial carpet, taking in Egypt and Babylon, but with the first port of call being the clay-red and black geometrically-designed, labyrinthine meander borders at the Aegean Sea.

As we have already discussed, the Greeks at the time of Plato used secret word ciphers, as well as number codes, to hide the meanings of the stories from the uninitiated. So, for instance, while to the ordinary market trader in the streets of Athens "melon" meant "fruit", to the astronomer priests it was secret word for "stars" and "knowledge of the stars".

Greek myths feature a Garden of the Hesperides that contains an orchard of trees bearing golden apples (melons or stars) which was guarded by a wise or wily serpent called Ladon, which Hercules, as part of his Twelve Labours, ends up slaying.

E. Valentia Straiton writes in *The Celestial Ship of the North*.

A symbol of sacred knowledge in antiquity was a tree, ever guarded by a serpent, the serpent or dragon of wisdom. The serpent of Hercules was said to guard the golden apples that hung from the pole, the Tree of Life, in the midst of the Garden of Hesperides. The serpent that guarded the golden fruit... and the serpent of the Garden of Eden... are the same.

Further, the Hebrew Tree of Life, or Tree of Knowledge of Good and Evil, must have been derived from the World Tree that features in so many cultures throughout the world and which confers immortality on those who use it as an *axis mundi* to journey up and down, in trance, and visit the Three Worlds – in other words, the shamans.

Mircae Eliade, the late professor of the history of religion at Harvard University, collated the reports of anthropologists who had interviewed shamans all over the Earth at the turn of the 19th century and found many commonalities in their experiences. However, it was a complete mystery to less-enlightened cademics why, say, a shaman in Australia reported such similar experiences in trance to one in Africa, when they had never met. But it's hardly surprising when you realise that they were all visiting the same timeless dimensions in trance, and it was their stories gained by "flying" up and down the Three Realms of the World Tree that gave rise to the primordial carpeting of wisdom, wall-to-wall across the Earth.

In his book *Shamanism: The Archaic Techniques of Ecstasy*, Eliade says of the descendants of Tabiti and Maya's people:

The Goldi, the Dolgan and the Tungus say that, before souls come into incarnation, they perch as children on the branches of the Cosmic Tree and the shamans go to find them and bring them through the portal. This mythical motif is not confined to Central and North Asia; it is attested, for example, in Africa and Indonesia. The cosmological schema Tree-Bird (or Eagle), or Tree with a Bird at its top and a Snake at its roots, although typical of the peoples of Central Asia and the ancient Germans, is presumably of Caucasian origin, while the same symbolism is found on prehistoric monuments.

So please bear this in mind as we step carefully through this tangled and overgrown garden until we reach the Tree of Knowledge of Good and Evil and the wily serpent there.

In the Genesis story, the name Adam is translated as "man", although one of the figures on the Mesopotamian cylinder seal is horned and thus obviously a god or goddess. Eve, we're told, meant merely "helper to man" but...

The figure of Eve is based upon much a much older mythological character who can be traced back to the ancient Mother Goddess or World Mother of the serpent cults of the pre-Biblical period. Closer examination of the name "Eve" reveals her serpent origins, for the Hebrew for Eve is *havvah*, meaning "mother of all things", but also "serpent". Likewise, the Arabic words for "snake", "life", and "teaching" are closely related to the word or name "Eve". – *Philip Gardiner and Gary Osborn in The Serpent Grail.*

We have already met the Mother of All Things in the Egyptian mythos, the cobra-headed Renenet who ruled the deluge in the Milky Way. There is also a Norse fertility goddess named Iðunn (pronounced Iden or Eden) who carried a box of apples that conferred immortality upon the eater. In other words, the box was a metaphor for knowledge of the stars.

Are you beginning to see the primordial carpet now? Right, I'll get the hoover out...

Have you ever looked up to the night skies around the Spring Equinox and seen a long wriggling serpent? You can't really miss it; it is so huge it takes up a quarter of the starry vault. This great serpent was known to the Greeks as Hydra and as the name implies, it was a water serpent.

Around the times when the aforementioned cylinder seal was so popular, the stars above were known to the Babylonians as the Celestial Ocean (the Abzu) and they named this great snake in the skies MUL.APIN, which simply means "serpent". The serpent's head was at the constellation of Leo and his tail dangled down and slightly to the west of Virgo and the Autumn Equinox.

The wise serpent god Enki (also known as Ea) was honoured in ancient Sumer; plaques show him depicted as a half-man, half-serpent creature that lived in the Abzu Underworld, and he was associated with wisdom and fertility. In stories about him, the association is made specifically between his life-giving semen and the waters.

In the Genesis story about the serpent that tempts Eve, the creature is called "the wiliest beast in the field". This has been interpreted as sly, which is one the adverse connotations of being cunning. However, it is just a play on the word; originally, the serpent was the wisest in his field and this connection between serpents and wisdom may be why the teachers of the Mysteries were also known as serpents.

So the wise, half-serpent Enki was the good god in the Sumerian flood myth who persuaded Ziusudra to build a great ark, to save his people from the vast floods that were being sent by Enki's brother, Enlil, who was angry at humanity. (This Sumerian deluge myth is thought to be the oldest one, and you can find it in **Appendix A**.)

In ancient Egypt, the cobra-headed "food-giving" fertility goddess Renenet was considered to be a wet-nurse to the baby pharaohs. They regarded her as a prime source of nourishment as the goddess who releases the flood from the Milky Way. The Egyptians believed that Renenet visited young women at the time of their "change", when their wombs shed their linings just as a snake sheds its skin. The snake was associated with rejuvenation and rebirth that came at the end of a cycle, signified by the fall of the womb's lining. In fact, this idea of reptilian visitation during the rite of passage into womanhood came from much older African tribal stories that sometimes exchanged the snake for a frog or a lizard as totem animals of fertility, which explains all those fairytales about princesses kissing frogs.

It is my view that the *New Testament* visitation of Gabriel to Mary and Elizabeth, which led to the birth of the sons, Jesus and John the Baptist, was a bastardisation of a story that originally came from serpent lore. Gabriel is portrayed as a messenger of God and all messengers in mythology are associated with the Greeks' wing-footed Hermes, which means "phallic". The Caduceus symbol, a short winged staff entwined by two serpents, belonged to Hermes but it can also be traced back thousands of years to the Sumerian Ningishzida, which translates to "lord of the good tree". We find Ningishzida portrayed on Sumerian libation vases as either a serpent with the head of a man or a double-headed serpent coiled into a double helix, the latter symbol reminding us of twin strands of DNA that represent the continuation of life or, in other words, fertility.

So I hope it is now becoming clear how dragons, serpents, trees and water are associated, on the mythological carpet, with fertility and sacred sex rites that are, in turn, connected with Virgo, who, if you go back far enough, was no virgin!

The brightest star of the Virgo constellation is called Spica. Spica translates in Greek to "ear of wheat", which is an ancient euphemism for "vagina" or "furrow". There's a fair bit of "ploughing of furrows" in the more erotic Sumerian texts and the ploughing of the land ready for the new seeding would be timed to the rising of the constellation of the Plough itself, meaning "penis" in that language.

For instance, there is a beautifully erotic song from that period about Inanna (the precursor to Ishtar) and her lover, Dumuzi. He represents the herdsman archetype and is also referred to as a wild bull and as a shepherd. The shepherd's crook is an image that has persisted to this day as a requisite accoutrement and symbol of leadership for religious heads. However, all leadership symbols, back then, were earned through the firing of the upper brain centres during sexual initiation in the arms of a hierodule, or sacred prostitute, who was shamanically connected to Inanna, Ishtar and Isis, to name a few of these erotically sensuous Grail protectors.

Here is Inanna's song to Dumuzi as he lays upon her bed:

My vulva, the horn,
The Boat of Heaven,
Is full of eagerness like the young moon.
My untilled land lies fallow.
As for me, Inanna,
Who will plough my vulva?
Who will plough my high field?
Who will plough my wet ground?
As for me, the young woman,
Who will plough my vulva?
Who will station the ox there?
Who will plough my vulva?
I bathed for the wild bull,
I bathed for the shepherd Dumuzi,
I perfumed my sides with ointment,
I coated my mouth with sweet-smelling amber
I painted my eyes with kohl.
He shaped my loins with his fair hands,
The shepherd Dumuzi filled my lap with cream and milk

> He stroked my pubic hair,
> He watered my womb.
> He laid his hands on my holy vulva,
> He smoothed my black boat with cream
> He quickened my narrow boat with milk,
> He caressed me on the bed.
> Now I will caress my high priest on the bed,
> I will caress the faithful shepherd Dumuzi,
> I will caress his loins, the shepherd ship of the land,
> I will decree a sweet fate for him.

Flying further north-west on the primordial carpet, we come to the swirling, gold-threaded knotwork stories of the Celts in which the same Plough is operated by Hu Gardarn. And so, when we are looking for poetic meaning as much as literal, we must pay close attention to the similar-sounding words for story elements that are in the same part of the sky - as in guardian, garden and Gardarn.

In the Celtic Welsh language, garden is gardd, guard is gwarchod and guardian is gwarcheidwadd. Travelling further on, into the icy north where the spirals become more runic, the suffix "gards" of the Norse Upper World and Middle World – respectively Asgard and Midgard - also meant "garden".

In the old Germanic myths, the dragon or serpent is a watch-keeper, a guardian, a vigilant warder of treasure. We see him in J R R Tolkien's dragon Smaug that guards the treasure of the smith gods, otherwise known as the Dwarves of Erebor in the Grey Mountains.

In *Sky Dragons and Celestial Serpents*, Alastair McBeath writes:

The spring or well guardian is a traditional dragon or serpent role of antiquity, plus the appearance of Hydra's head and body over the eastern horizon in the evening sky could be taken as a sign that the Sun was entering the region of the Upper Waters, bringing rain to fertilise the Earth for the new growing season. Hydra might thus be seen as guarding that important facet of the sky's activities in influencing human affairs.

Well, yes ... but it's about much more than just being able to predict the weather and the seasons. The water serpent is a symbol for the guardian that guards a garden of apples (knowledge of the stars) with his tail dangling down in the vicinity of the constellation of Virgo. This is why the teachers of the knowledge of the stars were known as serpents.

The motif of the serpent in sacred art and architecture worldwide goes back at least as far as the Bronze Age (3000–1200 BCE) and they are found worldwide as guardians in temple architecture and myths. There are too many to list them all here but, for instance, there are the hooded *nagas* protecting Angkor in Cambodia and in the Indian *Srimad Bhagavatham*, a Renenet-like cobra guards the baby Krishna in his crib.

So we can hazard an educated guess that the serpent also featured in much older star stories that Kroy-Khasis would have heard around the campfire, which were about the importance of sacred sex rites to fertility and wisdom, represented by the golden apples or knowledge of the stars jealously guarded by the wily serpent we know today as Hydra.

It seems highly likely to me that the melon or apple that grew on Genesis's Tree of Knowledge of Good and Evil was a metaphor for "knowledge of the stars" and that its Tree of Life was the ubiquitous World Tree, found in every culture worldwide.

I would then interpret the engraving on the so-called Adam and Eve cylinder as an Akkadian version of the Egyptian cobra-headed, melon-giving Renenet of the female menarche and wet-nurse of pharoahs, shown in both her human and zoomorphic form. It follows then, that the other figure in that illustration is a human about to receive sexual initiation. The image could have even been used in sacred rituals which, if we go by the fertility rites of the Mystery Groves of ancient Eleusis, would have taken place on the Autumn Equinox at the time of Virgo.

There was a clear association in the minds of our ancestors with serpents, wisdom, sacred sex and fertility because of their holographic understanding about how the creation regenerates itself. Sadly, the connection between the serpent and sex rites has been largely lost and buried because of the prurience of those responsible for translating the myths and preserving ancient lore. There are amusing anecdotes about the Victorian Egyptologists sawing off the huge erect penises of the statues of ithyphallic gods like Min before bringing them back to British museums. There are also some *lacunas* – gaps in the narrative – on the Sumerian clay tablets where, I would hazard an educated guess, the hero receives sexual initiation.

One assumes that these explorers would have preferred us to believe that our ancestors never had sex – or if they did, that it was of so little importance to them that they did not include it in their stories. This has created a huge *lacuna* in our understanding about what the stories meant and, probably for that reason, many today who are conditioned by a Western scientific viewpoint assume that the natural world just grows automatically, all by itself. While they may understand that Spring brings the leaves and flowers that fruit and then the leaves fall in the Autumn, they do not perceive Nature as needing any further help other than the odd judicious spadeful of manure.

As we learned from Inanna's song to Dumuzi, there has long been another kind of "manure" or "living waters" which are created by shamans in sacred sex rites. This more holographic approach to creation and re-creation is best depicted by the ancient Egyptian image of the coiled serpent eating its own tail, known as the Ouroboros. In devouring itself continually, the serpent gains enough nutrition to keep itself alive and so it goes on and on, in ever-repeating cycles of creation.

Shamanic sexual practices are an offering to the gods or the spirits with whom shamans make love and, together in this way, the Ages continue to turn on the Wheel and the world is able to regenerate itself.

My book *Reclaiming Sovereignty* goes into a lot more detail about how we find evidence of these sacred sex rites going far back into history and it also explains how shamans practice it today. It was the first book of its kind and so, as with all cutting-edge material, it has been treated gingerly. But now the world of archaeology is catching up. It has recently been discovered that many sacred megalithic circles like Stonehenge were built for the purpose of sacred sex rites thousands of years ago.

According to the archaeologist Professor Terence Meaden, the builders of Stonehenge and other megalithic circles had created a "play without words", in which one special stone casts a growing phallic shadow. This long, thin *umbra* would have penetrated an egg-shaped monument before hitting a central "female" stone that symbolised fertility and abundance.

Meaden also discovered that a similar light-and-shadow show occurs at Drombeg Stone Circle in Co Cork, where he spent 120 days photographing the sunrise over more than five years.

There used to be a similar arrangement at the Avebury stone circle in Wiltshire, England, which is probably older than Stonehenge. Before it was removed by the blushing Victorians, there was a phallic-shaped stone, now named the Obelisk, that would cast a long, narrow shadow at the time of Beltane (May Day) and which "penetrated" another stone, which is still there and has the appearance of a vulva.

Eric Edwards highlights the evidence in prehistoric cave art for ritual settings of sacred sex rites. In his article Avebury and its Environs as a Ritual Landscape, he writes:

The sexual metaphor in shamanic and fertility rituals is often shown with rock art motifs that symbolise the vulva, with the entry of the shaman into the spiritual realm regarded as a form of ritualised intercourse (Pearson, 2002). The Avebury complex has been described as the scene of a cyclical drama that took a year to perform with "…each edifice offering in turn a special setting for the celebration of a particular event in the farming year, matched to the corresponding event in the human life cycle." (Dames, 1977). In the Avebury area around 2600 BC the Neolithic inhabitants of the locale have left pottery

evidence for ceremonies of fertility and the ritual use of human bones (Burl, 1979).

The spirits that govern the lands are the spirits of Sovereignty, which, on the energetic level, is like a huge force that gushes forth from the Rivers of Blood or the DNA of the ancestors who are buried below. This chi-like or prana-like energy reaches the emotional intelligence of the people via the spiritual conduits of an Elder race whose role it is to guide the spiritual evolution of the human race. They are known in the British Isles as the Fae, the Gentry, the Sidhe or the Faeries. Other cultures have their own names for these spirits that appear to inhabit the betwixt and between – like the *aesir* of the Norse and the *devas* of the Vedics.

These spirits look like us to some extent, although they inhabit a timeless zone within the parallel dimensions. You may never have seen them because, these days, apart from the shamans, it is mainly only children who are able to perceive them – in other words, those who have not yet had their holographic, multi-dimensional perceptivity educated and ridiculed out of them.

From the evidence, it is clear there were specialised women shamans - high priestesses and sacred prostitutes known as heirodules, going back at least 10,000 years, who were in touch with these spirits of the land and so were able to transmit their wisdom to the king or pharaoh through sacred sex practices on his coronation night. These became known as the Sovereignty rites because the sexual initiation acted as a catalyst to raise the king's inner cosmic serpents to fire up his pineal gland and his higher brain centres, giving him the wisdom to rule.

The serpents arise from the genital region and then criss-cross the *djed*, or energetic spinal column, until they reach the chalice of the cup-shaped hypothalamus. The heads of the two serpents then rest upon the rim of the hypothalamus and from their mouths issue droplets of sweet elixir that stream down the inside of the chalice until they reach the pineal gland, which is nestled like a pine cone at its base. Once the pineal gland is bathed in these nectars, it fires up the crown chakra, opening up a portal to a huge library of wisdom akin to the Akashic Records, which the king then has access to. This in turn gave him the wisdom to rule – to bring order from chaos, just as the deluge hero of myth conquers the sea serpent and separates the land from the watery chaos.

Through these practices of bringing his energetic serpents under his control so that they can open the doors of his perception, the king, like the deluge hero, becomes the dragon slayer, comparable to the Greek Hercules, the Archangel Michael or the Babylonian Marduk, and he is thus deemed fit to bring order out of chaos and to rule his kingdom wisely.

This is the true meaning of the divine right of kings and the Holy Grail.

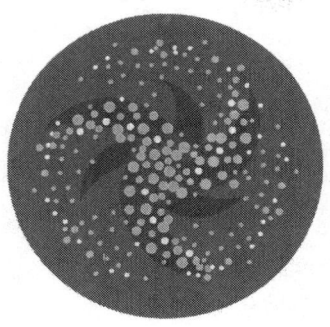

Practical exercise

Find your axis mundi

If you are already journeying, you will know your *axis mundi*. So this exercise is for those who have yet to undergo initiation as a shaman.

It's easy.

Just find a quiet place and relax.

Close your eyes and start to think about a tree that you know, or have known, and love. Most people have a favourite tree or one that remains dear to them, which is filed away in their Nation of Images, from their childhood. It may be the tree that is outside your window right now. Or it may be a tree you used to climb when you were younger.

It can be a tree anywhere on the Earth and even if it has since been chopped down, or you're not sure if it still exists, that doesn't matter. The only proviso is that it cannot be a total fantasy. It has to either exist now or to have once existed upon the Earth – because that means its spirit still exists in the eternal realms and it can therefore act from there as your World Tree.

Once you have found your tree, go and sit in it, in your imagination. From there, just relax and see what happens. You might just find it a great spot for some meditation and visualisation. If you feel like climbing down its trunk and exploring from there, go ahead. Or you may want to climb up its branches all the way to the top? That's fine. Just have fun with it. There is no right or wrong way.

Once you've found your *axis mundi*, you came come and go at any time, whenever you feel you need a quiet spot to feel centred and supported.

6. Camelot of the Polar Stars

KNOWLEDGE of the stars was a vital prerequisite for Maya and his fellow navigator shamans if they were to successfully guide their peoples across the oceans over several migrations that began at least around 33,000 years ago. But, as you will know by the now, the stars also had another, more esoteric use. Tabiti would have used them in her storytelling as metaphors for outer macrocosmic processes above, which – in a holographic way – resonated with the inner microcosmic world of the individual human below. It is this aspect of the serpent wisdom that we will be examining more deeply in this chapter and we will be looking through the lens of a polar hero who is closer to home, for most of us – Arthur Pendragon.

Today, we call the divination system that divides the night sky into 12 constellations arranged around the Sun astrology. However, those myths that feature the number 12 strongly – such as Jesus and his 12 Disciples or the 12 Labours of Hercules – are later solar myths, which were developed during the agricultural revolution that began in Mesopotamia after the end of the last major Ice Age. Before that time, we find that the number seven is predominant in the stories told to Kroi because it referred to the seven pole stars of the northern hemisphere which changed according to the precession of the equinoxes. They are Kochab, Polaris, Thuban, Deneb, Alrai, Cephei and Vega, and each one becomes the prime pole star for about 3,714 years.

Thus, the oldest myths are about the courageous hero who has to confront the fierce dragon or serpent of the firmamental seas, which we learned about in the last chapter, and defeat it in order to separate the land from the waters in the form of a mount or mountain upon which he erects the new pole star.

This huge dragon dominates the polar regions of the skies and it is the eighth-largest constellation in the night skies. In fact, this stellar sea serpent is so pivotal to the story of the deluge hero that he could be considered to be the head of the dragons; in other words, it is the Pendragon who surrounds the rotating polar stars of the northern hemisphere.

To the Greeks, the dragon was Draco and so that is how we refer to that wriggling and coiling line of stars today. There are a number of Greek myths which culminate in Draco being thrown into the skies. But to shamanic storytellers, Draco represented the deepest part of the work of fertility. From that perspective, this coiled polar serpent was the coursing stellar fire of the smith in the Underworld who forged the universal Spindle of Light between the Three Worlds to alchemically create the Marriage of the Sun and the Moon – and I'll explain more about the Alchemical Marriage that later on.

But for now, let's keep our feet on the Earth.

If you look up on a dark, starry night, you will see that the polar stars are made up of the constellations which, in some cases, were once pole stars such as Draco himself, Ursa Major (The Great Bear, the Plough, the Big Dipper, Arthur Chariot), Ursa Minor (the Little Bear), Lyra (the Harp), Cygnus (the Swan) and Cepheus (the Great King), Bootes (the Herdsman or Ox Driver), and Camelopardalis (The Giraffe). They all revolve "widdershins", or anti-clockwise, and make one full revolution in a 24-hour day.

Ursa Major is synonymous with Arthur Pendragon, who was named by the stargazing Welsh bards after their totem animal, the bear. The Cult of the Bear was prevalent across northern Europe in pre-Christian times and we find traces of it in the Old English epic of *Beowulf*.

Now, there are some notable worthies who insist that Arthur had been a local king and fierce warrior who lived in Britain around the fifth century and who fought 12 important battles. However, I find the evidence for his historical existence to be extremely thin and strained, to say the least. I used to enter into debates on this subject and from that I eventually learned it is a complete waste of time to throw down a ladder of logic and evidence to help people climb out of a position that they never used logic and evidence to fall into in the first place. I began to realise that some have an emotional need for there to have been a king called Arthur who once lived in Britain and who may come again on Earth, like an avatar, when the times are bad enough to warrant it. And so when emotion rather than logic underpins a position, people get stuck and refuse to budge - despite the paucity of historical evidence for such a character to have once fought in 12 battles, let alone there ever being a castle called Camelot, a beautiful wife named Guinevere and 12 knights seated around a circular table.

However, according to my research, the stories about Arthur hark back to a much older mythos, because in the earliest Celtic stories he appears to be a hero of the pole stars.

Let me explain further.

The most ancient instance of a mythological Arthur is found in a song of a

Welsh bard named Taliesin Pen Beirdd. Some have called Taliesin the last Celtic shaman of Britain although I think shamanism was long gone from these isles at the time he was composing his songs, in which he laments the loss of the "knowledge of the stars" among his fellow Christian monks in the sixth century. He is quite scathing about his sacerdotal colleagues in his poems and songs, even in his *Preiddeu Annwn* (which translates to *The Spoils of The Underworld*) which, to me, describes in metaphor Arthur's boat traversing the seven celestial stations of the poles around the firmamental seas of the Milky Way.

I would like to suggest that what is expressed in *Preiddeu Annwyn* indicates that the orally conveyed stories about Arthur are as old as those of the deluge heroes of the Egyptians, Indians and Sumerians. I have even found symbols and metaphors used in the Arthurian stories that can be traced back to the stories of Tabiti of the steppes of the last great Ice Age. There are people living today in the Caucasus mountains who count those of the Scythian tribes as their ancestors. They are called the Ossetians and they descend from the Sarmatians and the Alans who migrated south into Europe, thousands of years ago, and eventually settled in northern France and Britain.

The Ossetians tell us that their myths, which are many thousands of years old, feature a hero named Batraz who is at the centre of a circle or "round table" of warrior-like gods named the Narts. Apparently, Batraz owned a magical sword that could only be pulled out (from the roots of a tree) and wielded by a true king. In the same stories, we also find the equivalent of the Lady of the Lake and a magical cup, like the Grail, that only appeared to the bravest of warriors.

Thus, I would suggest to those who are hesitant to accept King Arthur as mythological rather than historical, perhaps you could just park that thought for now and allow yourself to objectively explore this new viewpoint? When we are being tossed and turned on the Wheel of Life, it is comforting to believe in a Second Coming of a great saviour. However, once we learn how to walk in the footprints of the hero, the teachings for which is being gradually unfolded to you in this book, we soon begin to realise we are the ones that we have been waiting for.

So as you already know, the earliest deluge heroes traversed the waters of the firmament to separate out the mound or mountain of land upon which they erected the pole to represent the pole star of that age. Now let us turn to Taliesin's poem about Arthur, which he recites in the Island of the Strong Door (Britain) on Earth (the four-square Caer), about King Arthur's voyage in his boat, which takes him around Caer Sidi, Caer Feddwit, Caer Rigor, Caer Wydyr, Caer Goludd, Caer Fandwy and Caer Ochren.

Preiddeu Annwfn
I praise the Mighty One, Pendragon of the kingly land,

Who encompasses the margins of the world!
Predestined was Gweir's captivity in Caer Sidi,
According to the tale of Pwyll and Pryderi.
None before him was sent into it,
Into the heavy blue chain which bound the youth.
From before the reeving of Annwfn he has groaned,
Until the ending of the world this prayer of poets:
Three ship burdens of Prydwen entered the Spiral City
Except seven, none returned from Caer Sidi.

Is not my song worthily to be heard
In the four-square Caer, four times revolving?
I draw my knowledge from the famous cauldron
The breath of nine maidens keeps it boiling.
Is not the Head of Annwyn's cauldron so shaped;
Ridged with enamel, rimmed with pearl?
It will not boil the cowardly traitor's portion.
The sword of Lleawc flashed before it
And in the hand of Lleminawc was it wielded.
Before hell's gate the lights were lifted
When with Arthur we went to the harrowing.
Except seven, none returned from Caer Feddwit.

Is not my song fit recital for kings
In the four-square Caer, in the Island of the Strong Door,
Where noon and night make half-light,
Where bright wine is brought before the host?
Three ship burdens of Prydwen took to sea:
Except seven, none returned from Caer Rigor.

I sing not for those exiled for tradition
Who beyond Caer Wydyr saw not Arthur's valour.
Six thousand men there stood upon the wall;
Hard it was to parley with their sentinel.
Three ship burdens of Prydwen we went with Arthur:
Except seven, none returned from Caer Goludd.

I sing not for those whose shield arms droop,
Who know not day nor hour nor causation
Nor when the glorious Son of Light is born,
Nor who prevents his journey to Dol Defwy.

They know not the brindled, harnessed ox
With seven score links upon his collar.
When we went with Arthur on difficult errand;
Except seven, none returned from Caer Fandwy.

I sing not for those of our companions,
Who know not on what day the chief was born,
Who do not know the hour of his kingship,
Nor of the silver-headed beast they guard for him.
When we went with Arthur of mournful mien:
Except seven, none returned from Caer Ochren.

There are other, longer versions of *Preiddeu Annwn*, but I'm sticking with the shortest and simplest version for our purposes here.

So let's analyse it.

"Caer" is Welsh for "fortress", "enclosure" or "circle". "Sidi" is cognate with "sidereal" and so Caer Sidi may mean the circle of stars, star-wheel or spiralling stellar enclosure. But that is as far as modern academic studies go. Researchers have so far not managed to match each of Taliesin's "caers" with its celestial circumpolar counterpart. However, there is a Rosetta Stone which will gradually become apparent as we go through this chapter.

What is the "cauldron … ridged with enamel and rimmed with pearl" and which "will not boil the cowardly traitor's portion"? It must be the round, starry dome of the sky that is flooded with the firmamental seas, which are kept boiling by the breath of the nine Moon muses, the numerical symbology of which you will learn more about in **Chapter 14: Interpreting Numbers in Myths**.

And, of course, it will not "boil the cowardly traitor's portion" because the timid and faint-hearted would be too afraid to venture there. To me, in this context, the boiling cauldron is a metaphor for the alchemist's cauldron or crucible and the seven caers therefore symbolise the rungs of the ladder of alchemical initiation, which I will unpack in more detail after we've taken a few more foundational steps. But we can note here that one of Taliesin's titles was the Son of the Cauldron – meaning he himself was such an initiate. Later on, I will explain how we can also become initiates "of the Cauldron".

The "brindled, harnessed ox" must be referring to the constellation of Bootes, which has featured as the Herdsman or the Shepherd or the Ox Driver in myths since at least Babylonian times, and he is the one who pulls the Plough (otherwise known as the Great Bear, Ursa Major or Arthur's Chariot), like Hu Gardarn. The "seven score links upon his collar" may refer to how the seven rungs of the alchemical Ladder of the Wise equate to the vertically spinning Law of Octaves, more about which anon.

Between the thighs of the Herdsman we find the star Arcturus, which means Protector of the Bear. Arcturus is the fourth brightest star in the galaxy and is a red giant 24 times larger than the Sun. His character is found in one of many Greek myths about the philandering Zeus who threw his mistress Callisto, with their offspring, Arcas, into the skies to become respectively the bear and the bear's guardian, who protects his mother from the lord of the gods' jealous wife, Hera.

In total, Taliesin's song of Arthur's harrowing of the Otherworlds sounds remarkably similar to Jason's quest in his ship, the *Argonaut*, which was to steal or gain in some way the Golden Fleece, except in the case of Arthur, the challenge is to gain the Cauldron of Inspiration - which, in later Norman Christian literature became the Holy Grail. Either way, in both cases and many more besides, the symbol of the Golden Fleece, or Cauldron or Grail, in my interpretation, represents the fulfillment of the path of initiation into the Mysteries of the Ladder of the Wise and the Teachings of the Cauldron.

In Taliesin's poem, Arthur can only win the Cauldron by becoming worthy. This worthiness seems to have nothing to do with the Christian dogma based on Original Sin; it is more about finding the courage to step "out of the box" to open up to new experiences that carry a risk of danger. This puts Arthur in the same boat (pun intended) as a whole raft (sorry!) of ancient mythological champions, from Gilgamesh and Hercules onwards, and he is worthy to stand alongside the champions of other heroic myths, such as Orpheus, who made the death-defying descent into the Underworld to rescue his lover Euridyce, or Theseus who bravely entered the labyrinth to kill the Minotaur.

After Taliesin's poem about Arthur's harrowing, there is nothing extant for a further three centuries. The ninth century monk Nennius, the *Annales Cambriae* and the *Historium Brittanicum* all have him winning 12 battles for the British against the Picts, in which there is no hint of a Camelot or of the 12 knights of a round table, nor of Arthur's dark, mysterious half-sister Morgan the Fae and his unfaithful queen Guinevere.

It then takes a further few hundred years for the Brythonic Norman scribe Geoffrey of Monmouth to compile his *Historia regum Britanniae* (*The History of the Kings of Britain*) and it is only here that Guinevere enters the story – more than half a millennium after Taliesin's composition of *Preiddeu Annwn*. What seems to follow then is a whole Arthurian industry which was supported from within the top echelons of Norman society in an attempt to give the British a feasible backstory with which to control them politically, and this is when the whole host of characters of the pageant of chivalry we are now familiar with begin to appear.

The 12 knights of the round table are first mentioned in the 12th century *Roman de Brut*, a verse literary "history" of Britain written, in the Norman language, by the poet Wace. Wace based his poem on *The History of the Kings of*

Britain. However, all scholars are more or less in universal agreement now that Monmouth's so-called "history" was based on the myths of the Celts, which in turn likely originally came from Tabiti's people.

Another of the folkloric texts that fired Monmouth's pen was a Welsh Mabinogion tale. The *Mabinogion* is a 18th century compendium of ancient Celtic tales dated to the 12th and 13th centuries. Most experts agree that the oldest of these, about an unlikely hero who was raised in a pig-pen, can be dated to about 1090 CE. But just as with all orally transmitted myths, this date is only when a written version of *How Culhwch Won Olwen* (Culhwch being pronounced Killhook), is attested to – much later than when it was first told and passed on from mouth to ear. However, there is a sort of virtual Way Back Machine. This is because it is possible to indicate the likely era in which a folktale was popular when, despite gloss after gloss, the bare bones of the skeleton of the deluge hero of the pre-agricultural Age are still poking through from where he's sprawled across the primordial carpet.

As medievalist Will Parker writes in his discourses on the *Mabinogion*:

The most archaic text in the *Mabinogion* collection is what is often referred to as 'the Oldest Arthurian tale': Culhwch and Olwen, written in the St David's area c.1090. Culhwch is worth examining in greater detail as many of the general problems we have in the interpretation of Medieval Welsh prose narratives are presented in stark relief by the structure and content of this particular tale.

There are a number of reasons why this should be the case. Not only is Culhwch the oldest surviving prose tale written in the Medieval Welsh language, it is also generally thought to be the closest to the oral background of traditional story-telling from which the *Mabinogion* originally emerged. The oral tale, by its very nature, leaves no direct trace on the historical record; so the precise form of these narrative recitals in the Middle Ages must remain a matter for conjecture.

Nonetheless, just as there are certain stylistic and structural features which are characteristic of the säge or oral popular tale in all times and places, so too are there also certain stereotypical plot structures and narrative elements which would seem to have their origins in the common prehistory of mankind. That such 'motifs' and 'tale-types' permeate both the structure and content of Culhwch and Olwen offers a strong indication of the proximity of this popular-oral background.

In other words, *How Culhwch Won Olwen* is a classic tale of fertility and Sovereignty. It features a hero who has to perform a number of tasks, including literally bearding a giant ogre named Ysbaddaden in order to win the hand of his beautiful daughter, Olwen, and replace Ysbaddaden on the throne. (The Celts were big on shaving and bearding in their stories. It was considered to be a symbol for renouncing and handing on of power, much as it was in the *Old Testament* story about Delilah ordering that Samson's hair be cut off.)

We realise instantly that the story is an ==archetypical questing myth,== when we hear at the beginning that the young Culhwch is being sent on a dangerous and likely unachievable mission by his evil stepmother, the queen, who wants her own son to succeed her. Heroes are often dispatched on Mission Impossible because the sender hopes that they will not return. The hero is often the nephew of the king and is due to inherit the throne – unless he is conveniently burned alive by a dragon first!

Culhwch's scheming stepmother waxes lyrical to him about the lovely Olwen, his cousin, whose head is "yellower than the flower of broom" and "whiter was her flesh than the foam of the wave; whiter were her palms and her fingers than the shoots of marsh trefoil from amidst the fine gravel of a welling spring... whiter were her breasts than the breast of a white swan, redder were her cheeks than the reddest foxglove... white trefoils sprang up behind her wherever she went and for that reason she was called Olwen."

No wonder Culhwch falls instantly in love with her!

His mother tells him that Olwen lives far, far away but perhaps his cousin Arthur would help him to find her?

And so it begins, as all heroic myths do, with a journey into the unknown:

Off went the boy on a steed with light-grey head, four-winters old, with well-knit fork, shell-hoofed, and a golden tubular bridle-bit in its mouth. And under him a precious gold saddle, and in his hand two whetted spears of silver. A battle-axe in his hand, the forearm's length of a full-grown man from ridge to edge. It would draw blood from the wind; it would be swifter than the swiftest dew-drop from the stalk to the ground, when the dew would be heaviest in the month of June. A gold-hilted sword on his thigh, and the blade of it gold, and a gold-chased buckler upon him, with the hue of heaven's lightning therein, and an ivory boss therein. And two greyhounds, white breasted, brindled, in front of him, with a collar of red gold about the neck of either, from shoulder-swell to ear. The one that was on the left side would be on the right, and the one that was one the right side would be on the left, like two sea swallows sporting around him. Four clods the four hoofs of his steed would cut, like four swallows in the air over his head, now before him, now behind him. A four-cornered mantle of purple upon him, and an apple of red-gold in each of its corners; a hundred kine was the worth of each apple. The worth of three hundred kine in precious gold was there in his foot gear and stirrups, from the top of his thigh to the tip of his toe. Never a hair-tip stirred upon him, so exceedingly light his steed's canter under him on his way to the

gate of Arthur's court.

I'm sure you're getting quite adept by now at picking up the metaphors and so you won't need me to point out that the apples referred to the knowledge of the stars, and the four elements, which are called in at the beginning of any magical operation, are represented by the sword, dew, axe and spear and cognate, respectively, with air, water, earth and fire. But you may not realise that the white (grey) horse is a Celtic symbol of Sovereignty and the swooping and weaving swallows represent the Rivers of Blood or DNA. So the crossing of the two greyhounds (brindled, like Taliesin's ox, beasts of the Underworld) from right to left like sea swallows sporting around the royal purple-garbed Culhwch on his white horse, and the four clods cut by the four hoofs of his steed that flew like swallows over his head, are no mere superficial literary flourish in his journey to find his Beloved Olwen – and thus graft his family line on to hers in the cause of Sovereignty.

There is a lot to this story and I recommend that if you get the chance, you read it in full. I'm just going to summarise it quickly here because I want to get us speedily to the part about the cauldron.

Culhwch eventually reaches Arthur's court where he goes on to stay with him and learn the arts of warriorship. Arthur then promises to help him find Olwen and so they set off together with a party of six others – making seven altogether, besides Arthur.

The first person they meet, on the way, is Custennin the sheep-herder and his wife and, as it turns out, Olwen is their niece. The motif of the shepherd or herder was a staple in these sorts of stellar stories because, in the language of the initiates of that time, the term "sheep" would alternate with "melons" or "fruit" as code for "stars". We already met the earliest known shepherd character in the last chapter, as the goddess Inanna's lover Dumuzi. The Herder or organiser of all the stars therefore has great power in this cosmology and as we already know, as Bootes it protects between its thighs Arcturus, the guardian of the Bear.

Anyway, we go on to hear that the lovely Olwen's father, the evil ogre Ysbaddaden, has persecuted the cosmic shepherd, causing him to lose "all but one of his 24 sons". Metaphorically, the 23 lost sons are likely stars that were drowned under the deluge. It could equally refer to the 24-hour day, meaning that only one hour remained to save his legacy? We use a similar expression today when we want to express the urgency of the need to complete a task when it is almost too late: five minutes to midnight.

Custennin, however, knows that there is a curse on his enemy, Ysbaddaden, and that is whoever marries Olwen will usurp her father and take his place as ruler over the land. So the sheep-herder is more than happy to direct Arthur and his party of seven to the ogre's fortress.

When they arrive, there is a fierce battle of poisoned stone spears, in which

Culhwch ends up injuring the ogre in the leg, belly and eye. This is a nod to the motif of the Wounded King – also known as the Fisher King in later Arthurian myths – and we will learn more about him later. But for now, suffice to say that he represents the death or dying old sovereign who will soon have to make way for the new, young ruler.

However, Ysbaddaden is not dead yet and so it's Mission Impossible time again. He agrees that Culhwch can marry the fair Olwen so long as he passes 39 utterly infeasible trials that culminate in the catching of the enchanted Divine Boar, the *Twrch Trwyth*, in order to retrieve the comb and scissors it carries on its head with which to beard the ogre.

Actually, the number of trials varies, according probably to how many nights the roaming storyteller wanted to stretch out his visit. I will not list them all here but to give you an idea of how unachievable they were, one of them was to pick the flax to be made into Olwen's bridal veil from a barren field and then gain the help of the mythical farmer god, Amaethon mab Don, to plough the land.

But it is when we come to the execution of another of those challenges – the stealing of the cauldron of Diwrnach – that we find a story that almost mirrors the one that Taliesin recounted in his song *Preiddeu Annwn*.

Arthur set out … and went on Prydwen his ship, and came to Ireland. And they set out to the house of Diwrnach … And after they had eaten and drunk their fill Arthur asked for the cauldron … When it was refused them, Bedwyr arose and seized the cauldron and placed it upon the back of Hygwydd, Arthur's servant … Llenlleawc the Irishman grasped Kaledfwlch (the sword, Fragarach) and brandished it, and slew Diwrnach the Irishman and all his host … After putting the armies wholly to flight, Arthur and his men embarked in their presence in the ship, and the cauldron with them …

Thus many of the elements of the sixth century *Preiddeu Annwn* are found in *How Culhwch Won Olwen*: Arthur and his ship of seven men, the voyage to steal the cauldron and Llenlleawc (Lleminawc) and his flashing sword all set in a story that features a draconic ogre and a protective herdsman. Surely Taliesin was referring back, knowingly or unknowingly, to the myth of the deluge hero when he entertained his listeners with it?

But where did Arthur's round table of 12 knights of Camelot originate from? Well, here we run into a bit of a mystery (by which I mean mystery with a small "m" – the Agatha Christie variety) that you might be able to help me to solve. I have most of the pieces of the jigsaw puzzle, which you will find here, and even all the blue sky bits. But first we need a brief potted lesson in the history of astronomy.

So here we go.

There are currently 88 officially recognized constellations today. Roughly half of them come from the *Almagest*, a treatise that was compiled in the first century of the Common Era by the Greco-Roman astronomer Claudius Ptolemy, while the rest were gradually added as astronomers discovered them over the following centuries. Most scholars reckon Ptolemy was having to construct his map of the night skies from a sort of devastated Ground Zero intellectual wasteland due to the previously mentioned earthquake of Santorini, a millennia-and-a-half before, the impact of which had wiped out much of the stored cosmological knowledge of the ancient Mesopotamian world. If you add to that the various destructions of the Library of Alexandria – one of largest collections of esoteric texts ever assembled in one place – it starts to make sense why the period that followed next became known as the Dark Ages.

In fact, it was not until comparatively modern times that archaeologists uncovered the star charts of the Babylonians, known as the MUL.AFIN lists, much of which were based on the astronomical knowledge of the Sumerians and the Elamites who lived 2-3,000 years before Ptolemy.

But anyway, during the Dark Ages, the Saxons and Norse called Polaris, our current Pole Star, the Nowl, meaning "navel" – although it wasn't the Pole Star of their times. Their Pole Star was known to them as the Lode Star and it was in the constellation of Camelopardalis. And this where we run into the mystery because, according to the official history of astronomy, a constellation with the name of Camelopardalis was not found until 1613, four centuries after the Norman Arthurian literature was written in which we find the first mention of Camelot. Astronomers also called Camelopardalis the Giraffe and if you look at it on a star map, that moniker makes sense; it does look like an animal with a neck so long it seems disproportionate to its body. It is also thought to be why amateur astronomer Lewis Carroll caused Alice in Wonderland's neck to stretch so high that her head was in the trees in his popular Mystery story for children, the surreal characters of which make up a virtual Victorian planetarium. But, curiouser and curiouser, it turns out the name Camelopardalis is actually a Greek-Romanised amalgam of "camel" and "leopard".

Now, the hired scribes in Norman times were all well educated in mathematics, mythology, astronomy, alchemy and astrology. And so is it possible the French poet Chrétien de Troyes knew the Lode Star was the erstwhile pole star of the Northern Tradition and thus used this location for his castle of Camelot in his 12th century poem *Lancelot, the Knight of the Cart?* It certainly fits with metaphorical stories about the turning of the pole stars where, as in *How Culhwch Won Olwen*, the son-in-law wins the castle and the rulership of the land, from the father of the bride. According to de Troyes, Guinevere's father Leondegrance bequeathed the castle of Camelot as a gift to his daughter and her husband Arthur on their wedding day. The name of Leondegrance sounds very leopard-like, so it could refer to the "pardalis" part of Camelopardis – or could it be referring to the constellation of Leo?

Anyway, I'll leave that mystery with you for now while we move on to Morgan Le Fay.

Morgan does not appear in the Arthurian mythos until Geoffrey of Monmouth introduces her in his *Vita Merlini*. In this book, he purports to recount the life of the magician Merlin although, as we have already surmised, Monmouth's so-called chronicles drew not on historical records but on the magical and mythological materials of the Druids that featured giants, heroes, dragons and sea nymphs. These stories were never intended as historical records. Instead, they are rather like arks that are designed to cross the Underworld seas of time and which carry in their submarine holds golden keys for opening up the streams of innate wisdom in the subconscious minds of listeners by watering the dreaming seeds within their own inner night landscapes.

We have already met one of those Druids, Taliesin pen Beirdd, who was the primary chief bard of the islands of Britain during the sixth century. There is a song attributed to Taliesin entitled *The Three Fountains* and in this extract we find what could be a hint to the Scythian origins of Morgan Le Fay and the Lady of the Lake.

> **There is an odious worm from Caer Satanas.**
> **It has conquered all between depths and shallows.**
> **Its jaws are as wide as the Alps.**
> **Death cannot conquer it, nor hand nor blade.**
> **Its weighs 900 stone, its paws are hairy:**
> **One eye in its head, green as the glacial ice.**
> **There are three fountains in its neck.**

Obviously, The Three Fountains is about a dragon and, most likely, it is a metaphor for Draco. But it is the term "Caer Satanas", or the Fortess of Satanas, that caused the hairs on my neck to stand up. As far as I'm aware, there is no other reference to Satanas or any similar-sounding name in the whole of the extant Celtic literature, both Welsh and Irish. However, there is an important fertility goddess that Kroy-Khasis would most likely have been familiar with. Her name was Satana and she was the aunt, midwife and eventually the lover of the champion Batraz, hero of the Narts, in whose stories we have already identified several Arthurian themes.

To me, there has always been something faintly erotic and incestuous about Morgan le Fay's relationship with her half-brother Arthur and, although it is not stated, when you hear about her taking his wounded body on a boat to Avalon for healing you are left with the impression that she remains with him there as his lover.

So could Taliesin have been referring to that Satana from some older Celtic stories no longer available to us? And might this be where, hundreds of years later, Geoffrey of Monmouth found his inspiration for Morgan le Fay – aka Morgan of the Fae peoples?

That theory becomes more credible when we realise that despite this chronicler's name of Monmouth, there is no record of him ever coming from Welsh stock. He is now thought to have been part of a Brythonic-Norman family. This is highly relevant to our search for his inspiration for Morgan of the Fae because as an official chronicler who wrote in Latin, he was almost certainly sanctioned by the land-owning aristocracy of Armorica in northern France, which was governed by a Caucasian war-like tribe that the Romans had installed there as a proxy force to keep order, namely the Alans, who were latter-day Sarmatians, aka the aforementioned Serpent People.

The Alans virtually ruled that part of France from the first century onwards.

For example, Emperor Maximus the Thracian (235-238 CE) was born of an Alan mother and a Gothic father. Another famous Alan, Alan the Red, was said to have accompanied William of Normandy in 1066 as he walked up the beach in Hastings under the banner of Rome. Successive popes of the Byzantine part of the empire, such as Theodosius II, Marcian and Leo I, relied heavily on the fierce Alan general Aspar in repelling the barbarians, and it was only after Aspar's death that Rome finally fell. Yet, despite that "fall", a powerful cabal continued the rule of empire under various covert guises, such an ecumenical proxies and foreign mercenary troops, with British kings all being sent to Rome for their education, until the 16th century Reformation in which Henry VIII declared independence and sacked the monasteries and abbeys of Britain.

But until then, a covert form of rule had been waged through trying to win the hearts and minds of the conquered people with stories that seemed familiar and resonated with those buried in their Rivers of Blood – once they'd taken hold, they were twisted from myth to history. This psychological warfare was augmented by a veritable industry of scribes and spin doctors, mostly based in Amorica and all having been briefed, it seems to me, to provide the British with a narrative to render them more accepting of their Mediterranean conquerors. One of those in their employ was Geoffrey of Monmouth, who drew on Welsh magical texts in order to persuade the Celts and the Irish that the original indigenous peoples were the descendants of a race of giants, like the Celtic god Bran. They were told that after the (mythical) battle of Troy, others came like Silvius, the grandson of the Greek hero Aeneas, to blend their heroic genes with those who fought under the banner of the Welsh Arthur. Monmouth would have been largely influenced, at the same time, by that literary mileu of Norman writers such as French poet Chrétien de Troyes, who would all in turn have plundered the seed beds of the stories of the Alans, the Serpent Peoples from the Caucasus regions.

In his *Vita Merlini*, Monmouth spells the name of Morgan the Fae as Morgen;

in the Old Welsh and Old Breton languages, "morgen" meant "sea-borne" and generally referred to water-sprites. Thus, from that information we can more easily discern her associations with the archetype of the Lady of the Lake, who raises the magical sword of the hero from the depths and who, some scholars believe, may be traced back to the Scythian fertility goddess Satana, who bestowed the faery-forged sword on Batraz of the Narts.

Kroy-Khasis would have heard about a Satana who was born to her dead mother within a tomb in "the otherworld" beneath the seas. She is credited, in these myths, as the discoverer of the power of the lifeforce of water. And while Morgan the morgen ferries the wounded Arthur to be healed in Avalon, the Isle of Apples, Satana discovers a gold and white apple that imparts immortality and everlasting youth to any who should be lucky enough to taste of it, rather like Iden in the Norse myths.

There is also a distinct possibility that both the Welsh Morgan or morgen and the Morrigen, the terrifying Irish Queen of the Fae who would often be seen on battlefields in the form of black crow, came from the same Celtic source.

So from all of this, perhaps we can start to understand how much of the role of the story archaeologist is the function of separation and discrimination. We have to look deeper into a story with a powerful microscope to find the different strands of the primordial carpet, and then untangle them and clean them up for public viewing. Sometimes we only get a few stray threads that seem to match a certain pattern and we know we need to find more to complete the picture. However, that doesn't prevent us from making educated guesses, which is my segue into the conclusion of this chapter.

There is an even older, orally conveyed myth which, if they had known about it, would have provided the Latin scribes with inspiration for the theme of Arthur's troubled relationship with Guinevere.

It was the 12th century Chrétien de Troyes who first introduces the queen's illicit dalliance with a paramour in his romantic poem *Lancelot, the Knight of the Cart*. After several steamy trysts with the dashing young knight, Guinevere is carried off, one presumes against her will, by King Maleagant, the ruler of the Otherworld of Gorre.

Lancelot is entirely an invention of Chretien de Troyes although, again, some mythologists believe he may have been inspired by the heroes from the Caucasus. However, the Celtic source for the story of Maleagant's abduction of Guinevere is found in yet another Latin-scribed story from the mytho-industrial complex of 12th century France, by the cleric Caradoc of Llancarfan.

His tale, *The Life of Gildas*, centres around a sixth century monk who was known as Gildas the Wise. Caradoc tells us that Guinevere's kidnapper ruled the Summer Country and his name was King Melwas. "Summer Country" was a common euphemism then for the Otherworlds; Taliesin referred to the other dimensions in his works as the Land of the Summer Stars and some believe it was from that term the county of Somerset in England took its name.

Anyway, Caradoc has Melwas abduct Guinevere from Camelot and carry her away to his fortress over-looking Glastonbury – perhaps on the famous Glastonbury Tor, a prehistoric earthwork that towers over the Somerset town.

It takes Arthur a whole year to find his kidnapped wife – in other words, as long as you would expect it to for any deluge hero traversing the 360 degrees of the circumpolar Cauldron, in line with the orbit of the Earth around the Sun, which was why the ancient Egyptians divided the year into 36 months of 10 days.

In the end, though, it was Gildas the Wise who negotiated Guinevere's safe release.

This myth, known as the Duel at Beltane, is played out in the night skies over Glastonbury twice every year and if we base it upon the constellations we think it is mirroring, the inescapable conclusion is that it could be as old as the fourth millennium BCE.

Let me tell you more about it so that can see the thinking behind the dating.

The hero of the Duel at Beltane is another staple champion of Celtic myths, Gwyn ap Nudd, who also features in *How Culhwch Won Olwen*. One of Culhwch's tasks, set by the ogre Ysbadadden, was to release Gwyn from his battle with Gwythyr so that he could give Arthur and his raiding party his hound, Drudwyn, to help them in hunting down the Divine Boar.

In this story, Gwyn ap Nudd, also known as Lord of the Wildwood and Leader of the Wild Hunt, represents the constellation of Orion that dominated the heavens between November and May. Orion the Hunter (Osiris to the Egyptians) appears in the Babylonian star lists as "The Heavenly Shepherd" or "True Shepherd of Anu". So we are back to our all-powerful shepherd.

Anyway, in Greek myths, Gaia becomes angry with Orion for threatening to hunt down and kill every animal on Earth and so she sends him into exile with a scorpion, Ophiuchus, the Serpent Bearer. So the battle at Beltane, just as Winter is turning into Summer, is between Orion the Hunter and the Scorpion king, Ophiuchus.

Each May Day, Gwyn ap Nudd (as the Winter King Orion) has to fight a duel with Gwythyr (as the Summer King Ophiuchus) over a beautiful woman who is still represented in fairs up and down the land as the May Queen.

Of course the Winter King, Gwyn, has to lose the battle against the Summer King, Gwythyr, at Beltane in May, otherwise it would be permanent winter. But then they get to fight over the beautiful woman in the skies again at Samhain (Halloween). This time, Gwyn wins her back and dominates the night skies once more as the Winter King.

So if the two duelling protagonists in the night skies are represented on the one side by Orion and by Scorpius/Ophiuchus on the other, what of the fair damsel? Which constellation was she? This puzzled mythologists and archaeoastronomers for some time until computer technology allowed them to reproduce the night skies over Glastonbury Tor 6,000 years ago.

In those days, the constellation of the Southern Cross, now only seen in the night skies of the Southern Hemisphere, was clearly visible in the north too. But how is the Southern Cross like a beautiful, fertile woman? Perhaps, instead of visualising it as a cross, they joined the lines up around it into a sort of diamond or almond shape with a star at its centre? (This will make more sense when you learn about the meaning of the symbol of the Vesica Piscis in Part 2). But it seems that she was a veritable celestial Sheela-na-gig.

As Nicholas Mann and Philippa Glasser explain in their book *The Star Temple of Avalon*:

> ... the recurring drama unfolding in the night sky during the fourth millennium BCE would have had at its heart a particular jewel: the Southern Cross, whose central importance would have been indicated by its relationship to the earthy feminine contours of the Chalice Hill. When, in 1501, Italian explorer Amerigo Vespucci became one of the first Europeans to see the Southern Cross for several thousand years, he did not identify it as a cross; rather he described its pattern as a 'mandorla', that is, almond-shaped. As a mandorla or a vesica, the constellation can now be recognised as an ancient symbol of the divine feminine. Did early British astronomers also see it in this manner, identifying its four stars with Creiddylad, perhaps envisaging the horizontal band of the Milky Way as her star skirt, or her golden or silver hair, or possibly even seeing the star-vesica as forming the goddess' vulva, in the manner of the Celtic Sheela-na-gig?

If you have read my book *The Bright World of the Gods*, you may now be hearing a ringing sound in your ears. Hopefully, it is not tinnitus; it's just that you are realising the hidden meaning to the part of the plot in which my hero, Gwyn, has to go down into the Underworld to fight a duel with the Summer King over the hand of Creiddylad.

So from all this, I hope we can by now understand that the so-called approved and authorised history of the British, which starred a conquering king named Arthur, came from a writing school that had been set up to support the covert Roman-Norman conquest of Britain, and that its classically-trained scribes were inspired by the oral folktales and songs of the Druidic bards, which in themselves were drawing on a very long oral tradition, going back into the mists of time to the the last Ice Age at least and, in some cases, stretching as far geographically as the mountains of the Caucasus.

And we can also now conclude that these myths contained allegorical teachings that reflected a far deeper and far more long-lasting truth than that of a mere historical event, which is as it should be. Historical events come and go, and the repeated posturings and posings of men on the world stage don't amount to much in the end. But we are made of stardust and the stars are always with us and within us, making every man and woman a star or a hero of their own life's path.

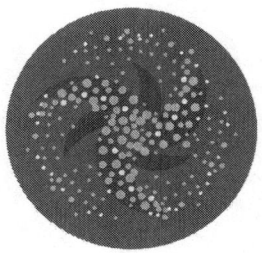

Practical exercise

Find the stories in the stars

It takes a lot of imagination to see a geometric shape as a giraffe or a cart, much less a bear. However, there are some very useful apps that you can get, these days, which will help you identify the constellations of the night skies. You just hold your phone or tablet up to the stars, and it will show you the nearest star groupings, and what they're called. So you can either use one of those, or you can trace them out by following my instructions and Figures 1 and 2.

Either way, I think this is a good time for us to start to become familiar with the natural planetarium over our heads.

If you are in the Northern Hemisphere:

Use **Figure 1** to help you find the Pendragon court of Camelot by searching for:

1. Draco (Olwen's evil father, the ogre Ysbaddaden)
2. Ursa Major (King Arthur)
3. Ursa Minor or the Lesser or She Bear (Olwen)
4. Bootes with Arcturus, meaning "Bear Guardian" (Custennin, Olwen's

uncle)
5. Camelopardalis (Camelot)
6. Hercules (Culhwch)
7. Lyre (Arthur's Harp)

It's best to wait for a dark and cloudless night and then go outdoors and look upwards to the north.

The most obvious constellation should be Ursa Major, otherwise known as the Great Bear or Arthur's Chariot.

The two stars that make up the back end of Arthur's Chariot are known as The Pointers, because they point upwards. The most northern star of The Pointers is Dubhe, meaning in Arabic "the back of the Greater Bear".

The end of Draco's tail lies roughly between Polaris and Dubhe.

Once you have found Draco's tail, just follow its serpentine course to its head and as you go along, you will find Ursa Minor (the Little Bear) in the east. If you follow the trajectory of Ursa Minor's "tail", you will come to the long-necked Giraffe of Camelopardalis. Draco's head points southward towards Hercules, which is a sort of square shape with wiggly lines extending from its four corners.

Now come back to Ursa Major (Arthur's Chariot) and follow its "tail" along in the opposite direction to its furthest star, Alkaid or Betelnash, both meaning "the end of the tail". At the end, continue along that trajectory and you will see the kite-shaped Bootes the Herdsman with its brightest star Arcturus, the Bear's Guardian, at its pointed base.

If you are in the Southern Hemisphere:

Use **Figure 2** as a guide so that, just like the marine navigators of old, you will be able to find "true south" by the lights of the five stars of the Southern Cross. This is not possible, by the way, using a compass, which will only give you "magnetic south" and not "true south".

Although it is one of the smallest constellations, this stellar cross, or Crux as it is also known, is easily visible south of the equator from April to June. However, don't confuse it with the nearby False Cross (1), which only has four stars. The easiest way to identify the true Crux is to look first for the brightest constellation, Centaurus (2). The Southern Cross (3) can be seen directly under the belly of the horned Centaur.

The Southern Cross is made up of five stars.

The star at the top of the cross is known as Gamma Crucis, or Gacrux (4), and the star at the bottom of the cross is titled Alpha Crusis, or Acrux (5). The stars that make up the arms of the cross are Beta Crusis, or Becrux, and Delta Crucis, while the small star in the middle of the cross is named Epsilon (6).

Once you have identified the stars of the Southern Cross, trace an imaginary line with your finger down from Gacrux to Acrux and then extend that trajectory downwards by about four-and-a-half times. When you reach the end of that line, you will be pointing close to the "true south".

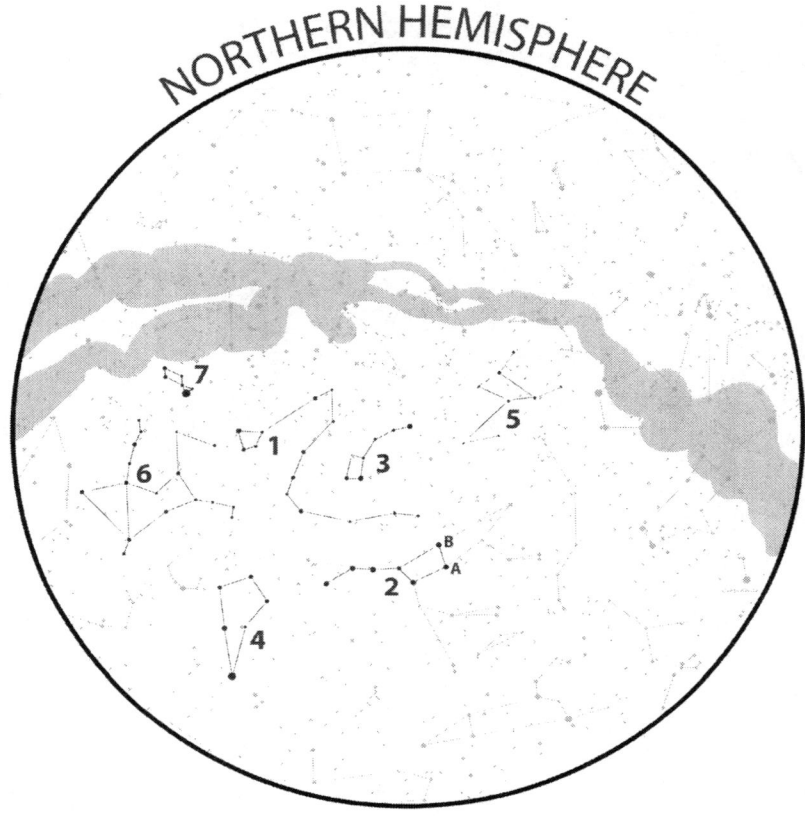

1, Draco (Olwen's evil father, the ogre Ysbaddaden)
2, Ursa Major (King Arthur), with Merak (**A**) and Dubhe (**B**)
3, Ursa Minor or the Lesser or She Bear (Olwen)
4, Bootes with star of Arcturus, meaning 'Bear Guardian' (Custennin, Olwen's uncle)
5, Camelopardalis (Camelot)
6, Hercules (Culhwch)
7, Lyre (Arthur's Harp)

Figure 1: Find Arthur's court of Camelot in the polar stars of the Northern Hemisphere

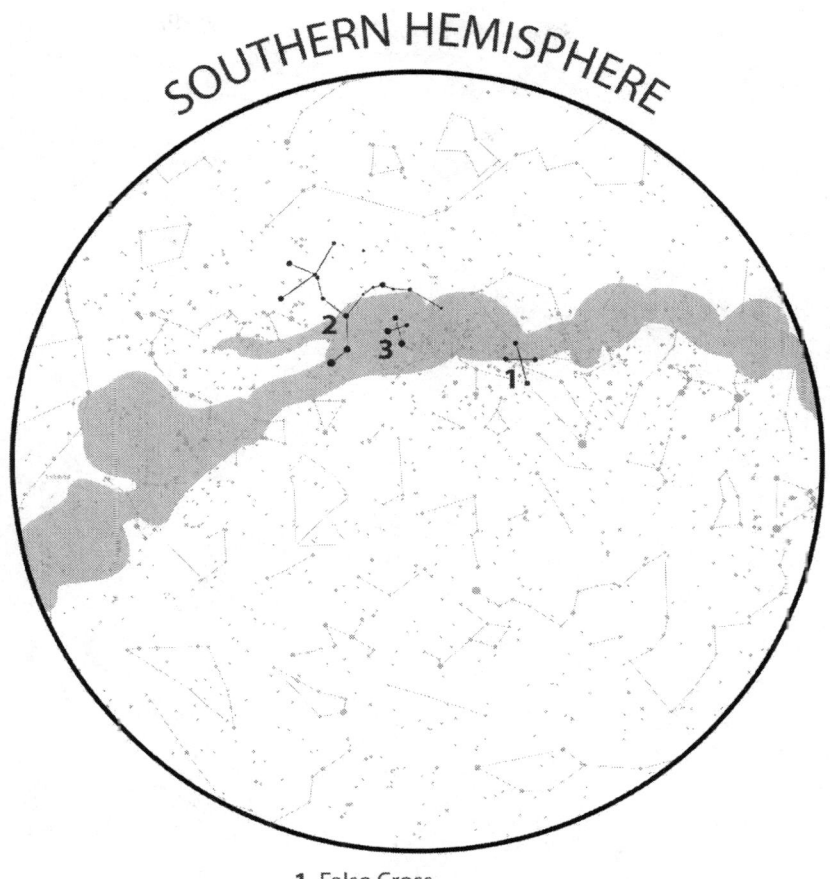

1, False Cross
2, Centaurus
3, Southern Cross with Gacrux top, Acrux bottom and Epsilon at the centre

Figure 2: Find "true south" in the Southern Hemisphere

7. Ladders and Cauldrons

IN THE last chapter, we discussed a new interpretation of Taliesin's poem *Preiddeu Annwn* as an account of King Arthur traversing the seven pole stars in his boat in order to steal or win the Cauldron. We learned that this sixth century Celtic bardic song was a metaphor for the process of initiation that transforms the hero into a "Son of the Cauldron". But what was that initiation? And can we undergo that rite of passage ourselves to help us evolve spiritually in modern times? The answer is a resounding "Yes" and what's more, it will radically change how you feel about your life.

In this chapter, we will start the process of learning what Taliesin and his fellow monks knew, and discover how we can use it as a mystic toolkit to transform our spiritual progress within our own lives.

The Cauldron is a symbol for the alchemist's crucible and once born into human life we ourselves become the subject of the work of the Great Alchemist. In other words, we are the First Matter, the crude material that has to be purified and transformed. Much of what our ancestors were trying to tell us in code is that all human existence proceeds up the seven rungs of alchemical initiation known as the Ladder of the Wise and it culminates, at the top, in winning the Cauldron, later known as the Holy Grail, which is the ultimate initiation of full enlightenment.

This process is not about the making of gods and goddesses. Those sorts of Otherworldly characters appear in these celestial dramas because they are the tour guides of the journey – and they are also, when needed, the paramedics, the magicians, the lovers, the tricksters, the adversaries and the midwives of our rebirth.

When we are in shamanic flight, we enter into our Higher Selves, temporarily, in order to communicate with these spiritual beings. In other words, we become a god. But that godlike status only holds while we are in those dimensions. The aim of the processes of the Ladder of the Wise and the teachings of the Cauldron is to become all that a real human being can be back here in the Middle World. Like the wooden puppet Pinocchio, who we will meet and examine in more detail later on, the aim of all the tests and travails that we, as the hero, have to face and overcome are to help us to become a "real boy".

So before we come on to the teachings of the Cauldron, we need to learn how to climb up the rungs of the Ladder of the Wise – and here it is.

7	Coagulation
6	Distillation
5	Fermentation
4	Conjunction
3	Separation
2	Dissolution
1	Calcification

Figure 3: The alchemical Ladder of the Wise

The Ladder of the Wise also mirrors the musicians' Law of the Octaves, because this seven-stepped process culminates in repeating the first step again but at a more elevated level. Putting that together with what we discussed in **3: The Holographic Universe of Music**, and then fed through your meditation should, hopefully, elicit a huge "Aha" moment. This Ladder of the Wise is alive and resonating vibrationally within every cell of our multidimensional Being. It is singing our way home with a song to which we are innately, instinctively attracted because it follows the rungs of ordered progression of a magical formula which was impregnated into our Rivers of Blood by our ancestors' stories many moons ago.

The roaming nomads of the steppes developed the metaphor of the seven precessing pole stars for their teachings about the Ladder of the Wise. In later times, after the agricultural revolution, when the polar hero was gradually replaced with the solar hero, each rung became identified with the seven planets of the solar system who were given governance of the 12 astrological houses.

The ancients were very aware of the importance of cosmological timing and so much of the teaching was merely for that purpose – to help them tell the time and the season. They would only begin their experiments when the astrological conditions were favourable. They knew that the influences abounding at specific planetary-influenced seasons, along with the position of the Sun, created the optimal conditions to bring each part of the seven-stepped process to flowering and fruition.

For instance, they would fire up the first stage of the Great Work on the Spring Equinox when the upthrusting flaming energies cause the sap to rise in plants and trees, and produce the necessary burning qualities for the first process of calcination.

You can find more details of the timings and astrological influences for specific parts of the operation below in **Figures 4** and **5**. Remember, this is a ladder going from the bottom to the top, so you need to begin on the lowest rung of calcination.

Rung	Process	Planet	Position of Sun
7	Coagulation	Sun	Leo
6	Distillation	Moon	Cancer
5	Fermentation	Mercury	Gemini, Virgo
4	Conjunction	Venus	Taurus, Libra
3	Separation	Mars	Aries, Scorpio
2	Dissolution	Jupiter	Sagittarius, Pisces
1	Calcification	Saturn	Capricorn, Aquarius

Figure 4: Positions of Sun and planetary ruler correspondences on the Ladder of the Wise

But how does enlightenment that is achieved through climbing the rungs of the Ladder of the Wise add value to human life today? What is the point of it? As one alchemist put it, quite brilliantly I thought, it is the process of reincarnating into your own life. And I would go further: the Time and Space into which we have incarnated forms the sides of the Great Alchemist's crucible, while the major events and landmarks of our lives provide the necessary conditions for the process of metamorphosis that turns us from merely being a subject or the material of the Great Work to actually becoming the Great Alchemist. Until that death and rebirth, we are just carbon with the whole weight of the universe pressing down upon us. Well, from our limited perspective it can sometimes feel like that. But the human heart is at the centre of the crucible of the cosmos and, as we know, under the right conditions, coal eventually turns into a diamond.

When you become the Great Alchemist, you will join the ranks of those whose actions impact on the lives of millions. You will have magnetic influence and magical power over your own life and, eventually, if you continue, over the times of man and the tides of history. Or you may just decide to renounce the whole lot for the ultimate liberation.

However, if all this is seeming like a massively tall order, you might be relieved to hear that it isn't really up to us to ensure that we evolve in this way. You know that so-called freedom everyone is always extolling? Well, we do have free will but only up to a point within certain parameters because the ==factors needed for our alchemical transformation were set before we were born.== The day, ==time and place of our birth were all carefully planned, right down to the second when we took our first screaming lungful of air,== so that the stars would be in a tailor-made alignment in the skies, thus setting off the Wheel at the right time and in the right place to provide the major landmarks, milestones, crossroads and waystations of our lifetime to come, all of which would create the needed challenges for our eventual transformation.

Rung	Process	Planet	Position of Sun	Best times
7	Coagulation	Sun	Leo	Gemini (Fixation) Aquarius (Multiplication) Pisces (Projection)
6	Distillation	Moon	Cancer	Virgo, (Distillation) Libra (Sublimation)
5	Fermentation	Mercury	Gemini, Virgo	Capricorn, (Fermentation) Leo (Digestion)
4	Conjunction	Venus	Taurus, Libra	Taurus
3	Separation	Mars	Aries, Scorpio	Scorpio
2	Dissolution	Jupiter	Sagittarius, Pisces	Cancer (solution)
1	Calcification	Saturn	Capricorn, Aquarius	Aries (calcination) Sagittarius (incineration)

Figure 5: Best times for specific parts of the alchemical operation

As R. J. Stewart says in his book, *The Underworld Initiation*:

In ancient, magical workings, specific planetary or stellar patterns were used to aid incarnation. This was not that certain conjunctions caused certain Beings to appear in the physical world. Rather, the conjunction was identical to the nature of the Being, enabling it to manifest in the womb at a harmoniously-related place.

You might want to read R. J. Stewart's remarks more than once, because it turns on its head everything that we have previously assumed about the who, why, where and how that we are.

There is nothing New Age about this teaching; in fact it's quite Old Age – older than the hills. These metaphysical processes are more ancient even than the multi-layered tales told to Kroy-Khasis, because they existed before the creation. They reflect, alchemically, what actually caused, and continues to cause, the creation, maintenance and eventual destruction of the universe and all lifeforms within it. So these metaphysical principles are certainly older than any religion. Alchemy follows the processes of Nature and that Lady of the Green Mantle is quite strict and precise in her production of forms which depend upon the use of hierarchies of sonar information, like the serried ranks of wind, string and percussion instruments in an orchestra pit, and which are organised according to delineated walls and borders, such as the lines on a musical stave. Therefore, in the same way, alchemy is a discipline in which the adept follows certain rules and correspondences as much as a violinist follows the score and the waving arms of the conductor of the Rites of Spring.

So how old is alchemy? When was it first practised? I'm going to give you a whistlestop tour of what we know of its history before sharing with you the very least you will need to get about how alchemy works in order for you to understand how to fire up your Three Cauldrons in traversing the Ladder of the Wise.

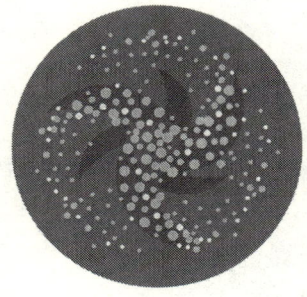

The earliest we can trace alchemy back is to the records of ancient Egypt, about 4,000 years ago, when the country was known as the Land of the Khem. In their writings, we hear about an alchemist, astronomer and magician, Imhotep, who became known as the Father of Medicine. The Greeks eventually copied Imhotep's works and called the practice *al-chemia* or al Chemia, from the Land of Khem; in other words, "the Egyptian science".

Back in Imhotep's day, healing was treated as one of the most secret and sacred sciences. Those who wanted to be physicians underwent severe tests and initiations. At this time, the study of the human body was much more holistic; the spiritual was not separate to the material and healers also learned about how the positions of the stars influenced and affected the individual.

According to Egyptian myths, Imhotep's alchemical wisdom came from the great god of scribes, Thoth. It was told that Thoth had preserved his canon of wisdom inside two great pillars "just before the Great Flood inundated the world". So as we now comprehend that deluges have been a regular feature of a warming and cooling planet for innumerable Ages and that the mythological Great Flood is a metaphorical Mystery teaching, that doesn't really help us with dating. However, a few thousand years ago, these two pillars were apparently "rediscovered". Egyptian priests claimed to find one outside the city of Heliopolis, while the other was unearthed near Thebes. They were both, it was said, covered with hieroglyphs and were named "The Pillars of the Gods of the Dawning Light". Eventually they were moved to a secret temple, which was dedicated to the earliest gods. Some texts indicate that this location was the Temple of Amun in Siwa, which is the oldest temple in Egypt, but we cannot be sure because only priests and pharoahs were allowed to view these sacred objects.

I hope, as you read those last few sentences you could hear the scepticism in my voice. My feeling is that even if they were "found", it wouldn't be the first time that priests buried an "artefact" only to uncover it later amid the unbridled awe of the assembled throng, and then remove it to a secret location. So I will leave you to use your own judgement on this whole issue.

However, the two pillars are described in scrolls dating back to 1550 BCE, which record them being put on public display periodically. Solon, the Greek legislator and writer who lived from 638 to 558 BCE, claimed to have told the grandfather of Plato's character Critias that he had studied them at first hand and that they memorialised the destruction of an ancient advanced civilisation. In other words, they were inscribed with the deluge myth about Atlantis, which we studied previously.

The fifth century BCE Greek historian Herodotus, who is infamous for being imprecise with the actuality, says that he encountered the two pillars in a secret visit to an Egyptian temple. "One pillar was of pure gold," he said, "and the other was as of emerald, which glowed at night with great brilliancy."

The Greeks later termed the science of alchemy Hermeticism after their god Hermes, who they equated with Thoth. The Romans came to call Thoth-Hermes Mercury and what was inscribed on the glowing green pillar became known as the teachings of the Emerald Tablet.

Bolos of Mendes, a sorceror of Alexandria who lived around 300 BCE, claimed that his renown alchemical treatise, titled *On Natural and Mystical Things*, was inspired by its words.

Around the same time, Alexander the Great specifically commissioned the building of the Library of Alexandria in order to house thousands of alchemical texts. The young Macedonian conqueror, apparently, had a great interest in this science, which he learned about from his tutor, the philosopher Aristotle and this led to what we now call the Alexandrian Gnostic system which is based on astrology and alchemy.

Sadly, the library was burned down - three times. The first two destructions by fire were claimed to be accidents that occurred as a result of war. But the third conflagration does seem to have been a deliberate act of arson, carried out at the command of the Christian Roman emperor, Diocletian, who had deliberately set out to destroy all the wisdom derived from Hermetic practices. Apparently, there were about 30,000 scorched and dog-eared manuscripts which the keepers of the scrolls rushed to retrieve from the flames and they were moved into a new building for safekeeping, which was finally destroyed by Caliph Umar in 642 CE, when Islam conquered Egypt.

It is said that Caliph Umar told his generals: "If these writings of the Greeks agree with the Book of Allah, they are redundant and need not to be preserved. If they disagree, they are blasphemous and need to be destroyed."

Thankfully, a fair number of those magical scrolls did somehow make it through the Islamic censor. The Arabs went on to become the sole preservers of the tradition for centuries. At the same time, all mention and practice of alchemy was banished and driven underground across the Holy Roman Empire, which, at its greatest extent, stretched from the Mediterranean countries in the south, including northern Africa and Egypt, eastwards as far as the borders of Persia and right up into Europe and Britain.

Many works by early Greek philosophers were later found among Arabian alchemical translations such as those of Plato, or "Aflatun" (as they called him), who the Muslims considered to have been a great alchemist because of his inventions for several devices for use in the laboratory. We also owe early Islam for preserving the records of Pythagoras who reputedly acquired his knowledge of mathematics and alchemy from the Emerald Tablet. Known as "Fithaghurus" to the Arabs, Pythagoras's *Book of Adjustments* was very popular among their alchemists.

They also preserved translations of the works of Archelaos, the teacher of Socrates to whom the great alchemical treatise *Turba Philosophorum* was attributed. The Arabians also conserved the oral teachings of Socrates, who was considered to be such an advanced alchemist that he had actually successfully generated an artificial lifeform. Socrates never publicly admitted to being an alchemist and he was opposed to writing down any teachings for fear they would fall into the wrong hands. Sadly, that didn't help him in the end when he was executed, by poison, for the crime of corrupting the minds of the young.

Plato was Socrates's student, while Plato's apprentice was Aristotle, who the Arabs called "Aristu". Aristotle wrote a book on alchemy for his student, Alexander the Great, which, by order of Heraclitus, was translated into Syrian in 618 CE. Several of Aristotle's works survived only in Arabic, including a discourse between himself and Alexander titled *Epistle of the Great Treasure of God*. In this book, Aristotle reviews the alchemical writings of Hermes, Asclepius, Pythagoras, Plato, Democritus and Ostanes.

However, the greatest Arabian alchemist was Jabir ibn Hayyan. Born in the eighth century, he wrote many books on alchemy and translated others that he claimed had been rescued from the Library of Alexandria, and put them into code form. For this reason, his works have been labelled "Jabir's gibberish".

But all this was before the Dark Ages – which we are barely emerging from now. The knowledge of the stars, in other words the Alexandrian Gnostic system of alchemy and astrology, would have been completely lost to mankind if it hadn't been for the Arabs preserving it and eventually passing it on to one Theophrastus Paracelsus in the 16th century, who brought it to Europe.

By then, the Dark Ages could not have been more stygian, especially when it came to medicine. The break between the holistic and the mundane had come in the fifth century, when Hippocrates segregated the knowledge of the stars from the healing disciplines, and this eventually led to modern-day medical science, in which doctors are trained to only accept that which can be observed objectively through the five primary human senses.

However, judging from the poems of Taliesin, it was still possible, in sixth century Britain, to keep the hidden Alexandrian science alive – albeit buried in complex riddling prose, a bit like Jabir's gibberish. Even after Rome had sent their emissary Augustine to Canterbury, to establish a more Roman type of Christianity that would banish any whiff of alchemical or magical thinking, the monks that lived further out across the country were more or less left alone to get on with matters as they saw fit. Thus the sort of religion practised outside the purview of its ecclesiastical centre in the south-east managed to retain a much more Celtic, and thus shamanic and bardic, flavour about it until at least the 10th century, when we know that the abbot of my own home town was an openly practising alchemist.

I live in Glastonbury, in Somerset, the land around which used to be considered the sacred heart of Britain under the stellar sword of the four nobles and to some of us, it still is. The abbey here then was huge – way out of proportion in size to the few hundred farming folk who scratched a living outside its walls. It now stands in ruins but there is evidence, to the trained eye, that it was probably host to a hive of magical activity, with tunnels snaking underground in which the monk alchemists would practice their craft.

As Christianity began to take hold in Britain, some of their scribes hid the codes for alchemical practices in gospel stories. This would have been easy to do because from the third century onwards, the monkish copiers were involved in the continual editing and re-editing of the New Testament, to suit differing political imperatives. Added to that, there is a Renaissance translation of an eighth century poem that is attributed to the legendary Irish bard Amergin. It's called *The Three Cauldrons of Poesy* and it describes an inner alchemical practice that has only survived today in the Three Bowls of Chi Kong – although it is also my intuition that it is the allegorical meaning of the Old Norse Edda's three wells Hvergelmir, Mimir and Urd, which are situated on Yggdrasil, the World Tree. Anyway, this would make more sense of the bard Taliesin's epithet of "Son of the Cauldron", because the practice of the Three Cauldrons or Three Bowls is all about incubating the inner secret fire that leads to the radiance of the brow, which is the true meaning of his name.

All this brings us to Glastonbury's most famous abbot, Dunstan, who was responsible for rebuilding the abbey after a fire destroyed it in the ninth century. He was also a bard and alchemist, and is famously depicted conquering the Devil through squeezing its nose with his tongs, which is obviously a metaphor for part of the operation of the Great Work.

Throughout medieval times, the role of the alchemist, who was often an astrologer too, was to support the monarch in one way or another. Dunstan was very close to King Edmund, and perhaps it is no coincidence that the male, solar, Michael ley line, which does a very potent fertility dance here with the female, lunar, Mary ley line, runs eastward across the country before ending up at that king's burial mound, Bury St Edmunds.

The name Dunstan is interesting and may have been inspired by much older strata of mythology. It is unlikely he was given that name at birth because it sounds like a title derived from an initiation. In this part of Britain, back then, "dun" meant "hill" and "stan" meant "cross on a hill". In other words, the name Dunstan could have been a title that alluded to the mythological deluge hero who battles the floods in the firmamental waters to erect the pole on the mound, thus winning the Cauldron.

Anyway, back in early medieval times, Glastonbury Abbey had been able to declare some autonomy from Rome by claiming that their foundation was by no less than Joseph of Arimathea, Jesus's uncle, hundreds of years before Augustine came to Canterbury. The legends claim that when Joseph arrived in Glastonbury, he had two vials containing Jesus's blood and plasma. In other words, he brought one vial of red liquid and another of white liquid. Alchemists will instantly recognise that metaphor and I will explain shortly about how these colours reflect the teachings of the Three Cauldrons as it weaves itself up the Ladder of the Wise.

But let's get back to our history for now...

In November 1539, Henry VIII tried to wipe out Glastonbury Abbey's autonomy and alchemical practices by sending his soldiers to hang, draw and quarter the abbot, Richard Whiting, and two other monks, on the Tor. Then he stood, with his royal courtiers, on an upper floor of the George and Pilgrim pub, still here today, to watch the abbey being burned and torn down.

Later on, Henry's daughter, Elizabeth I, made alchemy respectable again with her court being a virtual haven for astrologers and alchemists such as John Dee, who, hundreds of years after Dunstan's death, raided the former abbot's tomb in Glastonbury, looking for his alchemical recipes on how to make the Philosopher's Stone. Even today, the Queen receives sprigs from the Holy Thorn on Christmas Day, which are cut from a hawthorn tree in the gardens of the same church that Dee raided.

The Philosopher's Stone that Dee sought is the symbol used for the culmination of the Great Work: it is the ultimate outcome of surmounting the top rung on the Ladder of the Wise. It is sometimes referred to as the Philosopher's Child, or the Child of the Philosopher, and this Child is the fruit of the Divine Marriage, which is also known as the Marriage of the male Sun and the female Moon, and you will learn more about that in **Part 2: The Language of the Initiates**.

In Celtic or more Gnostic Christian alchemy, Christ was viewed as the Child of the Philosopher and many events recounted in the gospel stories about him and his deeds were perceived by medieval alchemists as a metaphor for an operation within the Great Work. For instance, the nativity in the stable under the star represented, to them, the birth of the Philosopher's Child or Stone, and the rest of the Messiah's life was interpreted as a metaphorical journey that represented the different rungs of the spiralling ladder and its cauldrons of initiation.

To me, the story about Joseph of Arimathea bringing the vials of white and red liquid to Glastonbury, once seen through the metaphoric lens of the alchemist, begs the question: where did he take the vial of black liquid?

But let me lay that out further.

The rungs of the Ladder of the Wise are divided into three colour-coded sections, Three Bowls or Three Cauldrons:

1. **Black** (*nigredo*) – the bottom two rungs consisting of calcination and then dissolution;
2. **White** (*albedo*) – the next two rungs consisting of separation and then conjunction;
3. **Red** (*rubedo*) – the top three rungs consisting of fermentation, distillation and finally coagulation.

Medieval alchemists regarded the three-day period of the death and resurrection of the Christ as a metaphor for the three stages – black, white and red - of the process of the Great Work.

In this analogy, the first stage of the crucifixion represents the black (nigredo) stage, when the Sun disappears. This is from Matthew 27:45:

Now from the sixth hour there was darkness over all the land unto the ninth hour.

The next two stages, white and red, are found in John 19:34:

But one of the soldiers with a spear pierced his side, and forthwith came there out blood and water.

In the Holy Communion ritual, red wine is consumed alongside a white wafer with the words "in re-memberance of me" because the two taken together represent the body of Christ. As you will see on the ladder, the re-membering (**conjunction**) takes place after the dismemberment stage of the **separation**.

Holy Communion or the Eucharist is also known in liturgical masses as "transubtantiation", while alchemists call it 'transmutation'. It's the same thing.

There is also a reference to the alchemical Divine Marriage in Gnostic Christian literature, by which I mean the Nag Hammadi gospels. These extra-canonical scrolls were so named because they were discovered in a cave in Nag Hammadi in the Egyptian desert in the early 20th century. Scholars believe that they had been hidden there in the third or fourth century, most likely from the fierce eyes of the censor. My two favourite candidates for the role of this inquisitor are the 1st century Bishop Irenaeus, who was the first to insist upon a literal version of the Jesus story for which he selected and re-wrote just four out of what must have been dozens of available gospels, and St Athanasius, who, in the year 367, sent out a letter banning non-canonical books.

Before the early centuries of the Common Era, those who believed in a historical Jesus Christ were few and far between and it was the Gnostic Christians, with their understanding that this literature was metaphorical and not literal, who made up the majority. There are some who believe – myself among them – that it was these Gnostic Christians who were thrown to the lions in the Roman arenas. Their beliefs and practices were certainly inconvenient to the new imperial narrative.

The Nag Hammadi gospels – such as *Pistis Sophia, The Exegesis of the Soul* and *The Gospel of Thomas* - are clearly allegorical, mystical accounts about a Christ who inhabited three different worlds, as are found on the shamanic World Tree. And once seen through the new perspective of the Nag Hammadi texts, Jesus's turning of the white water into red wine at the wedding in Cana, as recounted in *The Gospel of John*, takes on a very different meaning.

In *Exegesis of the Soul*, we hear about a sacred marriage that comes after a hierodule or sacred prostitute abandons her work in the marketplace to prepare the bridal chamber for the Christ/brother/husband.

"And when she had intercourse with him, she got from him the seed that is the life-giving spirit, and this is the resurrection from the dead."

Of course, you will know by now that resurrection in this context means rebirth or reincarnating not physically but into one's own life after reaching the top rung of the Ladder of the Wise.

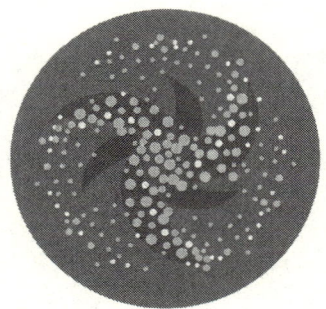

So now we've got to the end of the history lesson, you might be wondering whereabouts you happen to be in terms of this alchemically produced spiritual evolution? Well, I couldn't possibly tell you. Nobody knows whether the whole seven-stage process takes one revolution of the Earth around the Sun or one whole lifetime, or even 140 (seven score lifetimes), which could be the metaphorical meaning of the seven score links of Taliesin's brindled ox.

Of one thing, though, I'm pretty certain: this metaphysical ladder is not going upwards in a straight line. It is curling around and around like a serpent or a helix, which is why we sometimes feel we have to keep coming back and deal with knotty issues we'd thought were now safely done and dusted, and behind us. However, this usually isn't a reversal or deja vu; we have made progress up the spiral staircase. It's just that we are now approaching the issue from a higher, more refined and intelligent viewpoint.

It seems to me, though, that some people are starting out on this alchemical journey for the first time while others are old hands, and a few are probably ready for this to be their last lifetime on Earth. In other words, everyone is at different stages of development. I think that is partly what makes life so interesting but also, at times, so difficult, particularly if you don't have this understanding.

This stepped ladder, sectioned into the Three Cauldrons of black, white and red, applies as much to our own inner process of spiritual self-realisation as it does to our relationships with others because this same process is found in all and any kind of transformational growth that exists within Nature. And so whether you know anything about alchemy or not, the same three colours or Cauldrons and what they represent will apply to the major landmarks and waystations of your life. This is because the alchemical process follows universal laws that don't need us to acknowledge them to be at work any more than the Sun needs our permission to rise and set.

A lot of what goes on is in the submarinal deeps of what we call the subconscious mind, of which most of us are barely aware, which is ironic because, like the seven-eighths of the iceberg that lies concealed beneath the ocean, it doesn't need to be visible, on the surface, to steer this titanic "tin-opener" of our human existence.

However, once you learn more about the Great Work and the rungs which build one upon the other, you won't need anyone else to tell you how well you're doing because you will begin to get information yourself about the state of your own progress, and particularly if you are able to communicate shamanically with your spirit guides, who do know exactly where you are and who have been patiently hanging around waiting for you to realise that you need to consult with them on it.

There are also certain well-known characteristics to each step that you will be able to recognise. For instance, you will know if you are burning up – either with anger, envy or passion; you will also feel it when an ocean of tears douses those flames.

So let's get on to some very basic alchemical principles that will explain the wisdom teachings that all these illustrious bards, scribes and alchemists were trying to preserve from the Roman jackboot.

Here is a breakdown of the three major stages of the Great Work into their main characteristics, to help you recognise which stage you're going through in the Great Work of You!

Nigredo, *black - Calcination and dissolution*

The nigredo or black phase, the first stage, is regarded as the most difficult and painful. I encountered it early on during my shamanic practitioner training course and it was mortifying. Just when I wanted to create a good impression with a fascinating new circle of friends, the grinding down of my inner psyche began to expose horrible shadow parts of my personality I would normally try to hide - not just from others but also from myself.

I remember feeling as if I was being swirled or whirled in the crucible of my inner consciousness by unfamiliar and unwelcome emotions, and I will never forget the burning, red-faced inflammation of shame when I couldn't hide my faults and they were strewn all around on the floor, where everyone could see them.

So the *nigredo* is often a painful process and made all the more so when you don't realise that it is just the precursor to what will turn out to be a wholly beneficial transformation. Its aim is to reduce everything down to its barest essentials and then burn off all the dross. It is painstaking and arduous work - to face your demons in the form of the impurities that have usually been dumped into your emotional field by hitherto unprocessed emotions, some your own, some inherited. But they must be incinerated to the purest white ashes and then dissolved because if they crop up at a later stage, they will destroy the whole work.

We find the magician Myrddin (Merlin) experiencing the black nigredo phase in Geoffrey of Monmouth's 12th century *Vita Merlini* and that is why, in my own book *The Grail Mysteries*, I first introduce him at this stage of his life. Myrddin is undergoing deep shame and mortification after killing his nephew, accidently, during the heat of battle. So he is living as a hermit, like a wild man of the woods, with his mind almost completely lost in grief as he just follows the path of his small pig, which goes round and round the forest in what appears to be an unending and inescapable labyrinth of woe.

We find a synchronicity here with the Greeks with this unicursal maze. Their mythic labyrinth, on a more distant part of the primordial carpet, was built by the artisan Daedalus who, similarly to Myrddin, was living in the exile he'd been banished to after killing his nephew. The shame that would naturally arise from killing an innocent family member is classic *nigredo* phase stuff. It is a vital and necessary stage of spiritual growth and should not be Prozaced out of existence.

The first part of the black phase, **calcification**, is ruled astrologically by the planet Saturn and the second part, **dissolution**, is ruled by Jupiter. (But don't worry about planetary governors and what they mean for now, as I'll be explaining all that, in the simplest terms, when we get to **Part 2: The Language of** the Initiates.*)

Albedo, white – Separation and Conjunction

The white or *albedo* phase is essentially about purifying the material and this is achieved during **separation** (ruled by Mars) before the **conjunction** (ruled by Venus). All that nasty, shameful chaff which previously erupted into view in the black *nigredo* phase is divided and separated from the nutritious wheat you want to keep in an operation which is akin, esoterically, to winnowing.

In personal alchemy, there is no short cut around this stage. One has to sort through one's "stuff' just like one sorts through a sock drawer - and it is about as exciting!

In the white or *albedo* phase, you separate yourself, or are separated against your will, in order to rise above the quagmire of your broken personality and dreams to realise and recognise your true or Higher Self, with which you can then form a conjunction.

Rubedo, red – Fermentation, Distillation and Coagulation

All of the purification that took place in the white albedo phase generates an incredibly potent energy and this is all released during the three-stepped red *rubedo* phase.

After suffering through the *nigredo*, undergoing the intense purification of *albedo*, the matter – that's you! - can seem to be lifeless and devoid of energy. So medieval alchemists would "give it more blood" by reddening it in the fire.

Alchemists use the processes of **fermentation** (ruled by Mercury) and **distillation** (ruled by the Moon) to complete the *rubedo* red phase of transformation to produce the final crystallisation, or **coagulation** (ruled by the Sun), of the energy and matter to become the Philosopher's Stone.

In personal terms, the red *rubedo* phase should bring an infusion of new life to the adept. Any hidden impurities in our characters that somehow made it through the previous phases are finally destroyed as we go through the spiritual transformation of death and resurrection.

This final step on the ladder is about enlightenment, reanimation, revitalisation and rebirth. When we are undergoing this stage, we often receive vividly colourful visions of a wider and deeper manifestation of reality that involves a higher form of imagination - in other words, the visions gained from shamanic trance, or similar. It is so vivid and so psychedelic in nature that it is sometimes referred to as the Peacock's Tail.

Practical exercise

When one or more of the symbols shown in **Figure 6** below appear in your dreams or shamanic journeys, it could be indicating that you are going through the matching part of the process. So try keeping a dream diary and listing down the significant symbols and keys that are presented you while in altered states.

Rung	Process	Alchemical symbols in dreams and journeys
7	Coagulation	Peacock, phoenix, gold coins, balanced scales, egg-shaped stone, androgynous youth, eagle soaring, and Sun and Moon beaming down proudly on a child.
6	Distillation	Blooming rose, lotus, jasmine or edelweiss, fountains, waterwheels, dew, rain, snow, unicorns, white doves, owls, pelicans, winged serpents, and a dragon in flames eating its own tail.
5	Fermentation	Corpses, graves, coffins, massacres, mutilation, worms, dung beetles, rotting flesh and a snake crucified on a cross.
4	Conjunction	Cockerel, virile bull, ithyphallic images, rams and satyrs, binds around opposing entities, two streams merging into one, and a couple embracing.
3	Separation	Double-edged axes, swords hanging from above, knights wielding swords, dismemberment, parting of the Red Sea and the Apocalypse.
2	Dissolution	Lakes and pools, floods and deluges, underground streams, quicksand, tears, menstruation, fishes swimming and washing in tubs.
1	Calcification	Funeral pyres, hellish scenes, torture by fire, crucifixion, birds rising from flame, fire-breathing dragon, salamanders, and skulls and skeletons

Figure 6: Symbols that may occur during altered states, indicating your position on the Ladder of the Wise

After reading through all that, you might be wondering why on Earth anyone would want to put themselves through such harrowing trials? Who would willingly volunteer for burning, drowning, then being sent into exile, dismembered and boiled in a cauldron. What kind of masochist would want to have hellish dreams about funeral pyres, rotting flesh or getting sucked into quicksand?

But the Ladder of the Wise is not a voluntary option. It's not like deciding to buy an air ticket to fly to India to find a guru, or opting to retreat to a cool Buddhist meditation centre on a remote Scottish island. We don't have any choice. It is why we are here and we even planned it that way, before taking incarnation, so we can't blame anyone else. But if you find that a frightening thought, I invite you to consider this: I've found that not being taught that I was born on to this ladder is what has caused me the most pain and confusion in my life.

Anyway, so now we understand a little more about the seven-runged Ladder of the Wise, let's spend some time looking at the three-stepped teachings of the Cauldron into which the ladder is segmented.

Our knowledge about the inner alchemic practice of The Three Cauldrons derives from the poem of the Druidic Irish bard Amergin. Some believe he migrated to Ireland from the Basque region of Spain in the eighth century, although the earliest translation we have today was copied down by a monkly scribe in the 16th century.

Anyway, here is his poem *The Three Cauldrons of Poesy*.

My own existence springs forth from the Cauldron of Poesy,
Which was created by the gods from the dúile;
Enlightened is each inspiration
That streams forth in my speech and from my centre of being.
I am Amergin White Knee,
Ancient in years and grey of hair.
My inspirations are found within
The many forms of poetry
That are born within my Cauldron of Warming.
The gods do not orient each person's cauldrons equally
Or fill them with the same talents and abilities:
Some are formed upside down, some tilted or upright.
Some are empty, while others are half full,
Some are filled with knowledge like Eber and Donn,
Capable of creating chants of life and death,
Through a skillful combination of words
In the power of three genders: masculine, feminine, and neuter,
And possessing the strength of three measures: double letters,
Long vowels and short vowels.
My Cauldron of Vocation is trained
Through a study of the arts of poetry
And sustains me through proper composition.
I sing also of the Cauldron of Knowledge
That allocates the gifts of wisdom
According to the laws of each art,

And the work of each artist in general.

To break down Amergin's prose, he is saying that we are all born with these Three Cauldrons in various different states of functionality within our energetic fields. Some are in the wrong position or do not contain enough vital energy for us to fulfil the Great Work. The aim of a human lifetime is to get all three cauldrons facing upright and in alignment so they can provide a suitable alchemic receptacle to hold the heavenly mead or waters of life, which then start to "cook" from the secret fire contained in the liquid. Obviously, a tilted container or one that is upside down is useless as a crucible, as it will spill its contents.

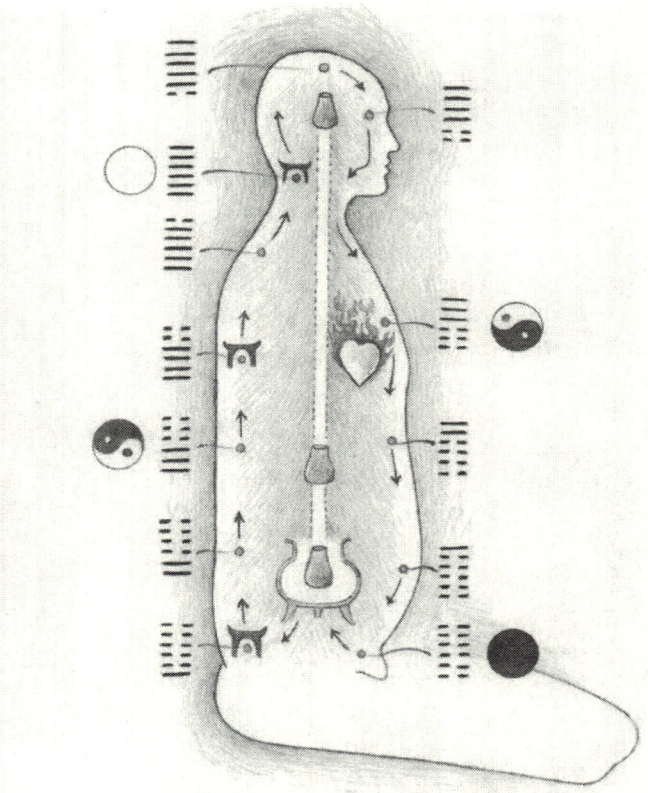

Figure 7: Traditional Taoist diagram showing the Three Cauldrons

The traditional Taoist system depicted above shows the energy rising up to extreme Yang behind the neck and then descends to extreme Yin in front of the groin.

The following illustration is Glastonbury artist Yuri Leitch's interpretation in which he shows the correlations with the shamanic, Celtic and Taoist systems.

This book was conceived in a year when I was journeying into the Norse World Tree in order to get information about how it is presented in the *Eddas* - the corpus of sagas that we have inherited from the Scandinavian peoples. It was then that I discovered that the three wells of the Norns of Yggsdrasil corresponded to the Celtic three cauldrons.

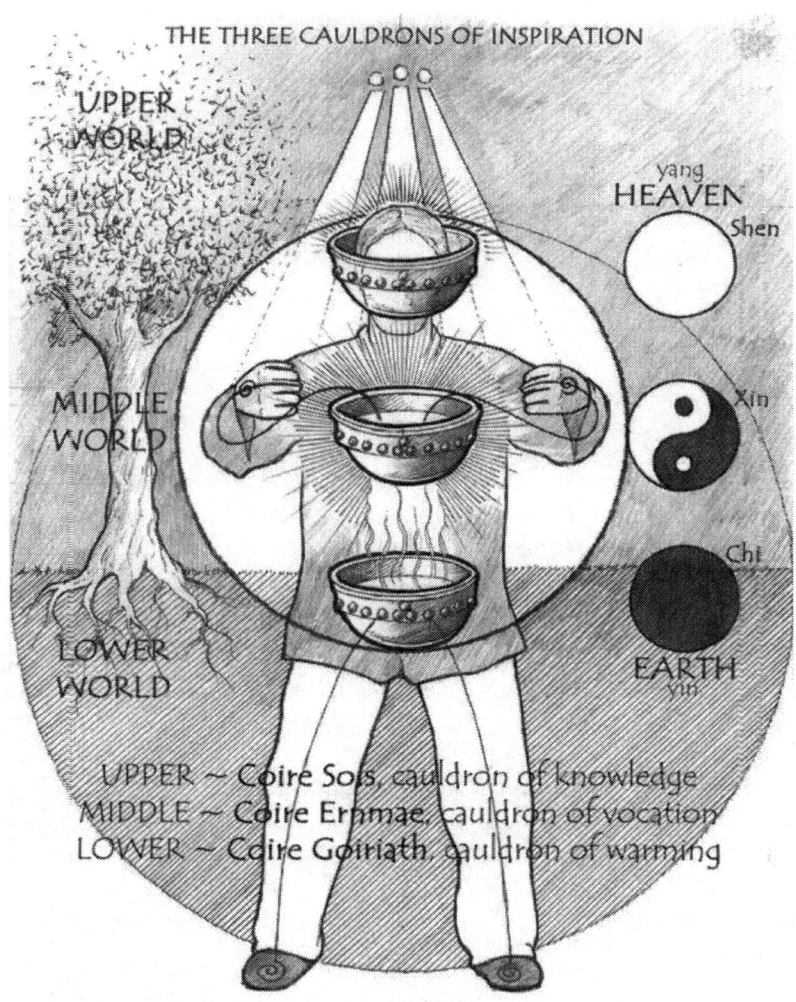

Figure 8: The Three Cauldrons of Inspiration by Yuri Leitch

A short while later, I journeyed again. I consulted with my spirit guide about a new book that would use this understanding as its basis. Since then, I have been inundated with realisation upon realisation about the metaphorical meaning of the myths that I have been studying for more than 40 years. And I only received the last part of the puzzle when I joined a Chi Kung class a few months ago and started practising the cultivation of *chi* within the Three Bowls.

Tradition	Celtic	Scandinavian	Chinese	Initiations
Source	The Three Cauldrons of Poesy	The Eddas	Chi Gung	Alexandrian system
Cauldron 1	Coire Goriath The Cauldron of Warming	The Lower World Well of Hvergelmir	The Cauldron of Incubation	Water: Scorpio Fire: Sagittarius
Cauldron 2	Coire Ermai The Cauldron of Vocation	Middle World Well of Mimir	The Cauldron of Motion	Water: Cancer Fire: Leo
Cauldron 3	Coire Sois The Cauldron of Knowledge	Upper World Well of Wyrd	The Cauldron of Inspiration	Water: Pisces Fire: Aries

Figure 9: Comparing the Celtic, Norse and Taoist systems

Thus, from all this experience, I believe that the practice of Three Cauldrons is part and parcel of the spiralling Ladder of the Wise, the metaphorical template found in the mythological hero's voyage around the pole stars and, more latterly, the zodiac. The alchemists of old coined the term "the human vessel" and so the sea-going vessel of the hero's submarinal ship is fuelled in its engine room, so to speak, by the secret fire in the water, which is represented in myths by three astrologically determined water and fire initiations, which you will find on zodiac charts further on into the book.

The Benedictine alchemist Antoine-Joseph Pernety wrote in the 18th century:

"In allegories and fables, the philosophers have given this secret fire the names sword, lance, arrows, javelin etc. It is the fire which Prometheus stole from heaven, which Vulcan employed to form the thunderbolts of Jupiter and the golden throne of Zeus."

Pernety could have added that it is also the mead that was stolen by Odin in the Norse saga and the nectar that was seized by the beak of the eagle Garuda in the Vedic story about the churning of the Ocean of Milk.

The 19th century German physician Franz Hartmann wrote in his book *Alchemy*:

"The secret fire of the alchemists is sometimes described as a serpentine working power in the body of the acetic. It is an electric, fiery, hidden power, an electro-spiritual force and creative power."

Initiates fire, like an arrow, this serpentine, hidden power up the "djed", or energetic channel that encases the spine, until it lights up the cup-shaped hypothalamus via the drowning of the pineal gland in red and white serpentine drops of nectar. This is achieved through shamanic sexual practices that are depicted by the symbol of the sword penetrating the chalice.

Mercury is critical to this inner alchemical process and he is found in the Celtic myths as Gywddion, in the old Norse sagas as Odin and in the Saxons' songs as Woden.

Practically, I recommend approaching this work holistically and that those who are shamans should follow guidance from their spirit guides about how to quicken the process.

But we are already proceeding, whether or not we even realise that we are on the ladder. This is expressed in the philosophy of the old Celts about the four joys and four sorrows of human existence, which naturally create the fuel to propel the human vessel along. Thus, the four joys and four sorrows are received by the hero through the help of the gods and the hindrance of the adversaries he meets along the way.

What follows is my interpretation of how the three Cauldrons or Wells fit into the three stages of the Great Work.

The Cauldron of Warming - Nigredo

Most of us are born with our lower bowl - the Cauldron of Warming (Celtic) or Cauldron of Incubation (Chinese) - in the upright position and it contains as much, or as little, energy as has been accrued over time by our ancestors. In other words, we are standing on some mighty shoulders. And once we understand what an incredible gift has been bequeathed to us, we begin to realise the extraordinary opportunity that human life presents us with. The aim of the work on the lower bowl is to replenish the energy in the Cauldron of Warming or Incubation. The purpose of the whole work of Three Cauldrons is advance enough in terms of spiritual evolution to make sure that the Rivers of the Blood are kept clean and pure so that future generations will be born with plenty of energy in their lower bowls.

The Cauldron of Vocation – Albedo

The middle bowl - known as the Cauldron of Vocation (Celtic) or Cauldron of Motion (Chinese) – is sometimes innately unright but it can also be tilted on its side, or even upside down. The aim of the work on the middle bowl is to get our Cauldron of Vocation in the upright position, so that it can act as a container and transmitter, upwards and downwards, for the energies coursing back and forth from the other two bowls.

The Cauldron of Knowledge - Rubedo

The upper bowl – known as the Cauldron of Knowledge (Celtic) or Cauldron of Inspiration (Chinese) – is often upside down at birth and thus the ultimate aim of the work is to get that Cauldron of Knowledge to turn around, so that it is upright to receive the "heavenly dew" of the energies.

Everybody can practice the alchemy of The Three Cauldrons and benefit themselves and their ancestral line – there is no-one on Earth today or in the Otherworlds who is beyond redemption.

The harrowing trials and tribulations, along with the joyful and pleasurable experiences we meet during our lifetimes, all contribute to the work of the replenishing and realigning the three cauldrons; to the Celts these were known as the Four Joys and the Four Sorrows. However, you can take direct action to quicken the whole process by practising Chi Kung or shamanic sexual magic.

I suggest you familiarise yourself with all the teaching materials supplied thus far before going on to **Part 2: The Language of the Initiates**, in which will I teach you some key words, expressions and formulae used in the secret codes so that you can start to recognise them when reading a story or watching a film in which the understory is hidden and only recognisable to those who have the understanding.

Then hopefully, once you've got all that information into your cognitive toolkit, you will be ready for **Part 3: Into the Zodiac**, where you will become equipped to recognise and benefit spiritually from the stories of the solar astrological hero.

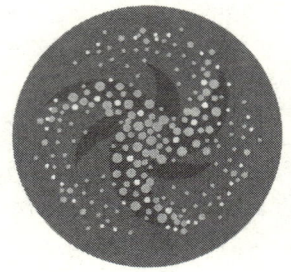

I want to conclude **Part 1** on what, to me, is a very important point. I'm not going to say "not everybody is meant to know these things" because I don't know if that is true. It is true, however, in my experience, that most people will not want to know these things and that's all well and fine because this may be their first time out on the ladder and they may need to spend more than one lifetime getting a firm grip on the bottom rung before they are ready to take on new information.

Initiates refer to those new souls as "children" and in my opinion, there's nothing wrong in being a "child"; far from it – we come from a society that values childhood. We frown on those Victorians who sent tiny young lads up sooty chimneys to sweep them, or forced children to slave in the Southern cotton plantations. However, this is not mere woolly altruism; it is also because we fully recognise and acknowledge the added value, in terms of creativity and invention, that it gives a society's development - intellectually, emotionally and spiritually - when its infants are allowed a period in which they are free to roam in their imaginations, to build sand forts on the beaches and castles in the clouds.

It is part of the role of the initiate to care for the welfare of these "children" as if they were their own offspring. In my view, that does not mean trying to make them face the Dark Night of the Soul when they should be going out into the sunshine with their friends to play football. We just have to use our tact, discretion and wisdom to steer the young ones away and protect them from those who barbecue toddlers on spits.

Part 2

THE LANGUAGE OF THE INITIATES

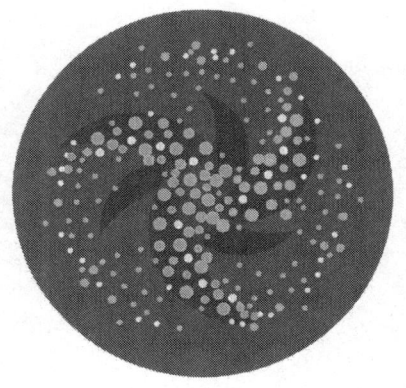

8. The Quickening

IT IS not my aim in this book to teach you how to do astrology, alchemy or Chi Kung. But if you want to take any of those aids to further enlightenment, I've recommended some excellent books written by those far more expert, in their specific field, than myself. You will find those works in the **Bibliography** at the end.

The aim of **Part 2: The Language of the Initiates** is to provide you with the least you need to know to be able to read the astrological and alchemical metaphors I've discovered buried in ancient myths.

Over thousands of years, these mystery teachings have been bastardised into fake histories in order to serve various and changing political imperatives, while their real meanings were kept hidden and only accessible to the initiates of occult societies based on a secret, priestly language, such as Latin or Sanskrit. But once we learn how to interpret the language of the initiates, we can unlock the doors of our perception with the metaphorical keys in these epic tales, which will help us understand how to make sense of our lives today.

In a nutshell, the passage of our lives naturally provides the means of alchemic transformation, with each of us being born at differing stages of progress in this work that has been accrued from previous lifetimes and from those who share in our Rivers of Blood. The state of our progress up the Ladder of the Wise is reflected by a) the positions of our three inner cauldrons and b) how much energy they contain. It is our role, while in a human body, to correct any misalignments and replenish that energy so that not only do we get the opportunity to carry on climbing the ladder but also help those who come after us, in our family line, to give them a good start in this process. In other words, this is the real meaning of the eternal life sought by the champions of many an ancient heroic tale.

So first, let's examine the characteristics of this path through the lens of modern literature and films, because it is possible to glean some kind of indication of our progress once we have understood how, even today, the storylines of films and plays are based on the inner workings of the process that leads to the Divine Marriage. One way is to examine our past romantic relationships through the lens of the Alchemist, because the process of how we meet, fall in love and wed follows the exact same template as the operation that culminates in the quickening that produces the Marriage of the Sun and the Moon – and I aim to explain more about this all-important, vital requisite of the quickening as we go on.

But being able to analyse where we ran into problems that we failed to resolve in the past can be enormously informative and indicative about our sticking points, showing us where further work is needed.

The mystical Sufis envisaged the steps of the ladder of the alchemical journey as the different stages in the development of a romance, from the first budding glimmers of infatuation to ultimately entering into permanent unity through marriage, and it might by why they produced such evocative love poetry.

The 13th century Sufi poet and alchemist Rumi wrote:

Love is that flame which when it blazes up, burns away everything except the Beloved.

That certainly sounds to me like the process that begins with the burning of **calcination**.

Similar morphologies are used in the storylines of Hollywood rom-coms and so I think this is as good a place as any to start learning more about the different steps that lead up to the Divine Marriage through our own relationships.

Many of these types of stories illustrate the old adage "the path to true love never runs smooth". To begin with, the couple are usually initially antithetical to one another and may even dislike each other on sight, even though everyone in the cinema can plainly see they are perfectly matched. However, at this stage, they are so affected by the other's bad opinion that it leads to the black *nigredo* phase, the Cauldron of Warming, and **calcination**, in which their perceived faults are slowly burned away in a fire of shame and anger.

Eventually, though, the couple meet up again and they eventually start to develop feelings for one another (**dissolution**). Our hearts, in the auditorium, begin to soar like larks ascending with the violins until suddenly, the couple are swiftly thrown apart in the **separation** of the white *albedo* phase, the Cauldron of

Vocation. The rupture cracks open suddenly and, seemingly, irrevocably, caused by a series of misunderstandings in a comedy of errors that is often woven through with deceptions or unworked-through baggage from the past.

The break-up is painful and each of them goes through an agonising spell of introspection, and long lonely hours spent in inner contemplation, in an effort to identify and unravel what went wrong. Well, that's what is meant to happen, unless one or both them of decides to drown their pain in drink, drugs, sex and rock 'n' roll and then, through lack of judgement, get thrown together at a wild party with Mr or Miss AN Other, in which case, they have to go back to square one, (**calcination**) and start all over again.

But for the purpose of this exercise, let's assume both are self-disciplined enough to take time out to work out their issues. The hurdles to the reunion seem to be insurmountable but just when the cinema audience is beginning to wonder whether all is lost, the two just happen to bump into each other again at a busy crossroads. There is a bit of an awkward conversation and then they decide to go for a cup of coffee, over which each admits their errors in the whole affair and, gradually, both realise that they want to get back together and form a **conjunction**.

However, this time, they have gained wisdom from their errors and are thus more sensible in their approach. As they enter the *rubedo* red phase, the Cauldron of Knowledge, they decide pursue the development of their relationship more slowly and thoughtfully this time. They need to chew over and digest the new situation (**fermentation**). They know they need to give each other sufficient time to adjust to the new person each of them has transformed into as a result of all that deep inner work.

Eventually, the pair find that because they have evolved enough, they feel more stable and secure in each other's love and are now ready to create a third thing (a child or a new home) between them, and so they become engaged (**distillation**) and finally get married (**coagulation**).

So now, after giving you that generic template, here is a specific example I think you'll enjoy.

The film *Bridget Jones's Diary* is based on the steps of this alchemical operation and is, in itself, a cheeky nod towards Jane Austen's *Pride and Prejudice*, a Victorian novel which also has a plot that is structured and organised along a rocky, up-and-down path that eventually leads to the Divine Marriage.

The material to be transformed – otherwise known as the First Matter – are the stars of the film, Bridget Jones and Mark Darcy, who appear to be total opposites when they first meet among their parents' bizarre social milieu at a Christmas party. They are actually quite repelled by one another. Bridget thinks Mark is a vulgar and arrogant fool, and is appalled by his garish Christmas jumper. Mark decides Bridget is a "verbally incontinent spinster who smokes like a chimney, drinks like a fish and dresses like her mother".

When Bridget hears his opinion of her, it causes her to enter the *nigredo* or black phase of **calcination**, which, as we know, is so often marked by shame and humiliation at having to face repugnant truths about oneself. She is so embarrassed she makes a vow to work on self-improvement and begins to keep a diary as a way of helping this process along. This diary becomes the record of the alchemical steps Bridget takes towards transformation as, over time, she moves up the rungs of the ladder.

Eventually, Bridget learns to imbibe less alcohol, smoke fewer cigarettes and eat more nutritious food, and her health and figure begin to improve. She gains in self- confidence and after a number of chance meetings with Mark, the old adage that opposites attract starts to come into play. Then, when he arrives at her flat to rescue her birthday dinner, which she had unwisely decided to cater herself, all her friends instantly see a real romance budding on the bough. However, its flowering is sadly prevented by a piece of baggage from Bridget's past, which turns up in the drunken form of the **dissolute**, self-centred Daniel Cleaver. Daniel is one of Bridget's former beaus and tells her a big lie that reflects badly on Mark's character – but which she has no reason to disbelieve.

Daniel and Mark then get into a hilarious fisticuffs scene that has become a classic of modern cinema, which ends with Mark knocking Daniel out. And as the bloody-nosed anti-hero lays sprawled in the street, Bridget feels such sympathy for his plight she chides Mark for being so mean – and taking his cue from those remarks, he instantly leaves. But then it doesn't take long for Daniel to show Bridget his true colours and so she sends him shuffling off into the night too.

But with Mark and Daniel now both gone from her life, Bridget is alone to reflect on events, which is typical feature of the *albedo* white phase, in which the purpose of the **separation** of the two components is to purify themselves further, individually.

Eventually, through her parents, Bridget finds out about Daniel's lies. She began to realise that Mark had great integrity and with all the misunderstandings swept away, she is able to start falling in love with him properly (**conjunction**).

Soon after she begins to realise her feelings for him, her parents take her Mark's parents' Ruby Wedding celebration – perhaps to signal that we are now entering the *rubedo*, red phase. Here, she finds out Mark has become engaged to another woman, Natasha, and that they are about to leave the country to live in New York. Bridget gives an impassioned speech in which she laments that Britain is about to lose one of its finest men. However, it doesn't seem to make any difference. We are given to believe Mark and Natasha left for America the next day and so Bridget has to return to her life still alone, sadly ruminating on what might have been (**fermentation**).

Then, out of the blue, Darcy suddenly turns up at Bridget's flat and offers to take her out for dinner. While Bridget is getting changed, he idly flicks through her books and then comes upon her diary. We see Mark then leave her flat and Bridget, upon hearing the door slam, rushes out of her bedroom in just her underwear to find him gone.

Then she realises her diary is open on the table. During the time she had been under Daniel Cleaver's influence, Bridget had scrawled several angry insults about Mark, so she is horrified to think he has read her earlier, mistaken views of him – opinions she no longer holds. Not waiting to dress, she rushes out into the street.

She finds Mark coming out of a bookshop, holding a new diary for her that is a symbol representing the new story of the new life the couple will now share together. Cue the snow and the surging violins as they finally kiss (**coagulation**) and the credits roll.

Now, you might be wondering what happened to the penultimate step of the ladder, **distillation**?

Well, it is quite typical of Hollywood films to rush us along to the Marriage of the Sun and the Moon at the point of the much-awaited passionate embrace. I should imagine it's because scriptwriters don't trust our attention spans not to wander off during the **distillation** stage, which does admittedly involve a degree of what an audience might deem to be boring diligence and attention to detail.

But there is another reason worth our consideration. It is difficult to show a metamorphic process in dramatic terms that nobody really understands. What I mean is, we know **coagulation** happens but we don't know how it happens because whereas the six previous rungs were surmounted, one after the other, by a gradual, steady process of evolution, achieving the seventh rung only comes about like a flash from the heavens on the road to Damascus, as experienced by Saul of Tarsus.

You are probably familiar with these two stories in the *Acts of the Apostles* from the *New Testament*?

In one, the religious inquisitor Saul of Tarsus is riding to Damascus to arrest the Christians there when he is suddenly hit by a blazing white light so powerful that he falls from his ass. In that instant, he undergoes an intellectual metamorphosis that changes him irrevocably and he goes on to become Paul the Apostle, one of the most powerful and influential missionaries of the Christian era.

In another story from the Bible, the disciples experience a fire initiation. This is from Acts 2, 1-4:

And when the day of Pentecost was fully come, they were all with one

accord in one place. And suddenly there came a sound from heaven as of a rushing mighty wind, and it filled all the house where they were sitting. And there appeared unto them cloven tongues like as of fire, and it sat upon each of them. And they were all filled with the Holy Ghost, and began to speak with other tongues, as the Spirit gave them utterance.

These are just two accounts of quickenings that occur through the initiation of fire, or of the Phoenix, the mythical sunbird of the Phoenicians. But they are found as golden keys buried in the holds of many a mythological vessel sailing the oceans of Time.

If you transpose the astrological house timings shown in Figure 5 on to a zodiac, it's clear to see that it takes about seven circuits of the Wheel to complete one circuit of the Ladder of the Wise. For instance, the first part of rung one, **calcification**, begins in Aries at the Spring Equinox but for optimum results, the second part of calcination (**incineration**) should not be begun until Sagittarius (November into December). This means we could spend the best part of a year traversing the first rung – and that is only if one journey around the Wheel represents one year in a human lifetime. We just don't know.

The Ladder of the Wise might represent one or more than one year in the story of the mythological hero and it is sometimes just one day, as was the case of Phil Connors in the film *Groundhog Day*. So it could be that it takes us one whole lifetime to complete and pass through just one rung of the ladder – and only then if the operation is a success. Failures do happen quite often, just as in the lab experiments go wrong; the material might get too wet or too hot. And so we might have to come back in our next life to the same class in the same school to re-take an exam. But given that all the operations are completed successfully, this model could require seven lifetimes at least to complete the ladder. And then there may be another ladder...

In addition, these quickenings are, in my own experience anyway, threshold experiences – by which I mean we are just given a small taster of ultimate enlightenment and then brought back down to Earth again. It's just as well we do come back, otherwise we wouldn't be able to function in everyday life.

My own experience of the full Phoenix initiation came a few years ago, although I believe I had already been impregnated with the "eggs" in 1971, when I came to Glastonbury for the first run of its eponymous music festival, now famous worldwide while back then there were just a few thousand of us. I ended up sleeping on the grass verge of Cinnamon Lane just outside the town, at the foot of the tor. I was very young and six months pregnant at the time. I knew nothing of the magic that impregnates the land in this Vale of Avalon and had no idea of the significance of sleeping outside under a full moon at Summer Solstice in what was, in effect, the "nest" of the great earthwork known as the Phoenix, the sunbird which incinerates itself before its rebirth in the wood of cinnamon.

After the festival ended, I returned to my bedsit in a houseful of art students in Canterbury, Kent, with its big picture window perfectly framing the tower of the cathedral that was always brightly lit up at night. I didn't know anything about the ley line then, which connects Canterbury to Glastonbury. I gave birth to my daughter... and then life went on, with all the ups-and-downs that you would expect in the life of the archetypical seeker, including the obligatory sabbatical spent in an Indian ashram. Then, four decades later and after a whole series of huge coincidences, I ended up coming to live in Glastonbury and the only house available and perfect for my small needs was nestled under the wing of the Phoenix.

Still completely unsuspecting of any overriding plan, one Autumn night I was drifting between dreaming and journeying when I suddenly awoke with a start. I realised my body was burning with an incredible heat I'd never before experienced. It was rising up my legs, quite slowly and gradually, and I felt it was asking my permission before going any further. So I gave it – and whoosh! The incredible fire swiftly moved up my torso, then my shoulders and then my neck... but then I panicked a bit. I feared that the incineration would send me into oblivion. However, it was too late and suddenly it was all over. In a way, it did send me into oblivion. Well, certainly into a dark abyss. I have no way of knowing how long I was in that nothingness. But then I was suddenly back, sitting upright in my bed and feeling absolutely fine and normal. I didn't start speaking in tongues or anything! I just felt completely complete.

But none of that – from finding myself in the right place at the right time, the "nest" of the sunbird, to the synchronicities that led to me living under its wing – was in my control. I had no idea any of it was happening.

As John Lennon once sang: "Life is what happens to us when we're making other plans."

However, while we cannot in any way direct our progress, it can be reassuring to recognise we are in a process, per se, and not just a random collision of chemicals in a helter-skelter chaos of meaningless phenomena. By understanding the metaphors and symbols in ancient myths that visit us at night in our dreams, we can feel supported and secure in our foothold on the ladder. We should also be reassured by the knowledge that alchemy must be at work in us because we are part of the natural world and that the same seven-stepped process is manifest in all of Nature. It is also within the workings of the Lady's Green Mantle that we find the quickening and because of this repeatability we have scientific evidence that the quickening is a "thing". For instance, biologists tell us that evolution occurs at a glacially-slow, grandfather-clock-ticking pace until just near the end of the process when, in an instant, there is revolution. I believe this is why the fossil record is littered with species that seem to come from nowhere; they have been produced by a rapid-fire quickening that occurs at the seventh rung of the ladder, at the point of transformation.

One of my favourite fictional examples of a quickening is found in the aforementioned film *Groundhog Day*. It portrays the inner journey to enlightenment made by sardonic, bitter and world-weary television news reporter Phil Connors, who is played by the inimitable Bill Murray. If you haven't seen it, I thoroughly recommend you do – in which case, I'd better give you a spoiler alert before you read on!

Phil and his camera crew are trapped in the small town of Punxsutawney in Pennsylvania following an unexpected heavy snowfall. They were there to record an ancient Dutch ritual centred on whether a groundhog, also named Phil, casts a shadow when it emerges from its burrow at Gobblers Hog on the February day that the Celts call Imbolc, at sunrise. If the groundhog does cast a shadow, the locals insist it means Winter will continue for at least another six weeks. Conversely, no shadow means an early Spring is on the way.

Of course, we know that "phil" was the ancient Greek word for "love" and so giving the two main characters the same name is an indication right from the get-go that this is going to be no ordinary movie – and it isn't. The snow becomes an unremitting blizzard, causing the whole crew to get trapped in the town, and the human Phil gets stuck in a time loop in which he is forced to experience the slow, plodding monotony of the exact same "groundhog day" repeating itself over and over again.

So how does Phil get himself out of this time prison? First, he tries being utterly hedonistic and runs rampant throughout the town, fulfilling all his desires, getting drunk and smashing up cars because he knows that he will not be penalised as there is no next day and thus no consequences to his actions. He tries many different strategies, all the time disparaging the "small town folks" who seem to dog his steps, day after day, with what he sees as the same petty, banal conversations. But each morning, when he wakes up, it is to same date and time on his clock and the same song, Sonny and Cher's I Got You Babe, playing on the radio.

Finally, he begins to lose his bitter, sardonic attitude and starts to appreciate each person he meets as an opportunity to exchange love - and that is when he is finally released. His transformation appears to happen almost overnight; we are not shown what caused it. So we never know whether the new Phil comes about through the auspices of a catalytic event or whether it was just he got so fed up with banging his head against the proverbial brick wall that he had nowhere else to go, metaphorically speaking.

I reckon he went through the quickening.

9. The Vesica Piscis

THE universe communicates with itself through pictures. Perhaps that is why we find, in shamanic practice, that symbols and metaphors are the main way in which the spirits talk to us and we also use powerful images to respond to them. A picture speaks a thousand words, as they say, and it utters those words through the vibrational resonance of its sacred geometrical dimensions with colour and sound frequencies.

All of the above is also true of symbols used on heraldic devices, like royal coats of arms. They are often, in fact, potent and protective talismans. A talisman is a magical design of symbols that is charged with the force it is intended to represent. In other words, sacred geometrical designs are used to represent the universal forces that are in harmony with what their owners wish to attract. The more it is in the "bandwidth" of those common cosmological principles, which are found in Nature, the easier it is to attract the force.

This means that for any enterprise or relationship to flourish, we need to use and abide by sacred geometrical symbols representing that force in Nature. We're required to talk to the universe, or Nature spirits, in a language they understand. And at the heart of this language is the Vesica Piscis, so named in Latin by medieval scribes because they thought it resembled the bladder of a fish, as shown in **Figure 10**. This is the symbol used for the part of the alchemical operation called, in the language of the initiates, the Marriage of the Sun and the Moon, which leads to the birth of the Child of the Philosopher or the Philospher's Stone. In other words, it represents the quickening of coagulation of the *rubedo* stage.

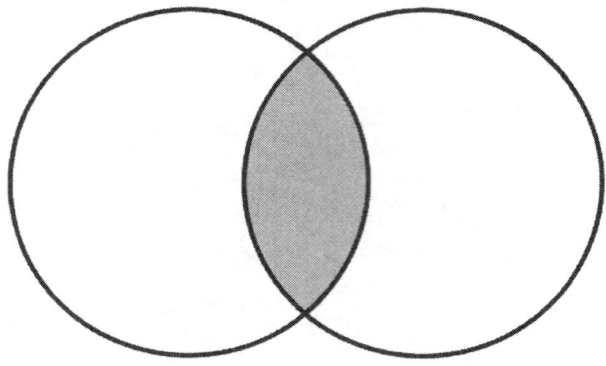

Figure 10: The Vesica Piscis

The two larger circles represent the male, or yang, solar force crossing over to fertilise the circle of the female, or yin, lunar force. Between them, they give birth to the perfectly balanced Child of the Conjunction, or the Child of the Philosopher – otherwise known as the Philosopher's Stone or Holy Grail.

Perhaps one of the clearest expressions of this alchemical operation within the Celtic body of myths can be found in *The Dream of Macsen*, in which the Emperor Macsen has a shamanic vision of the Elen, the Empress of Sovereignty, and falls madly in love with her. I won't go into all its twists and turns here, to avoid story overload, except to say that their path to true love and union was, for Mascen anyway, fraught with as much heartbreak and longing as that of Bridget Jones. Added to which, the three castles or fortresses that Elen asks for as her "maiden-gift" – Caer y n'Arfon, Caer Leon and Caerfyddrin – seem to indicate the teachings of The Three Cauldrons and that in that system, she represents Virgo, as shown in **Figure 11**.

But perhaps you'd like to read it and pull out for yourself all the allusions to this process based upon how the creation re-creates itself through the Marriage of the Sun and the Moon. It is an archetypal pattern that reflects how the metalworking smith in his forge deep below, which is fired by the inner Sun of the Underworld, "marries" or melds his material with the flaming stellar forces above to give birth to a seed of life that blooms into every living thing on Earth, in the Middle World. As Above, so Below.

Seen through the lens of The Three Cauldrons, the correspondences look something like this:

King	Prince (Radiant Child)	Queen
Solar	New star	Lunar
Underworld	Middle World	Upper World
Cauldron of Warming	Cauldron of Vocation	Cauldron of Knowledge
Caer y n'Arfon	Caer Leon	Caerfyddrin
Nigredo (black)	Rubedo (red)	Albedo (white)
Smith	Poet	Healer

Figure 11: The Celtic system of the Three Cauldrons as found in the Dream of Macsen

The Vesica Piscis has been described as the womb from which all of Creation is born, from the realms of spirit into the realms of materiality. It is transcendent in nature because its shape spirals outwards into infinity in ever-increasing circles and it also spirals inwards, into infinity, in ever-decreasing circles.

To quote Nicholas Mann in *Energy Secrets of Glastonbury Tor*:

The Vesica Piscis provides a simple way of arriving at the basic patterns and measures of sacred geometry, especially the fundamental ratio of the Golden Section... These are the ratios, proportions and harmonies found in Nature, in the form of plants, animals, crystals and the human body. They are also present in music and mathematics, and so form the underlying structures of creation.

The Vesica Piscis is a powerful symbol of the creation and growth of forms in the natural world... It is possible to imagine the progression created by the Vesica Piscis endlessly unfolding the inner dimensions of the Otherworld as it endlessly unfolds in the external world. The symbol is the expression of the ideal proportions of the archetypal inner world passing into visible manifestation, and the tangible proportions of the outer world returning into the world of the external.

The oval shape formed by the two circles overlapping is known as the *mandorla*. Mandorla is the Italian word for almond. The almond is an ancient symbol for the closing up of valuable contents in a hard, almost impenetrable shell. It is a metaphor for intense concentration upon the light that shines from within. During medieval times, the almond was interpreted as a symbol of the embryo that was enclosed within the uterus. Thus the centre of the Vesica Piscis represents the womb where the Seed of Life is birthed into the duality and then eventually evolves into the Wholly Trinity – it is the seedbed of all trigonometry.

We can trace the Vesica Piscis back at least 5,000 years in temple designs. Our ancestors during the Megalithic period built their sacred sites with the Vesica Piscis as the seed. Professor Alexander Thom discovered prehistoric quadrangles, derived from the alchemical, geometrical principles, were bases for the ground plans of many European stone circles, such as those at Avebury, Stonehenge and Carnac.

Egyptologists also believe that the Vesica Piscis was at the heart of pyramid building. The exterior angle of the Great Pyramid of Giza can be reproduced with the Vesica Piscis and there are many other indications that these great monuments to our ancestors' ingenuity were built on sacred mathematical lines.

Norman and medieval churches across Europe used the Vesica Piscis as the heart seed of their architecture and the *mandorla* also frames much of Islamic art.

The Vesica Pisces was used as a basis for the design of Glastonbury Abbey in the 12th century. The archaeologist and architect Frederick Bligh Bond discovered this information when excavating the Abbey, just after the First World War. It was probably what inspired him to design the new wooden lid of the sacred well in the Chalice Well Gardens at the foot of the tor with a stylised Vesica Piscis.

We can also see the dimensions of the Vesica Piscis clearly in Wells Cathedral, Somerset, just a few miles from Glastonbury. Described as "one of the most poetic of cathedrals" and a centre for excellence in music, Wells Cathedral's original 12th century design is said to have been based on that of Glastonbury Abbey, with the top half of the *mandorla* forming the soaring arch over the High Altar.

Many of the Christian Church's ecclesiastical paintings of Christ or the Madonna and Child are framed in a *mandorla* shape and I don't think this is a coincidence.

Going back to at least the time of King Alfred the Great, it appears that all the power regalia of the land – the geomancy, the ceremonies, the rituals, art, architecture and heraldry – seems to have come from hands guided by alchemists and seers who were aware of these natural geometrical principles. They knew that to encase one's vision in the *mandorla* of the seed of life is to create a talisman – or magical object – which sends out a very loud message indeed to the universe.

It creates a perpetual prayer or intention for abundance, fruitfulness and prosperity of your chosen object, which you depict therein. In addition, any royal coats of arms or heraldic device that places an object inside the talismanic *mandorla* is asking the spirits for that object to be protected, into perpetuity.

10. When You Wish Upon a Star ...

When you wish upon a star,
Makes no difference who you are,
Anything your heart desires
Will come to you.
If your heart is in your dream,
No request is too extreme,
When you wish upon a star
As dreamers do.

YOU may remember this hauntingly beautiful song from Disney's 1940 animated classic, *Pinocchio*? Never was a truer word spoken or sung. Our voices are all as unique as our fingerprints, so there is no danger of our own individual songs of praise or cries for help getting lost among all the other millions of prayers being transmitted daily, worldwide. Our word vibrates and resonates holographically with our inner stars - as Above, so Below - and we are heard.

In essence, the hidden understory of the cosmological journey of the hero or heroine is one long lesson in how to do magic – by which I don't mean becoming expert in sleight-of-hand conjuring tricks or brewing love charms. It is more a sort of holistic natural magic in which we are the subject of the enchantment that has, as its aim, the act of redeeming the ancestors and lighting a path forward for succeeding generations.

In terms of its scientific antecedents, it is actually inner alchemy that, when practiced properly, attuned with the stars Above and the ancestors Below, aligns the life of the practitioner with natural forces, otherwise known as spirits or gods and goddesses, which allow and show the human who consults them how to map out their lives according to their vocation or destiny.

The etymological meaning of the word "science" is "what is known, knowledge acquired by study; information". Alchemy was how science was practised before the scientists of the so-called Enlightenment threw the spirit out of the matter.

The sort of alchemy you'll learn in following the hero's journey as laid down in this book will not necessarily involve you having to invest in equipment like test tubes or Bunsen burners, although the original meaning of the word "laboratory" is derived from the medieval alchemists' *ora et labora*, or place of "prayer and work". Alchemy takes a much more holographic view of the universe than modern Western science by acknowledging the spirit or energy inherent in all matter and which can be consulted in inner space. The medieval alchemist had a prayer or meditation room within his *ora et labora* to retreat into, to quiet his senses and journey inwards, to commune with the inner spirit or god of the material he was working on.

So to whom would he have been praying? Well, it very much depended on three factors: firstly, the culture he was born into; secondly, the material he was working on and, finally, the aim of his operation. But whatever his intention, it would have always included petitioning the spiritual ruler of the material he was going to transform. This is because everything in Nature, right down to the smallest blade of grass, has what is known as a planetary governor – in other words, it is ruled by otherworldly gods and goddesses similar to those encountered by the mythological hero on his journey. This cosmic ruler is vital to any alchemical operation; without the willing co-operation of that planetary governor, no magic can take place.

As Marc Edmund Jones writes in *The Interpretation of a Horoscope*:

> **The planets are the dynamic bodies that distribute the forces of actual living and experience, setting up the strains and stresses of life and creating the basic complex in which you have your existence.**
>
> **You live by working against dynamic compulsions, struggling back and forth, interacting with the universe. You and the universe have a partnership in activity. You are shadow-boxing with the universe every minute of your existence. Even your dreams are the shadow-boxing you do when you are asleep.**
>
> **The planets are the bodies in the heavens which articulate the forces, or express the system of energy of which the universe is composed. The planets in your chart represent your distribution of this energy, or show what part of it you have made your own. By working from the planets you have a key to an individual's very livingness, and thus are able to help him much more than**

merely telling him that he has an open personality, a long body and a closed pocketbook.

We are born into human bodies or vessels which constitute our alchemical container for this Great Work, to take us through a form of an alchemical evolution. The planetary governors are arranged at our birth in a pre-determined and customised configuration which gives us our character, with all its specific strengths and weaknesses, and gives rise to our challenges.

The astrologers refer to the 12 sun signs as houses. The houses are numbered one to 12, beginning with the first house at Aries. And so, for example, if the Moon was in the eighth house of Scorpio at your birth, the house of sex and death, it could indicate that your vocation on Earth is to be involved with transcendental or sacred sex connected to life after death. If so, you should instinctively know how to work with sex magic because the knowledge is already in your Rivers of Blood, inherited from your mother's DNA.

Dreams or shamanic journeys about houses often carry astrological metaphors that give us messages about our progress. For instance, if your visioning involves a house which is littered inside with the detritus of a wild all-night party and is divided with the object of your love on the other side of the wall, this could be because Saturn is currently in your fifth house of Leo, which is usually a house of fun and lovemaking, and that you will therefore have to be a little more patient and humble about your abilities in making not just that relationship work but all others too, until the Father of Time moves on again. Perhaps clearing away the empty glasses would be a good start!

As we can see from that example about Saturn, the planetary governors sometimes teach us by adversity. So when we are resisting by fighting against our destiny, or feeling depressed and frustrated about an important part of our life, it is often an indication that we are at a crucial part of our spiritual development.

There are seven of these inner planetary spirits altogether and each is identified with a planet in our solar system. They also govern one day of the week and several hours of each day, which begins at the first hour after the sun has risen. For instance, if our aim is to align ourselves with our warrior spirit, we could pray to Mars on the dawn of the day that has Mars as its planetary governor, which is Tuesday.

The alchemical clock on Tuesday starts at dawn with Mars in control for the first hour and then each of the other planets takes over for their one-hour slot until Mars resumes again, and this sequence goes on until dawn on Wednesday, when Mercury begins that process after sunrise for that day. You can find more correspondences between the planets and the days of the week by consulting **Figure 12**.

Planetary god	Metal	Helps	Governs	Day
Saturn (Chronos)	Lead	Discipline	Capricorn Aquarius	Saturday
Jupiter (Zeus, Thor)	Tin	Expansion adventure	Pisces Sagittarius	Thursday
Mars (Tiw)	Iron	Assertive-ness, masculinity	Aries Scorpio	Tuesday
Venus (Aphrodite, Freya, Ishtar)	Copper	Receptive-ness, intuition, femininity	Taurus Libra	Friday
Mercury (Hermes, Odin/Woden)	Quicksilver	Transformation	Gemini Virgo	Wednesday
Moon (Luna)	Silver	Purification, memory, body and soul	Cancer	Monday
Sun (Sol)	Gold	Empower-ment, creativity, spirit	Leo	Sunday

Figure 12: The planetary rulers and their influences

You will already be familiar with the zodiac. But only by viewing it through a shamanic lens, which arranges it across the Three Worlds with the *mandorla* – or fruit of the Vesica Piscis - as the Middle World, will you be able to understand the fundamental landscape used in our ancestors' myths, a cosmological structure that was levelled into a sort of Flatworld in post-Roman era translations. As you will see from **Figure 13**, some glyphs have been added to the zodiac, next to the name of each house. Each of those glyphs represents the governing planet of that sign and there is a key to which planetary deity each one symbolises in **Figure 14**.

Other than the Sun and the Moon, each planetary governor appears twice in the zodiac and thus twice in the hero's journey. For instance, Mercury rules both Gemini and Virgo – both signs that are high in mental and intellectual activity. Saturn is the master of both Capricorn and Aquarius, Jupiter governs Sagittarius and Pisces, and Mars oversees Aries and Scorpio.

The glyphs that our ancestors used to symbolise each planet is derived from an extremely ancient system that bases its metaphorical language on the circle, the semi-circle and the equal-armed cross. The circle represents wholeness or holographic wholiness, the semi-circle represents the soul and the equal-armed cross, which is sometimes shown as an arrow, represents matter.

So by simply recognising that system and meditating on these symbols, a whole world of information opens up to us that is, at its base, about the bridging of the Underworld microcosm of man's Rivers of Blood with the macrocosm of the Above. In other words, praying to "idols" does work. Talking to, say, a statue or painting of Venus will activate the goddess of love in your inner space; she will hear you and even more clearly at certain hours of the day she governs.

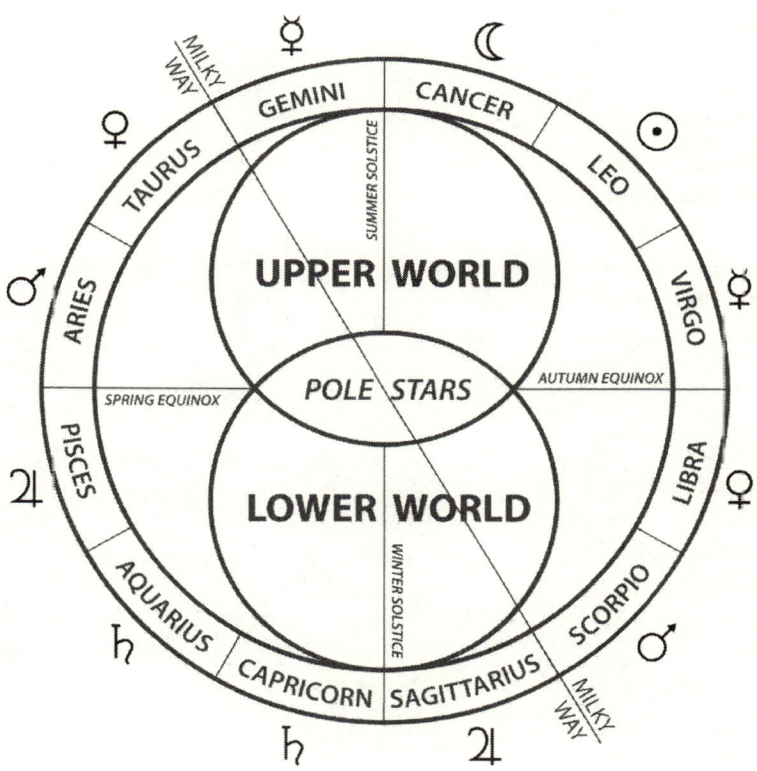

Figure 13: The zodiac of the Alexandrian system showing how the Milky Way is a river used by gods and goddess coming down into human incarnation from between Taurus and Gemini to between Scorpio and Sagittarius.

Figure 14: The ciphers of the planets

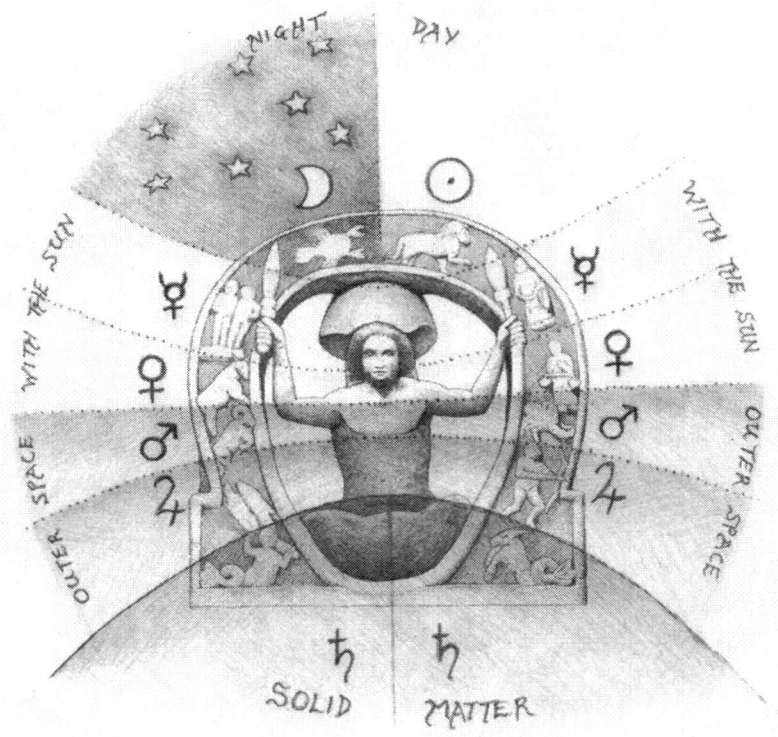

Figure 15: Yuri Leitch's interpretation of the Mithraic Rock Birth on Hadrian's Wall showing the mirrored planets

Figure 15 shows an illustration of this mirrored system by Glastonbury-based artist and writer Yuri Leitch. It is based on the so-called Mithraic Rock Birth sculpture found on Hadrian's Wall, which was built in the 2nd century to mark the northern limits of the Holy Roman Empire. We see the god Mithras emerging from the primordial egg amidst the mirrored planets. The iconography on Hadrian's Wall is generally attributed to the Romans. However, it was mostly Scythian – well, Sarmatian – mercenaries that patrolled it, and so this sculpture could equally have been their handiwork.

The following breakdown is to give you an idea about the characteristics of each planetary governor so you will recognise them when their personas crop up in ancient zodiac myths, and it may also help you to identify the stellar factors currently at play in your life. I will also describe my own subjective impressions of these spirits, arrived at by working with them shamanically and alchemically.

(I am not including the planets that have been discovered more recently, such as Pluto, Neptune and Uranus, because they are not found - or at least they have not yet been discovered by me - in ancient myths.)

We start with the Sun and the Moon, which are not technically planets. But they are the most influential stellar bodies in our solar system in myriad ways and the dance that they perform together at the times of eclipses – known in alchemy as the Marriage of the Sun and the Moon – makes them primary drivers of the most powerful catalyst for holistic and holographic transformation and fertility.

The Sun

> 1 The heavens declare the glory of God;
> and the firmament sheweth his handywork.
> 2 Day unto day uttereth speech,
> and night unto night sheweth knowledge.
> 3 There is no speech nor language,
> where their voice is not heard.
> 4 Their line is gone out through all the earth,
> and their words to the end of the world.
> In them hath he set a tabernacle for the sun,
> 5 which is as a bridegroom coming out of his chamber,
> and rejoiceth as a strong man to run a race.
> 6 His going forth is from the end of the heaven,
> and his circuit unto the ends of it:
> and there is nothing hid from the heat thereof.
> *Psalm 19, from the King James Bible*

The Sun represents the ego and it rules the astrological sign of Leo. Its perpetual flames are what give the leonine personality its magnaminous and warm-hearted genorosity of spirit. As the ruler of the solar system, in which even gravity itself is governed the Sun, this star beams down like a kind patriarch over all of his kingdom as he rides across the skies in his chariot, from dawn until dusk.

We often find a character that represents the Sun entering hero myths when the protagonist reaches the age of young adulthood, like Culhwch and Arthur. Sometimes, it acts as a guide and teacher to help him develop his courage, learn the virtues of loyalty, nobility and generosity, and to overcome his pride and selfishness. The Sun can take the form of a father or an older relative like an uncle, or even an earlier ancestor, who acts as a teacher to the hero, leading by example so that the young man has an ideal role model to follow as he begins to plot his path forward. Sometimes, though, the lessons can be harsh, like in the Epic of Gilgamesh when Shamash the Sun sends Enkidu a fatal illness for insulting the Lady of Fortune, Ishtar.

The Sun is found in Babylonian myths as Shamash, in Greek myths as Helios, and in Celtic myths as Graine, Bel or Lugh.

As a Leo, I am ruled by the Sun and so he is the planetary governor I'm most familiar with. He is there every day – albeit sometimes hidden behind grey English clouds. But I always sense his presence and he opens my heart, informs my warmth, friendliness and generosity, gives me self-confidence and qualities of leadership, and makes me bright – so bright sometimes that I have to turn down the dimmer switch, especially when around the sort of people who don't much like being dazzled.

I have worked magically with the Sun for a long time. I once made an alchemical tincture with the herb eyebright. But the most powerful solar work that I have ever done was to repeat, regularly over 40 days and 40 nights, a potent Vedic mantra dedicated to the Sun. The sounds made by Vedic mantras are built on the same geometrical frequencies and resonances I described in **3: The Holographic Universe of Music**. So I experienced, in this way, building an energetic Sun temple in the deeps of the Underworld, which ended up playing a pivotal role in my shamanic work on the land.

Orbit: The Earth takes one year to orbit the Sun, which is travelling through Space at 600,000 miles per hour on a fixed circuit that takes 200 million years to complete.

Herbs: Alchemically, the Sun governs the herbs bergamot, chamomile, cinnamon, clove, eyebright, feverfew, heart trefoil, lemon balm, lovage, marigold, meadow rue, passionflower, peony, rosemary, rue, saffron and St John's wort.

Body part: The Sun rules the heart, the spine and the spleen, the eyes and the

thymus gland, and the circulation of the blood.
Day of the week: Sunday.
Alchemical stage: The Marriage of the Moon and the Sun

The Moon

> "I am that soundless, boundless, bitter sea.
> All tides are mine, and answer unto me.
> Tides of the airs, tides of the inner earth;
> The secret, silent tides of death and birth.
> Tides of men's souls, and dreams, and destiny.
> Isis veiled, and Ea, Binah, Ge."
> *Dion Fortune – The Sea Priestess*

The Moon rules Cancer and is generally portrayed as the watery, reflective pools of energy that can act as a mirror for our lives, particularly as it holds all the memories – both consciously remembered and buried in the subconscious – deep in its subterranean depths. As governor of the tides of the seas and the bodily fluids, she is also the ruler of the times and tides of man. Her magnetic pull rules over world affairs as a whole and not just in the inner being of the hero – but he can keep in step with her dance if he aligns himself holographically to her three sides of maiden (new moon), mother (full moon) and crone (old or dark moon).

More recently, the Moon has been considered to be feminine because her liquid emotions are thought to be more characteristically female. Thus, the Greeks identified her as three different women – Phoebe, Artemis, Selene – perhaps to reflect her three faces, and the Romans called her Diana. However, in Babylonian times, the Moon god was male and named Sin.

In my experience, the Moon is definitely female. I have quite a shy and reverential attitude towards her because her cool beauty, grace and wisdom stun me into awed silence. She is utterly mysterious and yet immensely powerful and effective. In a way, she is the essence of femininity, which is quietly tenacious yet not overbearing or ostentatious.

Orbit: The Moon takes approximately 28 days to circle the Sun.
Herbs: Alchemically, the Moon governs the herbs aloe, arrowhead, daisy, dog-tooth violet, eucalyptus, hyssop, moonwort, moneywort, mouse ear, nutmeg, opium poppy, orris root, pearlwort, periwinkle, wild poppy, rattle grass, dog rose, saxifrage, speedwell, sweet flag, turmeric and water violet.
Body parts: The Moon controls the ebb and flow of all the fluids of the body.
Day of the week: Monday
Alchemical stage: The Marriage of the Moon and the Sun

Mars

Mars rules both Aries and Scorpio, and as we follow the journey of the zodiac hero we discover how those martial, warlike qualities develop through meeting our own challenges, over time.

The mythological protagonist sets out on the Spring Equinox at Aries as the immature, fiery, thrusting hothead who is far more likely to rely on pure brute force to overcome his adversaries than his wits and more subtle means of persuasion. However, as China's Sun Tsu pointed out in his sixth century BCE military treatise *The Art of War*, the wise warrior only goes into battle when all other recourses, such as intelligence and the arts of diplomacy, have failed and also, most importantly, when he knows not only that he will win but also how his victory will be assured.

Our warrior at Aries has not yet developed the wisdom of Sun Tsu. However, if all goes to plan, by the time he meets Mars again, at Scorpio, he will be better prepared to learn how to be a great spiritual warrior – which is just as well, because this is when he has to face his greatest trials.

The Roman Mars was derived from the Greek Ares, but the source for both was the Babylonian Nergal. As a fertility god of the Underworld, Nergal was responsible for the uprushing fire from the Earth at springtime, which forces the sap of the greenery upwards, and this is why alchemists always began their operations on the Spring Equinox, to take advantage of that flaming force.

Nergal was associated with the cockerel and his name meant 'dunghill cock' – which says it all, I think! He is also sometimes depicted as a lion and so I think he may well be the lion that is Ishtar's mount.

I once made a spagryic dedicated to Mars, in which I used nettle as the material. It was just a practice exercise. I had no occasion to use it and it sat in my cupboard for a long time. My life was so calm and peaceful then, I could not imagine I would ever need the qualities of a warrior. But one day, I did. Then I remembered the Mars spagryic in the cupboard. I took a few drops in a glass of water and it is no exaggeration to say that I was instantly transformed inside.

I felt, energetically, as if I was holding a sharp sword straight at my enemy's throat. When I spoke to him, he turned tail, as if on a sixpence, and ran, and never came back. Did Mars give me courage and the wisdom and discrimination to tackle him effectively? I think I was beyond courage; I was way ahead of needing to summon up any qualities like bravery in my clear, one-pointed, almost tunnel-visioned determination to succeed and 100 per cent certainty that I would, and I did. The residue of that experience remains with me, even today. Mostly, I keep my sword in its scabbard around my waist. Some people can see it glinting there and they know I wouldn't hesitate to pull it out, if required.

Orbit: Mars takes about two years to circle the Sun.

Herbs: Alchemically, Mars governs all-heal, allspice, basil, briony, broom, byrony, butcher's broom, catnip, celandine, coriander, cotton thistle, crowfoot, flaxweed, geranium, ground pine, ginger, nettles, masterwort, pennyroyal, saltwort, sarsaparilla, senna, tarragon, tobacco and woodbine.

Body parts: Mars controls the muscles, the red blood cells, the metabolism, the motor nerves, the gall, the rectum, the head and the left hemisphere of the brain.

Alchemical stage: Calcination.

Mercury

Mercury rules both Gemini and Virgo. His other epithet of Quicksilver Messenger explains his influence in those signs, which is largely about the lightning-fast processing and communication of information, whether across the synapses of the brain, the world via transport, trading routes and telecommunications or holographically, across the Three Worlds.

There are some who call Mercury a "trickster god" and compare him with Puck in Shakespeare's *A Midsummer Night's Dream*. I grant that he can be quite crafty and difficult at times – especially when he goes retrograde – but that is because he has to be and it is all for our own good in the end!

Mercury was known as Nabu to the Babylonians, Thoth to the Egyptians, Odin to the Norse and the wing-footed messenger Hermes to the Greeks.

In my experience as a writer, I have to admit I would be lost without Mercury. As a Leo with Gemini rising, he is always there, inspiring my words and often, when I'm stuck, coming up with the *bon mot* or the next cunning twist in the plotline. Mercury is also at the heart of [he just told me to change that to] plays a pivotal role in every alchemical operation, no matter which planet governs the material.

Orbit: Mercury takes 88 days to circle the Sun.

Herbs: Alchemically, Mercury governs the herbs acacia, agaric, buckbean, caraway, clover, celery, chicory, dill, fennel, fenugreek, flax, garlic, germander, hazelnut, honeysuckle, horehound, marjoram, mint, parsley, oregano, valerian and wormwood.

Body parts: Mercury controls the intellect, the nervous system, the thyroid, the ears, the vocal cords and the lungs.

Day: Wednesday.

Alchemical stage: Mercury is the prime catalyst of the whole operation but in my experience, he is particularly noticeable when we go through the **dissolution** stage, which is the penultimate step before the final Marriage of the Sun and the Moon at coagulation. It is as if a force has entered our lives and is spinning it out of control, and you find that you are living your life backwards. It can be a bit confusing when all kinds of weird stuff that you didn't knowingly intend or cause, in the past, starts popping up all around you, and it only starts to make sense when you realise it is just your future rushing towards you.

Jupiter

Jupiter rules both Sagittarius and Pisces and he is the judge the hero first meets when he falls into the Halls of Judgment in the Underworld. There, all the deeds of his life, whether well intentioned or not, rise like the dead from their graves to meet him. If he passes that trial and is pronounced fit to become a hero – otherwise known as Winning the Hallows - he will either release his father, who has been trapped there, to be reborn on the Winter Solstice or be reincarnated as a baby himself.

Jupiter reappears later on to guide the young child as it reaches Pisces, to help it widen its vision and give it confidence and vision enough to grab hold of new adventures and challenges in its first tentative explorations in trying to discover the meaning and purpose of life.

Jupiter was known to the Babylonians as Marduk, to the Norse as Thor and to the Greeks as Zeus.

My own experience of Jupiter is one of expansiveness and joy, and also the thrill that comes when starting a new venture – or adventure. If I want to call upon Jupiter, I burn juniper berries. When I had an important shamanic initiation on my own path in 2010, Jupiter was prominent in my astrological chart in such a way that he seemed to be leading the stars as a great cheerleader of my progress.

Orbit: Jupiter, the largest of the seven planets, takes 12 years to circle the Sun.

Body parts: Jupiter controls the liver, the arteries, subcutaneous fat tissue, the adrenal glands, the spleen, the kidneys, the digestive organs, the buttocks and the thighs.

Herbs: Alchemically, Jupiter rules anise, betony, borage, comfrey, coltsfoot, dandelion, eglantine, elecampagne, ginseng, juniper, liverwort, meadowsweet, mistletoe, myrrh, peppermint, sage, sandalwood, sorrel and tansy.

Day: Thursday.

Alchemical stage: Sublimation.

Venus (Ishtar)

> **Who is She who looketh forth as the morning,**
> **Fair as the Moon,**
> **Clear as the Sun**
> **And terrible as an army with banners?**
> *The Song of Songs*

Venus is probably the planetary governor we are most familiar with and so you'll most likely already know that the Lady of Fortune is associated with love, beauty, harmony, proportion and order. Venus governs both Taurus and Libra, thus first appearing to the young mythological warrior when he has not yet developed enough maturity to know how to handle a relationship with any woman, let alone a goddess, and he tends to go at her like a bull in a china shop. So he is usually swiftly ejected out of Taurus at the end of her delicate foot and, as a result of offending her, he suffers a Reversal of Fortune. This downturn in his luck leads him into a number of challenging tests and trials that help him to develop his wisdom and qualities of leadership, so when he gets to meet Venus again at Libra to receive her sexual initiation, he is more mature and considered in his behaviour, and thus matters are usually more harmonious and fruitful.

Venus was Inanna to the Sumerians, Ishtar to the Babylonians, Isis to the Egyptians, Freya to the Norse and Aphrodite to the Greeks.

I have a very personal relationship with Ishtar. I was shown, during the aforementioned shamanic initiation in 2010, a previous lifetime in which I had served as a priestess at her temple in Babylon. I find that Ishtar is not all sweetness and light, or rainbows and unicorns, which is how the Greeks, and later the Romans, used to like to portray, respectively, as Venus and Aphrodite. She definitely has a touch of Lilith about her at times, and it is Ishtar who is referred to in the extract from *The Song of Songs* above as "terrible as an army with banners" because she was the goddess of Love and War until the Greeks, as was their wont, broke her in half and then attributed her loving qualities to Aphrodite, who the Romans called Venus, while giving all her warrior qualities to Ares, the Roman Mars. I consider this to be an act of vandalism that emasculated the personality of the divine feminine and that women have had to struggle to rediscover their inner male nature ever since.

Orbit: Venus takes 225 days to circle the Sun and in her 10 conjunctions with it over eight years, she draws a five-pointed star.

Body parts: Venus rules the sexual organs, the umbilical cord, the nose, the neck, the palate, cell growth, the complexion, facial appearance, the abdomen, the thymus and the breasts.

Herbs: Alchemically, Venus rules the herbs alder, bramble, burdock, catmint, columbine, digitalis, dittany (white), dropwort, fleabane, figwort, foxglove, groundsel, goldenrod, moneywort, motherwort, mugwort, self-heal, skirrit, soapwort, thyme, vervain, vanilla, violet, wheat, willow, yarrow.

Day: Friday.

Alchemical stage: Conjunction.

Saturn

Saturn is the planetary governor that rules the death and rebirth of the hero in the Underworld at Capricorn and then the early life of the reborn hero during Aquarius.

Otherwise known as Old Father Time, he is a strict teacher, he has our own best interests at heart. Saturn's presence in our lives is only a problem when we rail against his discipline.

It can seem, when Saturn is around, that nothing is going right in your life while in reality it is because the stern disciplinarian has interceded to prevent your passage through human existence from falling off the rim of the Wheel. If Saturn tells you sit down and get on with your homework, it is best to just quietly obey and I actually do find there is a certain sense of satisfaction and almost relief in accepting and acknowledging such constraints.

Saturn is his Roman name, while he was Ninurta to the Babylonians and Chronos to the Greeks.

I have had many personal shamanic and alchemical experiences with Saturn, probably too many and too involved to go into here. Instead, I want to tell you a story about my Piscean granddaughter.

She had been given a smartphone for her 11th birthday and just like any youngster in possession of such a glittering and wondrous object, she could never put it down. She would set the phone's alarm for dawn, long before she needed to get ready for school, so that she could join in the group texting on WhatsApp with her friends, or explore the internet for the latest news on Taylor Swift or Ed Sheeran, and so on. It would be the same when she arrived home from school. The phone was the go-to object; it would be next to her, on the table, during dinner and she would even be glued to it during her favourite TV programmes.

It wasn't long before her parents realised "something had to be done". So they decided to talk her to about it. They were dreading the conversation, though, because they had heard tell of other children who had thrown terrible tantrums when it had been suggested that they reduce the use of their phones, forcing protracted negotiations over the whole business.

So they were expecting a huge storm to break out when her dad finally said to her one day at dinner: "Mummy and I have been thinking that maybe you are using your phone too much and were wondering whether you should limit your use of it."

My granddaughter just quietly replied: "OK, what do you suggest?"

They were so surprised that they were lost for words and it took them some time to recover enough to come up with a suggested timetable, which she accepted without a murmur.

You see, what we had all forgotten was how much my granddaughter loves rules. She would have no problem if Saturn turned up in her classroom when her schoolmates were being loud and unruly and called for order; in fact, she would be quietly relieved.

As a Piscean and a musician, she loves to roam far and wide in her imagination but at the same time she wants the rivers of her dreams to be bounded by firm banks and have a guiding hand at the helm of her boat. Nothing could be worse, for her, than completely unbridled freedom. It would be like her trying to play her violin to sheet music with no staves and the musical symbols all jumbled up. Rules make her feel safe and protected so that she can proceed with confidence on her path – and she is wise enough to know it.

Orbit: Saturn orbits the Sun every 29 years.

Body parts: The skeleton and cartilage.

Herbs: Alchemically, Saturn rules the herbs amaranth, bifoil, birdfoot, bittersweet nightshade, blackthorn, blue bottle, buckthorn, centaury, cypress, darnel, dodder, fleawort, water hemlock, black hellebore, horsetail, knotgrass, ivy, Lady's Slipper, mullein, patchouli, Solomon's Seal, wintergreen and tamarind.

Day: Saturday.

Alchemical stage: Coagulation.

To conclude this chapter, I'd like to add a word or two about the Earth. After all, not only is it a planet too but it is the fourth one from the Sun and the only astronomical orb that is known to harbour life. So what about its planetary governance?

In my experience, the Fae or faeries are the rulers here on this Middle World plant. They are the spirits of the lands and seas of the entire Earth, and there are almost as many different names for faery folk as there are countries.

For instance, they are the *fada* in Portugal, the *fee* in Germany, the *tylwyth tef* in Wales, the *vila* in Bosnia, the *nepi* in Kazakhstan, the *devas* in India, the *peri* in Turkey, the *zanash* in Albania, the *nang tiem* in Vietnam, the *diwata* in the Philippines, the *feetjie* in Afrikaans, the *patupaiarehe* to the Maori and the *juniya* to the Arabs, to mention a few.

So it is surprising to me that so many peoples all over the world have a name for a species of being that so few will admit exists!

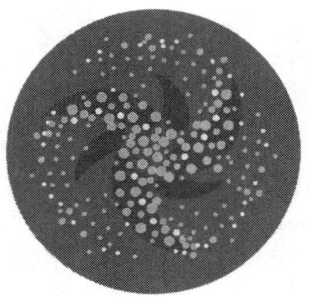

Practical exercise

Listen to the Planets

If you want to go beyond words, which I admit have vast limitations when it comes to trying to describe these vast cosmic influences, then do try listening to Gustav Holst's Planet Suite. It will give you more of a right-side brain feel for the qualities of each planetary governor.

It seems clear to me that Holst was skilled in the language of the initiate because this magnificent musical odyssey is organised into sequential movements that follow the planetary governors in their correct order of houses around the zodiac. Not only that but, to me, the whole suite is a musical tale of Sovereignty restored on behalf of the ancestors, which is the common metaphorical understory of all great myths.

It begins on an Aries Spring Equinox with the martian qualities of Mars and builds slowly from an ominously quiet start, with the drums of war barely heard in the background, but then, by turns, sounding louder and softer and then even louder again. It is as if a huge army is marching over the hills and dales towards the listener, accompanied by alternatively soaring and then diving violins, which mirror the surging fear in the stomach as war grows ever closer.

The next two movements sound to me like the aftermath. Now that the peace has been won, along comes the sweet and harmonious Venus at Taurus, restoring order, proportion and dominion. After Venus, we meet the quicksilver, spiralling, darting Mercury at Gemini, reinforcing again the spider's-web networks of transport, communication and trade.

Holst leaves out the Sun and the Moon at Leo and Cancer (probably because they're not strictly, scientifically, planets, although I'd love to have heard his interpretation of the alchemical Marriage of the Sun and the Moon) and he passes over Virgo and Libra because he has already provided the music for their governing planets, Mercury and Venus. He also skips over Scorpio, having already given us its ruler Mars at the beginning.

So then now we are at Sagittarius and his joyful, patriotic, chest-beatingly expansive Jupiter is proudly praising the Sovereignty of the nation, which reaches a climax at *I Vow To Thee My Country*. Then, finally, we reach Saturn at Capricorn, who is in his Grim Reaper guise and thus the whole piece ends with the church funeral bells on Earth that gradually and softly lead into the heavenly bells welcoming home the Deceased into the Realms of the Ancestors.

11. The Double Goddess of the Secret Fire

AS we go through the hero myths further into this book, it will become clearer how the Upper World gods operate at different parts of the journey, according to where the hero has reached in his passage along the "rim of the wheel".

We have already learned that five of the planetary governors - Mars, Venus, Mercury, Jupiter and Saturn – rule two houses each around the zodiac. For now, I want to concentrate on the mirroring of Venus, at Taurus and Libra. This is because, despite Baroque artists like Diego Velázquez hinting at their metaphysical understanding by painting the beauteous lady gazing into looking glass, I find that misunderstandings in the consensual consciousness about her performance of that doubled-up astrological function are at the root of many religious demonisations and pogroms.

So let's unpack the Mysteries of the double goddess of the secret fire.

I am pretty sure the double goddess would have had a role in the stories told by Tabiti's grandmother's grandmother, and even further back than that, because whenever she appears in the plot it means a pivotal and profoundly transformative initiation is about to take place. She is usually linked to sexual initiations as they apply to Sovereignty, fertility and the Milky Way, which, as you saw in Figure 12, descends on a diagonal between Taurus and Gemini, down into between Scorpio and Sagittarius.

Archaeologists have found carved double goddesses more than 25,000 years old in the form of double-headed figurines along with clay "Venuses", as they call them, dating from the Neolithic period (10000 to 2000 BCE) at Catal Hoyuk and Gozo, the tiny island off Malta.

We continue to find this same archetype of the echoing goddess as we examine the myths of the later Neolithic, although they are hiding behind the veil of astrological metaphor. However, for those who have the eyes of the initiate, she has been threaded, in this way, into the stories of the ancient Egyptians, Greeks and Indians, as well as the Kabbalah and Gnostic Christianity, until she has become so ingrained in our psyches we now respond in a sort of subconscious Pavlovian reflex to her presence.

Even Roman Christianity had its own mirrored goddess character and, very helpfully, gave them both the same name – the Virgin Mary and Mary Magdalene – so that there should be no mistaking the allusion. And today, she pops up again in one of the most popular ballets of all time, Swan Lake, with Odette and Odile as the white swan and the black swan.

So it all begs the question, what does it mean? While we are just innocently sitting in the cinema or the theatre, or at the ballet, why are the storytellers of our times, the scriptwriters and choreographers, at such pains to introduce us to the double goddess?

I imagine most of them have no clue as to what it means. They just realise it is an archetype that works, and has always worked, in a narrative that swells box office receipts. The modern-day mind is primarily utilitarian – unlike those of our bearded ancestors who had no use for Occam's Razor, which is probably why that tool is of no use to anyone trying to understand the deeper meanings of myths. Only a total and utter polymath, a Renaissance man if you like, who is also a shaman and an alchemist can wield Occam's Razor successfully. Sadly, there are not many such people around today and because these stories have become so corrupted, not least by the classical Greeks who many academics so admire, we have for the longest time been viewing the double goddess through a glass darkly.

Archaeologists and anthropologists who research what they believe were more matriarchal cultures during the Palaeolithic era, such as Marija Gimbutas and Vicky Noble, end up concluding that the double goddess represented the two halves of the Moon – in other words, the waxing and the waning, the dark and the light, the menstruation and the ovulation. Not an unreasonable theory, one might think. I've heard other researchers of the Neolithic period – in other words, the Age when man was gradually settling down to a more agricultural way of life – concluding that double goddess figurines dating from that time represented summer versus winter, dark versus light. Thus, the young goddess Persephone's abduction to the Underworld by Hades is thought, by them, to be a tale about the fertility of the land and the harvests, and that when Hades allows Persephone to return to her mother, Demeter, on the surface again each year, the crops will spring forth green from the land and the bull will mount the cow again, and so on.

But I believe there is more to it. I'm not the first to point this out but the trouble with experts who continually narrow down their specialised area of focus is they end up knowing more and more about less and less. They have no holistic, much less holographic, perspective.

In my opinion, the mythological double goddess does represent fertility but on a much more profound level than that which heals the barrenness of the land, which for these agricultural peoples was in itself as much a mythical metaphor as was the Deluge. What is at stake is a much deeper and deadlier sort of barrenness that is akin to the poisoned fruits of nihilism, as many experience today. Any post-hoc reasoning that comes from a culture obsessed with what it produces materially makes no allowance for the fact that to the ancients, the spiritual came well above the material in their to-do lists.

Even as recently as about 4,000 years ago, we can find evidence of this way of thinking in the Indian Vedic caste system, where the Brahmin priestly caste was ranked higher than the *ksatriya* or warrior caste from which the king was chosen by the priests. I also remember seeing some research about the Ainu a while back. The Ainu made up the indigenous tribes that peopled parts of what we now call Japan and Russia in the early centuries of the Common Era. But, apparently, every single action they performed in their lives had a ritual attached to it because, to them, everything was sacred, right down to how they disposed of their fish bones.

Similarly, I'd be amazed if our earliest ancestral Eve needed dolls to teach her about menstruation cycles or the cycles of the Moon. Natural processes were all ABC to the ancients. They're only mysteries to us because we have cut ourselves off from the wild woods and the night skies.

Because the Double Goddess has survived in our literature and is, in fact, the only female on the zodiac, and therefore a primary character on the Ladder of the Wise, I've come to the view that she is part of a process of spiritual initiation and later on in **Part 3: Into the Zodiac**, you will see how she acts and interacts with the astrological hero as his sister-mother-lover, in such a way as to facilitate his journey into full manhood through the three fire initiations of the Three Cauldrons.

In the Eleusian Mysteries, the Double Goddess took the form of Demeter and Persephone. Later on, in the Gnostic Mysteries, it was as Sophia – the Upper World Sophia and the Earthly Sophia. This spiritual concept is well explained by Timothy Freke and Peter Gandy in their *Jesus and the Goddess: The Secret Teachings of the Original Christians*:

Christ represents consciousness. His lover/sister the Goddess represents the psyche. Christ represents the circle of the self. The Goddess represents the radius. The radius is a line with two ends. One is rooted in the centre of Consciousness and the other lies on the circumference, representing the body in the world. The Goddess is therefore thought of as having two aspects,

sometimes known as the higher or incorruptible Sophia and sometimes lower or mortal Sophia. The first Sophia represents psyche in a state of Gnosis, united with Consciousness at the centre of the circle of Self. The second represents the psyche fallen into identification with the body on the circumference [of the circle].

As in the Pagan Gnostic tradition, the Christian Gnostic goddess is known by many names. Most commonly, she is called "wisdom". However, she is also known as Psyche, Zoe meaning "life", and Achamoth, from the Hebrew for wisdom.

The higher Sophia falls from being at One with the Father in the Heavens into the depths below and becomes the lower Sophia on Earth who, through forgetting her true identity, becomes trapped in material creation. However, no blame or sin is associated with this Fall because it was necessary, as we have learned in previous chapters.

In the Gnostic *Pistis Sophia*, Sophia wanted to know what it felt like to be in material creation. As we so often say now, we're not human beings walking a spiritual path but spiritual beings walking a human path. This would definitely have been Sophia's motto, had she been a real person. Her path and only purpose in this life is to realise her Oneness again. This is the path of the initiate.

The fallen Sophia is also associated with Venus, the "bright star of the morning", which makes her, according to my reckoning, the original Lucifer. This may come as a surprise. However, to nail one common fallacy, Lucifer is never depicted in the Bible as Satan. Lucifer is first associated with Satan in the 17th century poet John Milton's *Paradise Lost*.

"Lucifer" is a Latin word and was not, therefore, in the original Coptic Greek translations of the Bible from Hebrew. The Roman Christian scribes translated it from Greek into Latin and they came up with Lucifer to encapsulate the Greek "bringer of fire", in other words Venus, the bestower of the fire initiation. It comes from the words "*lux*" (light/fire) and "*ferre*" (to bear/to bring), which when put together mean "bearer of light" or "bringer of fire" – in other words, the secret fire.

The Greeks called this first star of the morning Eosphorus or Phosphorous.

At length as the Morning Star (Eosphorus) was beginning to herald the light which saffron-mantled Dawn was soon to suffuse over the sea, the flames fell and the fire began to die. *Homer, The Iliad, Book 23.*

And after these Erigenia bare the star Eosphorus, and the gleaming stars with which heaven is crowned. *Hesiod, Theogony.*

In the fourth century CE, St Jerome translated the Bible from Greek to Latin into what's known as the Vulgate version. By then, most of the Gnostics who understood the meaning of the double goddess in their Sophia had been rooted out, killed or suppressed and the Mystery Groves had been destroyed. So when Jerome replaced the Greek "shining star of the dawn" with the Latin name for the planet named after the goddess of fortune, its meaning changed from an Upper World being who fell to Earth into a Babylonian king.

How you have fallen from heaven, morning star, son of the dawn! You have been cast down to the earth, you who once laid low the nations! You said in your heart, 'I will ascend to the heavens; I will raise my throne above the stars of God; I will sit enthroned on the mount of assembly, on the utmost heights of Mount Zaphon. I will ascend above the tops of the clouds; I will make myself like the Most High.' But you are brought down to the realm of the dead, to the depths of the pit. Those who see you stare at you, they ponder your fate. *Isaiah 14.*

The Kabbalah also tells the tale of a goddess falling into incarnation before journeying upwards again, to regain her true self and state of Oneness with the True Bridegroom. This same heroine is found in the original understory to folk tales like Cinderella and Sleeping Beauty, forever awaiting the kiss of the Divine Lover who has to fight through adversities like evil stepmothers, ugly sisters or a forest of briar rose thorns to plant his awakening peck on her rose bud mouth.

Later on, we will meet her in the *Epic of Gilgamesh*, first in the form of the Upper World goddess Ishtar, the daughter of the moon god Sin, and then on the edge of the sea, in her "fallen" form of Siduri, the "divine barmaid" who is a common heirodule archetype across many ancient myths.

Here is a perfectly divine barmaid by the edge of the sea, called by many names in many languages. Her bar should be as long as the famed one in Shanghai, for she has along her shelves not only wine and beer, but more outlandish and antiquated drinks for many cultures; drinks such as honeymead, soma, sura (a kind of brandy), kawa, pulque, peyote-cocktail, decoctions of ginseng. In short, from everywhere she has the ritual intoxicating beverages ... Hamlet's Mill.

To learn more about this dispenser of the sacred intoxicant, we need only turn to Ishtar's prototype, the Sumerian Inanna. Hundreds of terracotta plaques have been found showing erotic engravings of Inanna and Dumuzi, and it appears there were two Inannas. There was an Inanna for the sex rites of the taverns and there was another Inanna for the bedroom.

In the engravings from the taverns, known as the *coitus a tergo* drinking scenes, there is a conflation of three ideas – of sex, beer and apparent seizure. Inanna is often shown drinking beer while Dumuzi is having sex with her and is standing completely erect. This may seem rather odd to those who take these ritualistic depictions literally. But when they are applied as metaphors to the act of shamanic sex magic, they take on a whole new meaning.

There is a blissful state of ecstasy that can be achieved shamanically by the raising of what the Egyptians called the *djed*, the energy coiled at the base of the spine. Djed meant "that which stays erect" and it is also symbolised by phallic-shaped obelisks that came from the serpent cults. Obelisks were not originally meant to represent the erect phallus – which in itself is sometimes used in ritual art as a metaphor, in ithyphallic figurines - but an erect energy which runs up the centre of the body in the form of *sekhem* (life force or chi) that is created when certain alchemical magnetics are aroused.

The energy takes a double-serpentine form and these are visualised as two serpents. The ancient Indians knew these two serpents in their tantric practices as Ida and Pingala but to the Egyptians they were the Gold Solar Serpent and the Black Lunar Serpent, and they are alchemical opposites with different paths through the alchemical container of the body to produce the Marriage of the Sun and the Moon at the crown.

Let me explain how this process works energetically.

The serpents arise from the genital region and then criss-cross the *djed*, or energetic spinal column, until they reach the chalice of the cup-shaped hypothalamus. The heads of the two serpents then rest upon the rim of the hypothalamus and from their mouths issue droplets of sweet elixir, known as the Red and White Serpentine Drops, that stream down the inside of this chalice until they reach the pineal gland, which is nestled like a pine cone at its base. Once the pineal gland is bathed in these nectars, it fires up the crown chakra, opening up a portal to a huge library of ancestral wisdom akin to the Akashic Records, which the king then had access to. This in turn gives him the wisdom to rule – to bring order from chaos, just as the deluge hero of myth conquers the sea serpent and separates the land from the watery chaos.

Through these practices of bringing his energetic serpents under his control so that they can open the doorways of his perception, the king, like the deluge hero, becomes the dragon slayer, comparable to the Greek Hercules, the Archangel Michael or the Babylonian Marduk, and he is thus deemed fit to bring order out of chaos and to rule his kingdom wisely.

We find stories containing metaphors about the initiations of this secret fire all over the primordial carpet, from Scandinavia to India and even in one of Shakespeare's most popular plays.

In the Old Norse *Edda*, Odin (Mercury) shapeshifts into a snake to steal the heavenly mead and then metamorphoses into a hawk and flies off with it, to take it to the gods, but manages, on the way, to spill a few drops which fall on to the Earth, for the use of mankind. This is a metaphor for the Wyrd, or the mead of destiny that flows through the World Tree known as Yggdrasil (Odin's horse), itself a symbol of the Ladder of the Wise, which has a serpent (Nidhogg) gnawing away at its roots in Hel, the Underworld, and a hawk (Vedrfolnir) at the top in the Upper World.

The mead, the Edda tells us, was produced as a result of a truce between the battling forces of the *aesir* (Upper World gods) and the *vanir* (the Fae). A very similar story is told in the Vedas, in which the warring *asuras* and *devas* agree to a peace treaty in order to help each other to produce the nectar of immortality, called *amrita*, by churning the Ocean of Milk (the Milky Way). They form two lines, rather like tug-of-war teams, on either end of Vasuki, the king of serpents, who they use as a rope wrapped around Mount Mandara which was employed as a rod to churn the ocean.

In this way, all manner of phenomena are dredged up including lethal poisons, healing herbs, a powerful bow, precious jewels, a tree with blossoms that will never fade or wilt, a wish-fulfilling cow, a conch, an umbrella, a pair of earrings, various nymphs and dancing girls… all most probably astrological symbols of a Vedic sidereal system which is far more complex than that of the Greeks. Finally, Dhanvantari, the divine healer, rises to the top of the ocean, and he is holding a pot of *amrita*. The *asuras* instantly break the truce and resume the fighting in an effort to steal the heavenly elixir. But in a flash, the eagle Garuda swoops down and snatches it up in his beak and flies off with it, only to accidentally drop three drops on the Earth – just like Odin the Hawk.

Shakespeare uses a very similar metaphor in his drama about the importance to fertility that is intrinsic to the relationship between man and the Fae. It takes a whole chapter of my book *Reclaiming Sovereignty* to explain the alchemical understory of Shakespeare's *A Midsummer Night's Dream* because it is quite involved and multi-layered, plus it also reflects the Elizabethan writer's knowledge of the *ashwamedha*, or horse sacrifice, of the ancient Indian sacred theatre. But in short, all the misunderstandings and mismatched pairings in the play, which are necessary to create the seven-stepped process of the Marriage of the Sun and the Moon, are caused by a wrongly applied love potion that had originally been dropped on the Earth accidentally by Cupid, the god of Love.

Here is the speech of the king of the faeries, Oberon, on how the nectar fell to Earth:

That very time I saw, but thou couldst not,
Flying between the cold moon and the earth,
Cupid all arm'd: a certain aim he took

> At a fair vestal throned by the west,
> And loosed his love-shaft smartly from his bow,
> As it should pierce a hundred thousand hearts;
> But I might see young Cupid's fiery shaft
> Quench'd in the chaste beams of the watery moon,
> And the imperial votaress passed on,
> In maiden meditation, fancy-free.
> Yet mark'd I where the bolt of Cupid fell:
> It fell upon a little western flower,
> Before milk-white, now purple with love's wound,
> And maidens call it love-in-idleness.
> Fetch me that flower; the herb I shew'd thee once:
> The juice of it on sleeping eye-lids laid
> Will make man or woman madly dote
> Upon the next live creature that it sees.
> Fetch me this herb; and be thou here again
> Ere the leviathan can swim a league.

By now you may be feeling that your brain is swimming with too much information and not enough containers in your mental library to store it in. But please do bear with me, because in **Part 3: Into the Zodiac**, I will be supplying you with enough shelving to fill the Library of Alexandria when you learn about the relationship of the zodiac hero with the double goddess and how he undergoes his trials and tribulations as he climbs the Ladder of the Wise via the three fire and water initiations of the Three Cauldrons.

For now, we just have a couple of chapters to go in this section which will arm you with sufficient understanding of the coded language used by the initiates for you to make the necessary connections and interpretations in ancient myths, and therefore, about events in your own life.

12. The Saturn Return

WHILE we are still young and on the lower rungs of the Ladder of the Wise, we tell ourselves children's nursery tales so that we don't feel quite so helpless and thus can fool ourselves into thinking we have a grip on reality. However, this grip is actually an illusion when we don't know what reality really is. Nevertheless, we comfort ourselves by unconditionally accepting the stories our adversaries tell us because it's so much easier than facing our own inner tuition, or intuition. We happily believe in the long and tangled yarns of the rams and ewes surrounding us, that we are lambs and that the Elder sheep just want what's best for us. They don't tell us that they are in fact wolves in sheep's clothing – and so are we!

So we docilely allow ourselves to be herded into sheep pens to be fleeced while being distracted with promises that we are all working towards paradise on Earth, when we only have to look around us at the "red in tooth and claw" processes of Nature, of one animal preying upon another, to realise the impossibility of such a false utopian dream, and that unicorns don't exist, the rainbow's end can never be found and even a rose has thorns.

So if we cannot be a part of creating everlasting peace on Earth, what are we here for? Well, it's a good question and one that can only be answered by following the lessons of Saturn, who returns every 29 years into our lives to toll the playground bell as a signal that it's time to return to the School of Hard Knocks.

Astrologers are aware that each time Saturn returns to the position it occupied at the time of our births it heralds a profoundly life-changing period and it can also feel like a most difficult and challenging stage.

The terms most associated with Saturn's influence are control, structure, limitations, practicality, discipline, sense of reality and responsibility.

In short, Saturn is the strict teacher who forces us to stop daydreaming as we gaze out of the classroom window, or passing notes and gossiping amongst ourselves in the back row, and sit up straight and pay attention. He directs our gaze to parts of ourselves we would rather not look at because we know they are our weaknesses. Some psychologists call it facing the dark side of our character. But it is only in the dark corners of our psyche until Saturn shines a light on it – and seeing all our faults lit up in such harsh lights can be shocking and daunting. But he does not send his Klieg lights into our consciousness because he wants to be cruel to us. It is because, whether we remember it or not, we incarnated with a destiny that like the gingham-patterned, cloth-wrapped package at the end of the wayfarer's staff, needs to unravel over time. And no-one knows better than the Father of Time when our time is up.

In my experience, the Saturn Return is one of the most important features in the path of the zodiac hero. When he appears in ancient myths, he represents the father who has to be redeemed by the son in the Underworld and the redemption of the ancestral line is a major part of the work for any shaman.

The zodiac hero is bitten by the scorpion at Scorpio and this causes him to fall down into the Underworld, where he finds himself in Sagittarius, and it is there that he has to face his demons – otherwise known as the Dark Night of the Soul. If he passes his trials there, his father is released from captivity and reborn as the Radiant Child at dawn on the Winter Solstice, while the son remains behind in the Underworld to await his own son who will hopefully eventually arrive, at some point, to release him... and so on.

This is not about a literal release and rebirth of a father – it is metaphor used to signify the process of eternal life, which is achievable for the family line through this alchemical process.

Redemption of the ancestral line, or the family DNA, by purifying the Rivers of Blood shamanically, is the equivalent of clearing and sanctifying ley lines, the practice of which has largely died out now or has been diluted into pilgrimages and other practices, such as "beating the bounds". The cleansing of all lines of holographic communication within the "above" and "below" is vital shamanic work, which some of us perform regularly. I have my own "patch" that I tend as lovingly as if it was my own flower garden and I use a combination of song, drumming and ceremony to keep the ways clear.

However, the fiery, egotistical zodiac hero at the beginning of the journey in Aries has no interest in such altruistic activities. He has no memory about why he has incarnated into a human body or the vital importance of the ancestors to his life's path and destiny. He has not been taught that he is standing on some mighty shoulders. Instead, he sees life through the lens of the separate ego and he only starts out on the study of alchemy and magic because he thinks it will lead him to the elixir of life and immortality, which will give him power over others.

It is one of Mercury's tricks on him (otherwise, he would probably never leave home) and it takes many twists and turns for the hero to eventually discover he already is experiencing everlasting life – but maybe not in the form he originally envisaged.

So you might want to work out when your Saturn Return is due, or whether you are now going through one? If it feels as if your life is "going wrong" at every step and you're not getting anywhere, it can sometimes be a relief to realise it is just your Saturn Return acting as it should and all is right with the world after all.

An astrologer can calculate the positions of the stars as they were in the skies at the exact time you came into incarnation in order to plot your birth chart, which is unique to each individual. The birth chart is, in effect, a map of your life and so an expert reader can deduce from that horoscope all the challenges you will have to face. They will find the position of Saturn at your birth to be very telling, particularly if you are just reaching your 30s or are just past your mid-50s or in your late 80s.

Technically-speaking, Saturn returns every 29 years to the place it occupied in the skies at the time of your birth and its influence can be felt for a year or so either side of the ages of 29, 58 and 87.

We find the derivation of the Hebrew Satan in the form of Saturn who appears in two stories in the Old Testament.

Firstly, he is the satan angel of the *Book of Numbers* that appears in the road and blocks the way of the shaman (or diviner), Balaam.

This story is set just after the Israelites had left the wilderness, where they had been wandering for 40 years. They went on to fight two important battles in which they had conquered, and thus occupied, the lands of their enemies. The king of Moab knew his kingdom was next on the Israelites' list and, possibly because he didn't think his army would be able to defeat this zealous rampaging force in battle, he thought he might resort to magical trickery. So he sent his messengers to the local shaman, Balaam, to offer him a number of inducements to put a curse on the Children of Israel.

Balaam told the messengers that he would have to consult with his spirits on this question. But when he did so, his spirits advised him to refuse the bribes of the king of Moab and have nothing further to do with him. Balaam sent the messengers back with his refusal. But the king just sent more messengers with further bribes, entreaties and finally, when none of that worked, resorted to outright blackmail. In the end, our shaman was tempted to agree and he did what no shaman should ever do; he set off on his ass to perform this magical work of a curse on the Israelites without receiving the permission of his spirit guides.

However, he had barely gone a short way on his ass, down the lane, when it suddenly halted. Balaam shouted at his charge and then whipped it soundly. But the ass refused to move another step. Balaam was utterly bewildered. He couldn't understand what was causing the animal to be so intransigent. However, it was because the ass could see what Balaam could not – a gigantic angel was barring their path with a flaming sword. It was the satan spirit, the spirit of obstruction, and it was so huge it took up the whole width of the road. The poor beast was riveted to the spot, awestruck and petrified by this terrifyingly shining apparition. But its rider, who was out of touch with the world of spirit, was oblivious to the otherworldy intervention and remained confused as to what was causing his vehicle to halt.

This story of Balaam and the Ass has gone through innumerable iterations since it was first told and in current Bibles it reads as if Balaam was ignoring the advice of God. But it is well understood that during the course of the many and varied rewritings and re-presentings of these stories to suit differing political purposes, especially the move from polytheism to monotheism under the Judaic king Hezekiah (c. 715 to 686 BCE), that the term "the gods" was usually transcribed to just "God" and ever since then, readers have been about as bewildered as Balaam by what this story is actually all about.

Knowing as we do now that many of these formerly orally transmitted stories began as cosmological metaphors and allegories, the similarity between the words "satan" and "Saturn" cannot be coincidence, especially as this satan angel was acting just as Saturn does when he exerts his stern headmaster rule to the point of being obstructive.

The traditional astrologer, Peter Stockinger, describes Saturn thus:

> Saturn's action is principally binding, chastening, chronic, cold, crystalising, denuding, hardening, depleting, hindering, limiting, magnetic, obstructing, retarding and suppressing. Also known as Kronos, or Cronos, Saturn is known as the malefic and 'The Greater Infortune'. However, Saturn in himself is not evil, but is chastening, corrective and untiring in his efforts to arouse humanity to better and right living, and by bringing sorrow, suffering, sickness, trials and tribulations upon people that they may learn by their experience and reap what they sow.

Saturn is also been named "The Reaper", "The Tester", "The Chastener" and "The Initiator". I think this last epithet describes his role best in his second appearance in what most scholars agree is the oldest book in the *Old Testament*. The story of Job reads just like a classic shamanic initiation story in which the hero has to lose everything to gain enlightenment.

During Winter in the Northern Hemisphere, the Sun is in the constellations of Capricorn and Aquarius, which are both ruled by Saturn. The death of the mythological hero occurs in Capricorn and then he is reborn into Aquarius. So as we traverse the revolving mill wheel that churns the Milky Way ocean of our subconscious that is mirrored above in the sparkling night skies, the planetary governor Saturn represents the first and the last in this octave and thus was known as the Alpha and the Omega of the cosmos in the Alexandrian system.

However, since then and over the course of several thousands of years, we can chart this gradual deterioration of the character of Saturn, the satan angel, who is just doing his job in trying to correct our trajectory when we are about wander off into sheep pens to be fleeced.

In the next and penultimate chapter of this section, I will explain how the co-opting and twisting of one particular myth is still keeping many of us penned in as lambs to the slaughter.

13. The Anunnaki and the Star Peoples

WE live in a world in which indigenous tribes – even those who still have some sort of medicine man wearing strings of beads and feathers in his hair – have forgotten almost everything their ancestors ever knew.

Strange diseases they had no immunity to decimated the Native Americans when Columbus and his men landed on the continent. But even before the 15th century Spanish conquest, the native population had been rendered wafer-thin on the ground by century upon century of climate change and vicious tribal warfare.

Some managed to hold on to their traditions longer than others, notably the Apache tribes whose war shaman leader, Geronimo, was able to protect his people with his brilliant manipulation of the dull, blinkered, one-dimensional minds of the invaders. But even he was co-opted, in the final analysis.

Many Native American leaders have been corrupted by alcohol, drugs and the lure of tax-exempt gambling casinos. In the forests of the Amazon, most of the ayahuasca retreats are now run by rogue CIA operatives while the indigenous Mayans are banned from conducting shamanic ceremonies on their own sacred pyramids, which have been given over to faux spiritual tourism.

The forced driving of shamanism underground has been going on since the invention of Christianity/

In Tibet, Bonpo shamanism were deliberately replaced by Buddhism in the 11th century.

From the 16th century on, Jesuit missionaries made sure the Roman Christian dogma replaced shamanic practices across the whole continent of Africa by abducting young boys from their villages and putting them in seminaries where they were abused by monks who knocked all their inherited junglecraft out of them.

The suppression of the beliefs and customs of the Scandinavian Sami shamans, known as noaides, began in the 17th century with the Sami women being sterilised.

In 18th century Australia, the aborigines were herded into reservations on badlands with poor water sources and then kept in the direst poverty while being corrupted and weakened by cheap alcohol.

These are just a few examples but there are many more. To me, it is sad to see young people, who are so desperate for spiritual guidance, turning for advice to the dispossessed who often, despite bearing the headdresses of the archetypal sage Elders, are now largely ignorant of the real alchemical and astrological metaphors within the star stories of those who went before them. The cognitive dissonance is so strong in these impressionable seekers that they fail to see the obvious – that if the otherworldly spirits of shamans really do have such wisdom to dispense, how did they allow these peoples to lose their lands and their self-respect?

The harsh truth is, once a race loses touch with its totem spirits Above and its ancestral spirits Below, the World Tree in their consensual reality is easily felled and sent to the lumbar yard, rendering that land ripe for the taking.

But the worst mistakes come about when Western anthropologists are sent out to learn about indigenous tribes and, in the absence of any other evidence or rationale, reinterpret their ritual artefacts and stories, which inform their sacred lore, as a record of their history.

For instance, the Dogon of Mali still repeat an ancient creation story about the "star peoples" who were half-fish and half-human and that came down from the heavens to teach them all they now know, from sowing and hoeing to metallurgy and weaving. This is similar to the account inscribed on the Sumerian clay tablets, known as the Enuma Elish, from a culture also claiming to be founded by a mythical fish-people known as the Seven Sages. However, the scientifically minded French anthropologists working with the Dogon realised the tribes had astronomical records about stellar processes that Western science hadn't yet caught up with. This convinced them the Dogon stories about the fish people must also have been true.

So does this mean that extraterrestrial fish people once came down to Earth? Well, it can seem like that in a world in which a vastly overbloated leviathan of a military-industrial complex tries to hide the *in vivo* testing of its advanced technology by encouraging a belief in little green men and UFOs.

However, this is nothing new.

The priests of old Babylon would famously tell their citizens that God – the ultimate ET - was unhappy with them because they were not paying enough taxes to the temple. They would proclaim that to prove his displeasure, God was going to make the Sun go dark at midday in three days' time when, of course, these priest-astronomers knew an eclipse was due. Today's carbon taxes to ostensibly offset climate change are just a more modern iteration of the same scam, which is only possible when people are kept in ignorance about reality.

Anyway, at the beginning of the 20th century the social engineers were presented with a really big problem that was almost as bad as the Sun going out. The story of the judgemental God in the sky, which had gripped the consensual reality for more than 1,500 years, was beginning to lose its hold. In a way, the eugenicists had created this problem themselves, because their own so-called Enlightenment thinking had led to an exodus away from blind faith in an omnipotent, omniscient and omnipresent God to only accepting forces that could be proved objectively in material reality.

So a new narrative was needed to corral and pen up the flocks. Thus the modern mytho-industrial complex began to develop one by using the work of Egyptologists and Akkadian scholars – a couple of whom I knew personally – that was based on texts carved on the Sumerian clay tablets which, at that time, had not been widely translated.

At the forefront of this new pseudohistory was senior Freemason and American author Zecharia Sitchin, and he tried to persuade us that the Sumerian writings told of a superior race of space beings, known as the Anunnaki, who come to Earth every 3,600 years to steal all our gold and our women, and take their ill-gotten haul back to Nibiru, their planet beyond Neptune.

Up until he died in 2010, his aim was the completion of his own "Goddess of Ur Genome Project", which had been petitioning the Natural History Museum in London, housing the bones of the Sumerian queen Nin.Puab, to allow them to be DNA tested. This, Mr Sitchin was sure, would reveal that Nin.Puab, whose skeletal remains had been found in the Royal Tomb at Ur, was not human but from another planetary system. In fact, he stated, she was likely to be one of the ancient astronauts of the Anunnaki race from the planet Nibiru.

Anyway, I'm sure you won't be surprised to hear that my own understanding about the Anunnaki is very different. I have come to the view that the belief in an imminent invasion of ETs is piggy-backing, within the consensual consciousness, upon one of the most successful psychological operations of all time – one that cemented together a whole empire for more than a thousand years by getting people to believe that a mythological dying and resurrecting Sun god had actually lived on Earth.

When you dig down far enough to the primordial carpet, you discover that many of the events in the so-called "life of Jesus", including his death and rebirth, had been told over countless ways and times; some are even dated to thousands of years before he was supposed to have lived. The dying and resurrecting Sun god was both an astrological metaphor for the redemption of the ancestors on the Winter Solstice and an astronomical metaphor in which the Sun, having reached its northernmost zenith, "dies" or stands still for three days before returning again. It came from a story passed on in the oral teaching traditions of the priest astronomers across Mesopotamia, Egypt, Greece and India during their Mystery initiations, the practice of which began about 6,000 years ago.

At that time, alchemists found no difference between spirit and matter except in how it manifests itself. During modern times, we have been taught to separate a sort of angry, vengeful Jehovah figure, who rips out an eye for an eye and a tooth for a tooth, from the more considered and rational studies of cosmological processes, otherwise known as science. It is, to my thinking, a false dichotomy in which there is no God like Jehovah, while the infinite starry fields surrounding us and within us could not exist without the Great Alchemist or Spirit which is made up of the universal, multi-dimensional mind.

Man seems to have gone full circle today, however, in his search for God. Quantum physicists are now able to see or sense the holographic nature of a creator, or self-organising principle of life, within the creation. There are scientists in Switzerland who think they have found this "God particle" through bashing bits of matter together in a 17-mile long tunnel called the Hadron Collider. I wonder if they realise our early ancestors already knew about this self-organising principle or Great Spirit of which we are all a part – and not by beating up atoms in a tunnel but by quietly seeking the answers within.

How do I know this? Well, by studying, at first-hand, the source material that Mr Sitchin got his Annunaki astro-bandits from. When we go back to the most ancient of texts available to us, we discover that *anu is the oldest word for God currently known about*. It is the self-organising principle, the spirit at the heart of all matter, and thus it is the name of highest god in the Upper World of the Sumerian pantheon, Anu, alongside his consort, the goddess Ninhursag.

Anu and Ninhursag gave birth to offspring who were collectively known as the Annuna. They were Inanna/Ishtar (queen of the heavens) Enlil (god of the Middle World), Ea, later Enki, (god of the Underworld), Utu or Shamash (the Sun) and Sin (the Moon). This makes seven gods altogether – the aforementioned Seven Sages - and I should imagine the choice of that number probably stemmed from the number of pole stars.

The word *anu* is so old it is found in the most ancient Sanskrit texts, as well as the artefacts and writings of all the peoples that conquered that most fought-over of fertile lands between two rivers, the Tigris and the Euphrates, beginning with the Sumerians from around 3100 BCE, then the Akkadians from 2334 BCE, the Sumerians again from 2150 BCE, the Old Babylonians from 1830 BCE, the Kassites from 1530 BCE, the Middle Babylonians from 1125 BCE, the Assyrians from 727 BCE, the Chaldeans from 612 BCE, the Persians from 539 BCE and the Macedonian Greeks from 331 BCE.

However, much of what the Babylonians wrote about the stars had been copied from the earlier Sumerians and pretty well everything the Chaldeans knew was copied from the Babylonians – and that is before you even get to the Macedonian Greek vandals of Alexander the Great who, after conquering Babylon in 331 BCE, not only stole all the star lore but cut their zodiac and their goddess in half in the process.

The original Babylonian zodiacs showed a heraldic animal and a god alongside a more rustic worker and animal for each of the 12 astrological houses. In other words, zodiacs then mirrored the spirits of the Upper World and those of the Lower World or Underworld. However, as if purloining wholesale the myths of the Babylonians and then slapping them together, willy-nilly, to construct their own cosmological narratives wasn't enough, the Greeks also cut out the Lower World's rustic figures, leaving us with only the Upper World gods and animals. In this way, we have the Greeks to blame for losing the connection of the Below, in our consensual consciousness, to the Above and also for Mr Sitchin's ignorance – or at least being able to play on the ignorance of the masses – in misconstruing the highest guiding spirits in the inner space of the Sumerians into outer space invaders.

In old Indian Sanskrit, the word *anu* as a noun denoted an atom of matter; as an adjective, it meant atomic, fine, minute. Anu is also one of the epithets of Brahma, the creator god, and it is conceived as both infinitesimal and universal, thus pointing to the pantheistic character of divinity. Hence, every *anu* is a centre of potential vitality containing latent intelligence. In the *Bhagavad-Gita*, Arjuna is enjoined to meditate on the "seer", that is the enlightened, omniscient One, who is "more atomic than the atom" (*anor aniyamsam*) and yet "the supporter of all".

In the *Rig Veda*, the Anunnaki were known as the Aryans. Both Annuna and Aryan can be translated to Fair Noble Ones – in other words, they were the inner space spirits the Indian shaman rishis consulted on agriculture, smithery, astronomy, geomancy and sacred geometry. The visionary leaders of the Dogon would also have gained inner guidance from these otherworldly beings but just as the French anthropologists misunderstood the African myths, so too did the British Raj, which ruled India between 1858 and 1947, miscomprehend those of ancient India.

These upper class, Oxford-educated translators of the *Vedas* were convinced that the Noble Ones must have meant literal aristocrat nobles of a fairer-skinned race, rather like themselves, who had invaded and conquered the South Asian subcontinent about 3000 years ago. They credited the sublime prose of these texts to more European and thus better-educated immigrants, finding it difficult to believe that the indigenous peoples they considered to be so much more primitive could have produced such remarkably deep philosophical literature. This was because they failed to take into account the fact that most of the traditional culture of northern India had been systematically eradicated over previous centuries by Mongol invasions and Muslim sultanate rule. Thus even as recently as about 10 years ago, academics still clung, white-knuckled, to what they called the Aryan Invasion Theory until they were finally persuaded otherwise by the overwhelming archaeological and linguistic evidence to the contrary.

Anu was also a popular "god word" in Egypt, where many priests were named Anu or Anubis. The city of Heliopolis, which was called the City of the Sun by the Greeks, had originally been named Anu. The Egyptian counterparts of the Annuna and the Aryans were the first company of Upper World gods known as the Aaru and they were hailed by these words which can be found today on the Louvre Papyrus 3283.

Hail to you, ye gods, ye associate gods, who are without body [my italics], ye who rule that which is born from the Earth, and that which is produced in the house of your cradles. Ye prototypes of the image of that exists; ye forms, ye great ones, ye associate gods, ye mighty ones, first company of the gods of Aaru, who generated men and shaped the type of every form, ye lords of all things. Hail to you, ye lords of everlasting.

In other words, the Annunaki, the Aryans and the Aaru sound much more like the incorporeal eternal spirits who guided the likes of Tabiti and Maya than gold-raiding, wife-stealing space invaders. To me, they did not have to come to Earth on rockets because they were, and are, already here and they probably will always be on this planet because they exist in the timeless parallel dimensions.

The Egyptian Underworld counterparts of the Aaru were the seven divine Uraei, or serpents of life, which represented the sovereignty of the land. These serpents were not considered to be good or evil but to represent the power of the elements in Nature.

There is also a Biblical story about the Judaic equivalent of the Annunaki. They were called the Nephilim and were said, in *Genesis* 6, to have been on the Earth before the Great Flood:

And it came to pass, when men began to multiply on the face of the earth, and daughters were born unto them,

That the sons of God saw the daughters of men that they were fair; and they took them wives of all which they chose.

And the lord said, My spirit shall not always strive with man, for that he also is flesh: yet his days shall be an hundred and twenty years.

There were giants in the earth in those days; and also after that, when the sons of God came in unto the daughters of men, and they bare children to

them, the same became mighty men which were of old, men of renown.

People who know no better often cite these verses about them as clear scientific evidence that mighty beings from other planets in our galaxy came to the Earth and made love with the "daughters of man". It is probably where Mr Sitchin got his wife-stealing theme from. But I read this as a metaphor for the sacred sexual sovereignty rites that take place between the Earthly shaman and her spirits, which you can learn more about in my book *Reclaiming Sovereignty*.

The word Nephilim comes from the Hebrew verbal root *n-ph-l*, meaning to "fall", and so we are back to the deluges of the primordial carpet. In ancient myths, the spirit is usually depicted as the male principle of the Upper World (Anu) and matter (*mater*, maternal) is represented as the Earth Mother female (Ishtar), fertilised by the serpent or fish god of the Underworld. This would make the Genesis story about the Nephilim a metaphor for an act of fertility that is at the heart of the creation, which the Judaic scribes almost certainly developed from older Sumerian/Babylonian stories about the serpent god Enki, who was one of the Children of Anu and was thus one of the Annunaki.

Enki, previously known as Ea, was the serpent god who inhabited the watery deeps of the abyss and in whose cube-shaped, submarinal house the fish people, the Seven Sages, slept. All the Sumerian gods were allotted parts of the sky and Enki's area of governance was to the south, around the Underworld constellations of Capricorn, Aquarius and Pisces.

We find images of Enki on Babylonian milestones in which he is associated with a double-faced effigy. From that, I would extrapolate that the double-faced god Janus, who gave his name to the month of January, was the Roman version of the Sumerian Enki, who governed the winter months in the skies of the northern hemisphere. Effigies found on cylinder seals and boundary stones show Enki with two rivers running from his shoulders – an early precursor for the Aquarian man carrying water. He was also symbolised by a goat-fish but now only the goat remains in the Capricorn house of our Greek-derived zodiacs, whereas the fish has become two in the house of Pisces.

In the *Enuma Elis*, we hear that far from the Annunaki's planet only appearing in the night skies every 3,600 years, Nibiru is permanently stationed there, like a star.

Nibiru, which is said to have occupied the passageways of heaven and earth, because everyone above and below asks Nibiru if they cannot find the passage. Nibiru is Marduk's star which the gods in heaven caused to be visible. Nibiru stands as a post at the turning point. The others say of Nibiru the post: 'The one who crosses the middle of the sea without calm, may his name be Nibiru, for he takes up the center of it.' The path of the stars of the

sky should be kept unchanged.

In this passage, Nibiru sounds like a pole star, which "stands as a post at the turning point" and from which sailors always take a reckoning. In Akkadian, Nibiru meant "river crossing", like a ferry boat, and in the extract from the *Enuma Elis* above, it has associations with wayfinder or a guide to travellers at sea. In other words, it represented a navigator's god, like the Greek Hermes, the Egyptian Thoth and the Roman Mercury.

So I reckon our women and our gold are safe!

Mr Sitchin's copious works on this subject are full of his made-up translations and he makes glaring omissions; his truncated quotes and extracts are taken out of context and from the amount of repetition and redundant pattern recognition, his works could also be an early form of neurolinguistic programming.

Whenever Mr Sitchin was asked to provide references for his "beliefs", he would insist that "it's all in the books". True, he does provide references and a bibliography of sorts in his vast *oeuvre* but not a jot to serve as evidence for the more sensational part of his story, about the Anunnaki coming to Earth from outer space on rockets every 3,600 years.

Perhaps one day our spaceships will be able to travel much further, to the Pleiades or to the Andromeda Galaxy or to Sirius. It would be fascinating to explore our universe. But however much we learned from that experience and however thrilled we were to see such off-world phenomena close up, we would still be in this dimension and therefore our consciousness would be the same as it is now.

However, if we were to learn to journey like a shaman into the other dimensions, there would be an opportunity for self-transformation and spiritual evolution through enhanced consciousness, as well as a greater understanding about the alchemical building blocks of all life.

Of course, it is very easy to persuade those who do not have a holographic consciousness that the devils and demons featured in ancient myths are just up there somewhere in outer space, waiting to pounce.

I hope that one day many more will realise that, while in the shamanic trance state, it is easy to reach other worlds, in the blink of an eye, where one can obtain guidance and information from the entities one meets there, including help with understanding the deeper meanings of ancient myths.

Before the World Tree was felled, this was a common practice of our ancestors and their otherworldly spirits – both gods and animals – are shown in their zodiacs, one of which, the oldest known to us, is from the Hathor Temple in Dendera, Egypt, and can now be seen in the Musée du Louvre, Paris.

A zodiac is sometimes known as a Wheel of the Year or Medicine Wheel because it connects the four cardinal points with the seasons, deities, elements, colours and creatures of the sacred holistic and holographic healing lore of a culture.

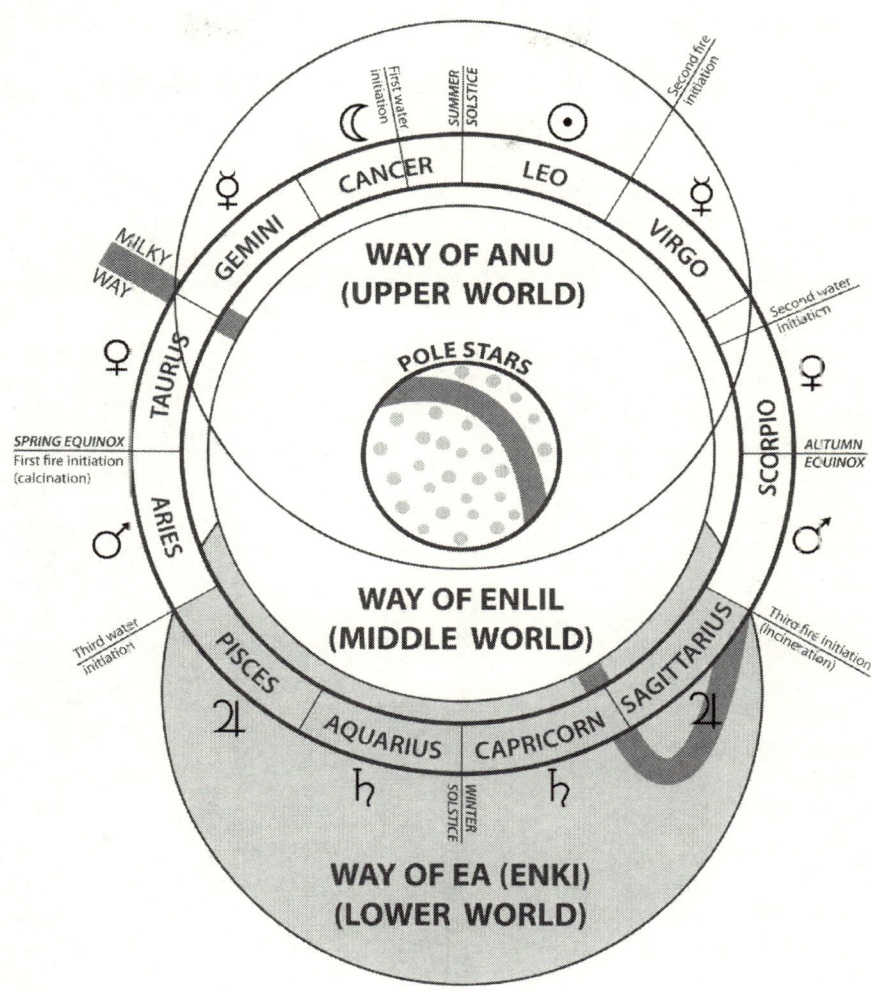

Figure 16: The inner cosmology of the Babylonians, when the Spring Equinox was at Taurus

I developed **Figure 16** from the information found in Babylonian stories, which, like all ancient myths, are set across three worlds. Although the diagram shows flat circles, it is a two-dimensional map of a serpentine spiral reaching out and coiling up from the deepest inner microcosm to the furthest outer macrocosm.

In this way, our access to the "star peoples" or the Anunnaki is instantaneous through a holographic vortex. Thus, there was, and still is, no requirement for spacecraft that can travel faster than light because nobody needs to go anywhere when the "star peoples" are already here. We just need to open our doors of perception to see them.

14. Interpreting Numbers in Myths

BY now you will hopefully have a picture forming in your mind of an ancient people who told metaphorical stories about a hero of the pole stars whose adventures took place on a circular celestial passage similar to the one they traversed in their nighttime wanderings below with their flocks. Eventually, after the agricultural revolution, the starry protagonist morphed into the solar hero at the centre of the zodiac. However, just to make things more interesting for the poor story archaeologist, the two systems – stellar and solar - and their champion often bleed through into each other on the primordial carpet which means that the coded numbers used in the older myths were either jettisoned entirely, or changed and repurposed for the later Sun-based myths.

So please do bear all that in mind as we go through this last chapter in **Part 2: The Language of the Initiates** and I promise to simplify it all down to the most basic level. What follows is just the least you will need to know about numbers in myths for you to be able to carry on enjoying this book.

1

As you know, the earliest stories are deluge myths and are about a hero who sails his barque or ark around the circle of pole stars, braving the terrors of the water serpent and the stormy flood of the firmament in order to fix the new pole in place after the old one has been submerged in the flood waters.

For instance, in the Egyptian Book of the Dead, the god Taht sails in his crescent-shaped lunar barque across the floods to fix the new pole star of that age. In the sixth century, the Celtic poet Taliesin composed *Prieddeu Annwn* (*The Spoils of the Underworld*), which is about the hero Arthur's sea voyage around the seven celestial stations of the deeps.

If these myths were composed today, the hero's vessel would be depicted as a submarine because his magical mystery tour that leads to full enlightenment is within the watery subconscious deeps of inner space. The outer one, twinkling above, was used to create a picture language as mnemomics for these stories, and circular monuments were engineered on the ground below as a constant reminder of these teachings for those that continually followed this passage behind their grazing reindeer herds.

The pole is the most important or prime symbol in these stellar myths and for that reason it is represented by the first prime number, one. (I agree that we were taught in school that one is not a prime number but, for reasons too long to go into here, I disagree.)

In the Northern tradition, the pole star was called the Lode Star and the Nail. The Finnish Kalavela myths feature a hero smith, Ilmarinen, who forges the dome of the sky and hammers it in place with a nail.

So the number one represents the pole star and it is symbolised variously by the tent pole, the World Tree, the masthead of the barque/ark, the primordial mound that is rescued from the floodwaters, the pillar or the pyramid.

The primordial mound eventually becomes the mountain that the barque or ark settles upon in the flood myths of many cultures, such as Mount Ararat (Judaic), Mount Meru (Indian), Mount Nizir (Babylonian) and Mount Hetep (Egyptian).

2

The number two represents variously a) night and day b) the male and female principle and c) DNA with its two twin strands, and these two themes are linked in that the conjoining of a man and a woman creates new life in their shared Rivers of Blood.

For instance, in the *Genesis* story of Noah's Ark, all of the animals went in two-by-two, male and female, as Noah's mission in this story is to save them from extinction and preserve their DNA for future generations.

At the same time, his wife is with him on the Ark, as well as his three sons, Ham, Japheth and Shem, along with their wives so that, once the floods had receded, they could create further generations.

The ark-building patriarch of the older Egyptian Deluge story – probably the source for the *Genesis* one - is Nnu with his sons Shu, Taht and Seb of the serpents, and they also all have their wives with them. There are no animals in that original but we find the two-by-two of night and day represented by the two sisters of Isis, the lady of the dawn, and Nephthys, the lady of the blackness. Isis was responsible for the deluge of light at daybreak while Nephthys governed the deluge of darkness at night.

(There are many more of these deluge stories in **Appendix A: Flood Myths** from Around the World).

In the 11th century Welsh story *How Culhwch Won Olwen*, Culhwch sets off on his quest to find his queen and take her father's throne with a pair of swallows swooping around his feet. Swallows represented sovereignty in Celtic literature and there is a saying: "He who holds the reins of the land, reigns over the land." Hence the Tarot figure of The Chariot.

3

The oldest tales refer back to a three-in-one godhead, such as the Hindu Brahma-Vishnu-Shiva trinity, respectively the creator of the universe, the one who maintains it and the god who eventually destroys it at the end of the Day. A Day just means a cycle in myths – it can refer to the cycle of the 24-hour day but it can also mean the Great Day and Night of Brahma, which lasts trillions of years.

The number three is more prevalent in the earlier stories, when the tales of the pole star hero were set against a backdrop in which the Moon had a more prominent role. The Alexandrian system was developed from a cosmology that was derived, in Mesopotomian countries nearer the equator, from three strongly defined seasons in which the best way to measure time was the passage of the Moon around the constellations, which took 27 days. Thus the year was also divided into the three water initiations and three fire initiations of the teachings of The Three Cauldrons.

The number three can also be about the number of days the lunar disc is dark before the new Moon appears. It is sometimes envisaged as a crescent-shaped Moon boat bearing a newborn child. Then in later solar-based stories, three refers to the number of days the Sun stands still on the Winter Solstice, the shortest day of the year, before "rising again" as the Radiant Child, a metaphor for birth and rebirth that is found in the stories of all cultures worldwide, and a popular carol that begins: "I saw three ships come sailing in, on Christmas Day, on Christmas Day..."

4

The number four is more prevalent in myths deriving from the beginning of the Agricultural Age, when the lunar-based three seasons gave way to four solar-governed ones, and thus lunar-solar calendars came into use. So the number three was multiplied by four, giving the 12 sun signs of the zodiac.

Symbolically, four can also refer to the four quarters of the universe, which is envisaged as a square. The four corners are governed by four characters; in the oldest myths by the bull (Taurus), a lion (Leo) an eagle (Scorpio) and a man (Aquarius), then later on, into the Common Era, by the four Christian apostles

Matthew, Mark, Luke and John.

In this way, the number four represents the establishment of dominion, empire and worldly power with its attendant system of laws. Four plus four makes eight and an octagon, which represents imperial rule over all the heavens and the Earth.

5.

When five appears with eight and 13, it is usually a nod to the sacred geometry produced by the celestial dance of Venus – known to the Greeks as Aphrodite and to the Babylonians as Ishtar. In her comings and goings over a period of eight years, or 13 Venusian years, she and the Earth perform a dance that draws a huge five-pointed star around the Sun.

Five generally represents feminine power and it is often in the shape of a pentagram or pentagon. The Hebrew word for "five" is "Hé", which is symbolised as a womb.

6

Noah is 600 years old when God tells him to build an ark in order to prevent his family and the animals being drowned in the flood. So six is about the final stage of the process of the perfection of man through his heroic trials – but it can also be shown as 66 or 600 or 666.

Six is the number of pole stars are drowned under the flood before the hero goes on to establish the seventh. Bible scholars say the name Noah meant "rest" and that explains the line from *Genesis* about the end of the creation: "And on the seventh day he rested." In other words, the pole star god can finally rest following his labours after heroically establishing the seventh pole. The Egyptian Nnu meant "lord of the celestial inundation" as well as "rest and repose".

In the later solar-based myths, the number six came to be associated with Time and its ruler, the Sun. In Sumerian myths, the Sun is female and called Shamash, with the Moon considered to be masculine and named Sin. After the agricultural revolution, the Sun becomes masculine with the Moon feminine and he is represented by the six-pointed Star of David – otherwise known as the Seal of Solomon.

7

Seven is probably the most prolific number that crops up in all kinds of sagas worldwide and deluge myths are no exception: Noah's ark came to rest on Mount Ararat on the seventh month.

There are the seven lost islands of Atlantis, seven-headed serpents, fishes with seven fins, trees with seven branches, poles with seven horns, the Sumerian and Vedic Seven Sages and the seven Samothracian Kabiri aboard the ark.

These sevens represent the circumpolar stellar bodies that take turns to be our pole star, changing every 3,714 years over a "Great Year" of almost 26,000.

8

Eight is the number of humans on the Ark in the Hebrew, Egyptian and Vedic versions of the Deluge myth and it is because eight is the holiest number, representing the foundation stone of the creation.

The eight humans on the ark – four men and four women – are required to generate the human race anew from the octagon of a regenerated foundation stone.

The number eight is often expressed symbolically as 888, making 8: 8 x 8 = 864. The late geomancer John Michell described it as the number of the foundation stone in the building of Jerusalem:

The number 864 is prominent in the temple measures, most of all in the 864-cubit distance between the two sacred rocks, the Rock of Foundation and Golgotha, or Place of the Skull.

In the language of symbolic number, 864 pertains to a centre of radiant energy, the sun in the solar system... the inner sanctuary of the temple, the altar and the corner stone on which the whole sacred edifice is founded.

864 is called the 'foundation number' ... and in the gematria of *New Testament* Greek, 864 corresponds to words or phrases such as 'altar', 'corner stone', 'sanctuary of the gods', 'holy of holies'...

The number eight could not be more holy in terms of being not only wholly holistic but holographic. The DNA of the human consists of 64 (8 x 8) codons and even our hearts beat in time with the macrocosmic heartbeat of Time and Space. The average heart rate for a human being is 60 beats per minute; multiply that by 60 minutes and it gives us 3,600 beats per hour, which is 86,400 every 24 hours – in other words, the time the Earth takes to travel each day around the Sun, which is 864,000 miles across.

On top of that, 88 is the number of days it takes Mercury to orbit the Sun.

This sacred cosmology is not just expressed in ancient stories; our early ancestors also created plays, dances, artworks, architecture and even board games and divinatory tools like the *i-Ching*, which use the number 8, or 8 x 8, as their foundation. That is why there are 64 (8 x 8) hexagrams in the *i-Ching*, 64 sections to the Eye of the Horus and 64 squares on a chess board. The Hindu Lord Shiva has 64 manifestations and there are 64 *dakinis* (female nature deities) mentioned in the *Vedas*.

The Mayans used an eight-by-eight square, for a total of 64 units, and the same eight-by-eight square was known in ancient Indian temple design as the Vastu Parusha Mandala with eight ruling gods.

Sixty-four is also the atomic weight of copper, which is the metal associated with Venus, previously known as Ishtar. Her city, Babylon, meaning "gate of the gods", was similarly built on this cosmological principle. The eighth of the eight gates (8 × 8) of Babylon was known as Ishtar's Gate, dedicated to the goddess with her eight-pointed star.

9

The number nine comes from the much older lunar-based mythos of the pole star hero, and is therefore more prevalent in Vedic mythology, which is based on sidereal astrology and astronomy. Some believe it was the ancient rishi Indians who invented the idea of using numbers to represent cosmological deities who in themselves feature in stories full of metaphors for cosmological processes, and they are also expressed in the Indian dance form that has its roots in the third-century *Natya Shastra* texts attributed to Bharata Muni.

Sidereal astrology is based on nine planets known as the *navagrahas* – the nine states of being. They are the Sun (Surya), the Moon (Chandra), Mars (Managala), Mercury (Budha), Jupiter (Brihaspathi), Venus (Sukra), Saturn (Sani), Rahu and Ketu.

The ancient Indian deluge is called *pralaya*, which means dissolution. It does not have the same judgemental connotations as the Biblical and Egyptian Deluge myths but is considered to be the natural end of a cosmological cycle, after which the world is renewed. But this story is similar in that it features a great patriarch called Manu who has three sons, like the Biblical and Egyptian patriarchs Noah and Nnu, and the god Vishnu appears to Manu and instructs him to build a boat and fill it with animals and seeds to repopulate the Earth:

> "O kind-hearted man, you have care in your heart, listen now. Soon the world will be submerged by a great flood, and everything will perish. You must build a strong ark, and take along a rope on board. you must also take with you the Seven Sages, who have existed since the beginning of time, and seeds of all things and a pair of each animal." Matsya Purana

In more Western mythology, the number nine is found in the nine Muses of Greek mythology, who are the maidens of the three multiplied by three-fold Moon seasons of the older Mesopotamian system. They are also featured in Taliesin's *Preiddeu Annwn* as the "breath of the nine maidens" that keep the seas of the cauldron boiling.

10

The only real value of 10 to be found in ancient myths is in the Egyptian stories that brought together Time and Space by dividing the 360° of the circle of the cosmos into 36 "decans" of 10 days each.

The ancient Greeks tried to develop that idea but not in a way that will be useful to us here, because those myths are often not the best place to begin if you want to understand the symbolic meaning of numbers in astrology, given that they often did not understand the original deeper meanings themselves. Alexander the Great's scribes purloined most of the myths they encountered when conquering countries like Babylonia, Persia and Egypt, for the purpose of controlling the new populations. By allowing the masses under their governance to retain their own tales with characters and plotlines they recognised, they could keep the peace. Then, at a later stage, they would twist that story in the service of their own political agenda. The Romans learned a lot from the Greeks!

But even so-called Pythagorean numbers – which are listed from one to 10 - were not actually invented by Pythagoras; evidence can be found for Pythagorean mathematics in 5,000 year-old Vedic fire altars.

12

The number 12 is found in so many myths because it refers to the 12 divisions of the heavens that make up the classic 12 houses of the zodiac. An animal or god-like being represents each of the 12 divisions and that is why the Greeks named that celestial circle a "zodiac", which meant "circle of animals".

15

In the Noah's ark flood story, the waters covered the Earth to a depth of 15 cubits.

In Egyptian mythology, 15 is the number of death and resurrection. The god of the watery flood in the Underworld, Osiris, was murdered and hacked into 15 pieces by the god Set and the 15th piece, the phallus, was thrown away and lost. However, Isis recovered 14 parts and put him back together again, then gave him a wooden phallus through which they conceived Horus.

17

Noah's ark sailed on the 17th day of the month and then came to rest on Mount Ararat on the 17th of the month, five months later. This means that the ark was afloat for 150 days and if you divide 150 by 17, it is surely no coincidence you get 8.8. This makes Mount Ararat the foundation stone of the "temple" for the new world to support the next generations.

36

The number 36 comes from the ancient Egyptian and Vedic system of timekeeping, referring to the 360-degree universe of space. In Egyptian myths, the year was divided into 36 decans of 10 days, giving 360 days in total.

40

In the Noah's Ark story, it rained for 40 days and 40 nights. Then Noah waited a further 40 days and nights before sending forth the first bird, a raven, to look for land.

The number 40 is found throughout the Bible. For instance, in the book of *Exodus*, the Children of Israel were in the wilderness for 40 days and 40 nights, as was Jesus of the New Testament, who had to face temptation by the Devil. In *Exodus* and *Deuteronomy*, Moses goes to the mountain to talk to God twice, for the same time period.

In Kings, *Elijah* fasted for that number of days and nights on Mount Horeb before he heard the voice of God. In *Jonah*, the prophet warned Nineveh that if the people did not repent, God would overthrow their city within 40 days and 40 nights.

Biblical scholars have no idea why the number 40 is so prevalent in these Hebrew texts. However, I have a couple of theories. It could go as far back as Vedic sidereal astrology, which is based on the 360-degree circle of the universe. If you divide that 360 by the nine Vedic planets, you get 40. Another way of looking at it is 40 days plus 40 nights equals 80 periods of time, or 8 – and we are back to the foundation stone.

50

I haven't yet figured out the symbolic meaning of 50, except that it may be a higher order of five. I've heard that zeros were used to denote a refining of a position on the spiralling Ladder of the Wise – for instance, in coming round again to deal with a situation you've met before but this time from a higher and thus wiser perspective.

We also know five usually denotes the feminine and from that we might be able to perceive why 50 is so often the number of mythological ships' crews – whether of deluge or zodiac heroes – because they are all aided, in different ways, by women in the form of the double goddess.

The original voyage in the *Epic of Gilgamesh* told of a crew of 50, although this has been lost to more modern translations. Fifty is the same number Jason took with him to man his ship, the *Argo*. There were also 50 men in the Greek tale of *The Odyssey*. After leaving the island of Circe, Odysseus divides his men into two boats carrying 22 each. If you add a further six, lost on the previous raid against the Cicones, it makes 50.

However, as the latter two myths – *Jason and the Golden Fleece* and *The Odyssey* – are Greek myths they could just have been blindly copying the Babylonian one about Gilgamesh, as they did with their 12 labours of Hercules. So it may not have been about women. It may be about 7 x 7 + 1 being the hero, in which case this is the same number the Celtic Arthur took on his voyage, as recounted in Taliesin's *Preiddeu Annwn*.

Part 3
INTO THE ZODIAC

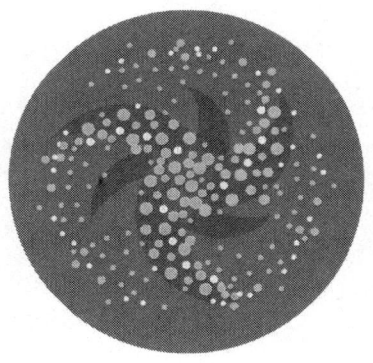

15. The Zodiac Hero

Row row row your boat
Gently down the stream,
Merrily merrily merrily merrily,
Life is but a dream.

THIS traditional English nursery rhyme sung by children as a light-hearted ditty contains enormous wisdom. Life is but a dream. The rest of it is true too and yet it tends to be ignored. There is a stream of Wyrd, as it was known to the Norse shamans; you are meant to row your boat down it and we would be "merrily merrily merrily merrily" doing so if humanity had not been rendered into such a state of ignorance over the centuries that most don't even know that they are equipped with oars, let alone where they are and how to use them.

Some try to make a virtue out of this disastrous state of affairs. "That's cool, man, chill," they insist, "I'm just going with the flow. Pass the chillum." Well, that's all fine during a lazy, hazy Summer of Love. But what happens to you and your vessel when you suddenly find that you're in the white water rapids and being thrown from side to side violently? How cool is it really when you hit the jagged rocks or get sucked down into a whirlpool?

In earlier chapters, we met the pole star hero who braves the wild, raging seas of the deluge in his ark, or barque, to win the Cauldron or Holy Grail. To me, these pre-agricultural-age, lunar-based stories of our nomadic ancestors from the Steppes carry perfect metaphors for this scenario and through working shamanically, as they did, we can learn from our spirit guides how to find our oars and navigate by the stars.

And so now that you've learned about some of the symbols and numbers used in myths, and their meanings, you're hopefully ready to meet a later version of the hero who traversed, instead of the pole stars, the fixed constellations around the Sun.

He is the zodiac hero, the starring character in many myths, in one form or another.

However, the astrological protagonist is not always clearly visible because these star sagas have become quite corrupted over time. Sometimes, he's unearthed from lying buried under the hills of the Ages with only an arm or leg poking through, like a fallen statue. That said, the trained ear can recognise a story about the mythological Sun god, even when only a few events in his life are present, because the older the mythological strata from which they derive, the more likely they are to be set in a certain sequential arrangement as much as doe, a female deer, leads to ray, a drop of falling sun, and so on to mi, fa, sol, la, ti, do in the solfeggio scale.

The mythologist Joseph Campbell called our champion "the hero with a thousand faces" and he described the universal journey he follows as the monomyth, which is his term for the primordial carpet.

Campbell summed this basic storyline up thus:

"A hero ventures forth from the world of common day into a region of supernatural wonder: fabulous forces are there encountered and a decisive victory is won: the hero comes back from this mysterious adventure with the power to bestow boons on his fellow man."

In his collected works, published under the title *The Hero with a Thousand Faces*, he goes on to cite dozens of examples of this same super-protagonist, from Krishna and Odysseus to Arthur and Jesus.

In other words, once you get down deep enough, there is only one story at its basis. And any differences in these peripatetic tales about the hero and his journey around the pole stars, and later on the zodiac, only arise because roaming storytellers tailored them to suit the local people and their specific mytho-poetic tribal customs and traditions.

To the ancients, whose lives were taken up with following the "trods" of their herds across the grasslands, the hero represented the archetypal man following the twists and turns of their own trods mirrored by the sparkling night skies, which were set in place at the time of his birth. The story told is about transformation and spiritual evolution but it is not to become a god. What religions never tell you is that godhood is not the highest calling. The spirits themselves are full of admiration for the one who passes through the third and final fire initiation at Sagittarius, making the hero a true and worthy human who is capable of joining the higher ranks of the initiates and thus lead others along the pathways of the trods, as Above, So Below. This is achieved through a quickening that is developed as a consequence of having to perform one after another of seemingly impossible trials, just as, like the White Queen through Alice's looking glass, we sometimes have to do "16 impossible things before breakfast".

This brings me to a key in these myths that has been lost over time but is a vital requisite if our champion is to win through against his adversaries in the face of seemingly insurmountable odds. It can only be achieved with the help of the gods, the goddesses, the ancestors and the animals – the spirits known to the shamans, in other words. The key is to unlock the doors of perception, so that he can be in contact with these otherworldly guides.

Therefore, the message that has come down to us through these stories is that to transform into a real human being, we have to learn to ask for help. But as they always say, pride comes before a fall. So most of us only drop to our knees in surrender when we have tried every other stratagem and have run out of options. However, this is the only way to receive divine intervention and it means our so-called failure can lead to unimaginable success, if we only know how to tackle the situation. In other words, while you're going through the white water rapids and your boat is slowly filling up with water and about to sink, the gods can use that volatile energy to spin your vessel up into the air. Admittedly, it can feel a little bit discombobulating at first but then you realise you're in a flying boat, which opens up myriad options.

I don't believe our ancestors were so reluctant to ask for divine intervention because, from what I can understand about them, they don't seem to have been afflicted with the modern concept of the ever-upward trajectory of progress. They acknowledged failure or falling as a means of learning the lessons we need, as humans, in this incarnation. In addition, they didn't have to pretend to be perfect in the eyes of a jealous god, or stop themselves from falling because they were under the false impression that the Fall is synonymous with sin and that the shaman's spirits are demons stoking the fires of an eternal Hell. Thus they knew that the hero does not become great on his own devices but only through the humble acceptance of his failings and thus gratefully asking for, and receiving, the help of otherworldly entities who know better than he does the lessons his soul needs – and how to learn them.

Today, we are hampered by faulty interpretations of these myths and for that reason we can be under the misapprehension that the hero receives divine help almost automatically, as if it is his right. Maybe it is because these stories were considered to be "pagan" by their Christian translators and thus assumed to be meaningless tales man told himself because he had nothing better to do before Jesus Christ "saved" him. But Jesus with his 12 disciples, who carried to Mount

Calvary his own cross to plant, just as the deluge hero would erect his pole on the mount he'd recovered from the floods, was just one in a long line of mythological heroes and so he wasn't the first son of the gods whose story was told to show us how much we can be guided, loved and supported.

In other words, what is actually missing from the latter-day, priestly translations of ancient myths is the ecstatic experience of the shaman.

Through journeying shamanically, my experience is that there are spirits in the heavens, the land and the Underworld that have held back their own liberation in order to stay and help humans evolve into their highest potentiality. And far from being judgmental, like a green-eyed Jehovah-type god, they are our biggest fans. They celebrate our anniversaries, they cheer our successes and they mourn with us as we suffer through our failures and losses, knowing all the while that these hardest of lessons will cut the deepest.

However, our guiding spirits are not in attendance to us through some kind of decreed duty or karma written in cold, hard stone. It is only because of their unconditional love for human beings. It matters not who we pray to – whether Jesus, Buddha, Krishna, Mohammed or any other spirit. All it takes to be able to make a holographic connection to those whose role it is to listen and respond to our prayers is for our heart to be sincere.

We were never meant to feel that we had to walk this path alone.

And so my unravelling and transcribing the zodiac stories of old has not been born out of some sort of intellectual curiosity about the past. On the contrary: I wanted to know how their messages could help us today in providing what is currently lacking in consensual reality. This is why I set out to read them so many decades ago now – not because I wanted a university degree in comparative mythology but because I realised our ancestors had left us these important messages in bottles that had somehow survived the crossings of the oceans of time, albeit smashed and fractured from the rough passage and, in some cases, the message having faded to the point of invisibility.

It was virtually from the lips of these storytellers of old that I learned in what way the vicissitudes of the winding alchemical path of the zodiac hero are similar to the ups and downs met by the human being as we try to find a way to make our lives meaningful. We know in our hearts that we are not just "consumers" content with merely eating, working, procreating and sleeping. We want to know why we are here and then use what we know in order to progress. To me, it does not seem like much to ask. People rarely just leap into their cars for the sake of it and drive them around willy-nilly because they like the sound of the engine. In the same way, few show up at the airport with a random ticket to anywhere or are content with a ride in a plane that merely circles the runaways. So why would we expect to live a whole human life, from the cradle to grave, without knowing its purpose and where it is going?

In order to understand what the zodiac hero has to teach us, we need to go back to a time thousands of years after Maya had led his people out of the Steppes region and they had fanned out and settled across Europe and the Mediterranean countries. Those peoples who had previously preferred to travel in the cool of the night, using the stars and the Moon to guide them, gradually adopted more of a fixed, agricultural lifestyle. Thus the Sun became more important in their mythologies and so the solar hero was put at the centre of a circle of 12 constellations.

We find evidence for the use of this 12-fold zodiacal system all over the Earth, at this time, in the form of cosmological stories, cylinder seals, pottery decorations, boundary stones and important ritual structures, like fire altars and stone circles, that were built on sacred geometrical principles.

For instance, there are:

12 primordial gods in Hesiod's Creation
12 Babylonian gods
12 mandarins of Emperor Yao in third millennium BCE China
12 Vedic Solar gods
12 Kami or stages of creation in the Shinto religion
12 Akhtars of the Zoroastrian (Persian) stars
12 gods in the Greek pantheon on Mount Olympus
12 tribes of Israel
12 disciples of Jesus
12 councillors of Asgard in the Norse Eddas
12 elders in the Council of the Dalai Lama
12 labours of Hercules
12 exploits of Gilgamesh
12 knights of King Arthur
12 followers of Odysseus

In those days, this lore was passed on through the Mysteries teachings, as they were known, which took place in various sacred groves around the Mediterranean every year on two important dates. The first Mystery Rites was held on the Spring Equinox and the second one on the Autumn Equinox. These two events had been known respectively as the Lesser Mysteries and the Greater Mysteries.

Thousands would flock from far and wide to attend the Lesser Mysteries at the Spring Equinox. Many of the teachings would be given in the form of stories and plays that were in allegorical form. To help people remember the names and the qualities of all the various spirits or gods who were portrayed in the plays, they were moulded into models or statues, and their likenesses were reproduced and painted on to pottery.

One of the plays performed at the Lesser Mysteries featured a Sun god who died and then rose again from the dead three days later.

Eventually, the whole event would culminate in a mass baptism, or water initiation.

However, the purpose of the stories and dramas of the Lesser rites were to prepare those who were ready for the Greater Mysteries, the fire initiation, which would take place on the Autumn Equinox. It was only then the advanced initiates were shown that these tales and plays were allegories that had a dual purpose – as both a holistic and holographic cosmological teaching. In other words, they were taught the true meaning – both astronomical and astrological - of the dying and resurrecting Sun god.

The scribes of the day would write down these metaphorical stories on papyrus and vellum which they stored in libraries all over the world, like the one at Alexandria – which eventually received its own fire initiation at the hands of the Romans and thus was the final conflagration before the lights went out to herald the advent of the Dark Ages.

Because of this tragic loss, Western or tropical astrology is derived from the later, Greco-Roman geographer and astronomer Ptolemy's interpretation of incomplete and faultily transcribed source material. In other words, it is a bit like a broken clock set in aspic. This sky map therefore is not a realistic facsimile when the heavens – and the Earth – are spiralling through space at 600,000 miles an hour and because of the precession of the equinoxes, the 12 constellations appear to "move" backwards, over time, roughly every 2,000 years or so.

However, I invite you to consider this viewpoint. It's my thinking that like all true divinatory systems, the astrological wheel doesn't have to be a realistic representation of how we are connected to the cosmos through Time and Space for it to work as a guide. Astrology is rather like the Tarot in that way. Both methods are based on universally understood archetypes and symbols, and in working holographically we are establishing, through the actions of these multi-dimensional archetypal characters, a different connectivity – a connectivity of meaning that was written in our Rivers of Blood by storytellers uncountable millennia ago.

So with that understanding, let us now familiarise ourselves with the astrological houses in the order that the zodiac hero traverses them on the Wheel, for you to begin to understand how each one provides different challenges and lessons to be learned for our hero. It is not meant to be the final word on this aspect of astrology by any means. I just want to give you the least you will need to know in order to be able to find this understory yourself, running as a subterranean seam of gold through ancient – and not.

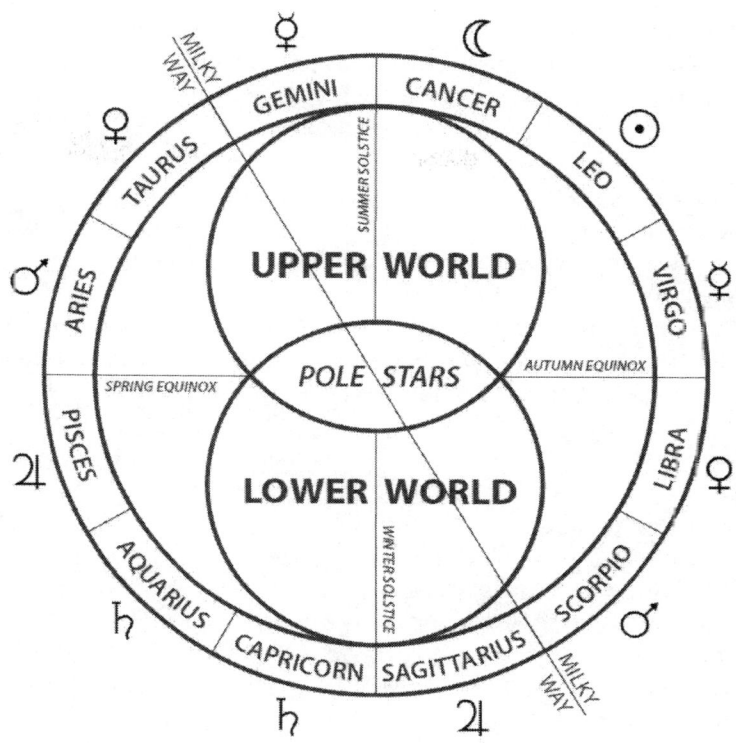

Figure 17: The Alexandrian system

so ancient – myths. In addition, the meanings of the astrological houses that I'm going to describe here are not meant to be taken personally, as a horoscope would be, which is drawn up to show all the other mitigating factors that accompany your Sun sign.

As you will see in **Figure 17** (which is a repeat of Figure **13** and also another version of Yuri Leitch's illustration towards the front of the book) I've divided the zodiac into the Upper World, Middle World (*mandorla*) and Lower World, because this is the shape that emerges from Babylonian myths, and further research shows me that the Alexandrian alchemists and astrologers of the last centuries before the Common Era viewed it in this way. It is not literal; it is meant to indicate that the travails on the first part of the hero's journey, which begins at Aries, are about the development of the conscious mind after birth and the individuation of the ego. He doesn't start to learn about the deeper facets of what really drives him – in other words his subconscious mind – until he is stung by the scorpion at Scorpio and then tumbles down into the Underworld at Sagittarius, after which he proceeds through further trials in the Lower World until he is eventually reborn on the Winter Solstice at Capricorn.

He has not yet evolved in wisdom sufficiently to intuit that some of the worst adversaries he encounters on his path will be his best teachers and that brute force is not always the best way to settle an argument. He is ignorant to the finer benefits of diplomacy and so assumes that grabbing what he wants, and brutally suppressing any opposition to it, will be the best way to achieve his goals. In other words, he has a lot to learn about the finer arts of diplomacy and rulership.

So with all that mind, let us venture forth into the zodiac from where the hero commences his cosmological journey, which is at the Lesser Mysteries on the Spring Equinox. This is currently set at Aries the Ram and governed by the god of war, Mars.

Aries the Ram
First fire initiation

Just as the sap is rising up through the Earth and spurting forth with a sudden uprush of flaming energy, so the blood of the adolescent, hot-headed, butting ram warrior is up and raring to go. Our Martian champion is the archetypal "young man a hurry" who has not yet acquired the virtue of patience. He intends to be a millionaire before his 30s. So he has no hesitation about dashing into situations on the spur of the moment, without forethought, and he can often come dashing straight out again.

Taurus the Bull

Our rampaging ramrod is, so far, deaf to the inner tuition of his intuition – in other words, his gut feelings. So he usually gets a few hard lessons when he reaches the Earthy bull of Taurus – and often too at the hands of a sensuous woman who represents the first appearance of the double-headed Venus, the planetary governor of Taurus.

If he is not wise enough to recognise the diamond he's being offered, he mistakes it for a shard of glass and throws it away. Or he is so dazzled by her beauty, he makes a self-entitled grab for her without showing his desired one the respect she deserves. This is more about his own real low opinion of himself than of her but as he has not met his true nature yet, he projects his own sense of unworthiness on to the woman. He is behaving a bit like a bull in china shop and thus the bovine creature seems an appropriate symbol for Taurus.

However, insulting the goddess of luck brings quickly forth a reversal of fortune and this sets off a whole raft of miseries and misfortunes. Thus, he is rapidly introduced to one of his first real experiences of the suffering that life can bring and it provokes great agony within him that he is cognitively incapable of dealing with. So he blunders on, angry at the world and completely frustrated at other people's stupidity for not recognising his greatness – and this creates even further turmoil all around him.

Gemini the Twins

The next astrological house in his path is Gemini, where the mercurial twins appear, just like Lewis Carroll's battling Tweedledum and Tweedledee, to represent the conflict raging within and without the hero.

> **Tweedledum and Tweedledee**
> **Agreed to have a battle;**
> **For Tweedledum said Tweedledee**
> **Had spoiled his nice new rattle.**
> **Just then flew down a monstrous crow,**
> **As black as a tar-barrel;**
> **Which frightened both the heroes so,**
> **They quite forgot their quarrel.**

I think the black bird here must represent Mercury, which rules Gemini. Mercury is the great communicator and so here the hero may, if he learns his lessons well, understand how to articulate and to put his thoughts into words that he can use to calm himself and make sense of others' antipathy towards him. However, even if he is successful in achieving a more rational approach, it can present another problem in that he may now struggle with making the right decisions for himself and others through being always able to see both sides of every argument.

Cancer the Crab

First water initiation

These mental travails, however, are soon to be subsumed by the salt water of tears at his next port of call, the feminine Cancer, which is ruled by the changeable moods of the Moon.

Because of the events caused by the reversal of fortune, he now feels like he's drowning in a sea of emotions. However, the Moon keeps him treading water until he learns to find his self-worth in his own reflected feelings about himself rather than in the vanity mirrors of others. At the same time, becoming aware and more sensitive to his feelings serves to get him in touch with his gut instincts, which he finally begins to learn to trust.

It is this unbearable pain that is often the precursor to him realising that he needs to continue on his quest, to look for deeper answers about life, even though he has no altruistic aims and just selfishly wants to use what he learns to gain power. However, the realisation that one is lacking power takes us back to the hidden message in the nursery rhyme at the beginning of this chapter. He is now waking up to the fact that he needs to row his boat. He must first though find the oars, in other words, gain the knowledge of the stars for the purposes of navigation. And as such, he has now reached the Summer Solstice and the beginning of the path of wisdom.

Leo the Lion

Second fire initiation

It is a great relief for our determined but damp protagonist to leave the feminine and changeable Vale of Tears and reach the heat of the midday Sun, ruled by the indominantly-male, straight-talking lion at Leo, which soon dries him out. The Leo character is often a relative or ancestor of our protagonist, rather like Arthur, Culhwch's cousin. As the generous, magnanimous Sun king, he enjoys teaching his new apprentice, by example, how to transmute his newly learned sensitivity and self-confidence into the wisdom, strength and courage that he will need to become a successful leader of men.

Leo is all about great, openhearted, heroic visions painted in bold and colourful broad brushstrokes. However, with all those big, bright, vivid markings upon the canvas of life, you do need somebody to clean the paintbrushes afterwards and this is where the next sign comes in.

Virgo the Virgin

After learning his lessons at Leo, our champion carries on to the next stage, which is Virgo. Here, he is set an endless list of tasks – just as the ogre Ysbadadden laid down for Culhwch 39 tasks and Hercules was given 12 labours. Some of the trials require enormous courage to complete; others are deadly in a different sense – deadly dull and montonous, with a requirement for great attention to detail, but which all help the hero to develop his powers of discrimination and administrative decision-making.

It is here that Mercury, the winged messenger of the gods, appears again to tutor our hero in transmuting the broad brushstroke approach of Leo into appreciating the small things where the *"deva is in the details"*.

Libra the Scales

After satisfying Mercury in Virgo, he reaches full adulthood and comes next to Libra – well, he does if the zodiac post-dates the Babylonians who did not have Libra and thus went straight to a double-dipper Scorpio. It was only later on that the Greeks took the claws of the scorpion and turned them into the scales of justice for Libra.

Libra, though, is where our champion has to face the final judgement. The metaphor often used in myths takes the form of a court scene, rather like the one in the closing chapter of Alice in Wonderland. It is also in Libra that he meets the double goddess Venus again and this time, assuming he has the learned the lessons of the previous tests and trials, he is better prepared to make sweet music with her.

Scorpio the Scorpion
Second water initiation

The Venus figure acts as a kind of initiatrix to provide help through the Death Gate of Scorpio, which is ruled by Mars. Scorpio is the sign of sex and death – which may sound a little intense until you realise that sacred sex is a multi-dimensional experience, meaning part of it takes place "through the portal". In addition, the scorpion dives down deep into the darkest depths, emotionally, where others would fear to tread, and thus brings back the black plutonian gold of illumination.

This ability to delve into the unfathomed, Neptunian submarinal realms gives the hero a greater capacity for honesty, intimacy and empathy. However, all that intense navel-gazing is bound to create ripples up in the surface world, which is why our champion now comes into his midlife crisis. He is stung by the tail of the scorpion and tumbles down into the Underworld, or Lower World.

Sagittarius the Centaur Archer
Third fire initiation

Here, under the tutorship of Jupiter, the hero has to confront his deepest and darkest fears in order to achieve transformation. This means he is compelled to face his shadow side, which often takes the form of his father – hence Darth Vader's immortal reveal to Luke Skywalker: "I am your father."

The mythological father is waiting to be released by the son's heroic actions. Once the father is freed, the son then takes his place to wait for the next hero – his own son, in some cases – to get stung by the scorpion in his turn and tumble down into the Underworld to face and pass his own trials and thus release him. This is a metaphor for the role of the shamans in their work of redeeming their ancestors.

Capricorn the Goat

Next, we come to Capricorn and the Winter Solstice or Saturnalia, where the redeemed father is reborn as a baby in a coracle or ark – rather like Moses in the bullrushes. In some traditions, this baby in the boat is known as the Radiant Child because when the heroic journey is performed well, the resulting children from that line carry great destinies and thus hope for the world.

You may have heard one of the Greek myths about Saturn in the form of the

Father of the Gods Chronos. Chronos is so fearful one of his children will try to supplant him on the throne that he eats all of them at birth, until finally one, Zeus, manages to survive and in turn, kill him and inherit the kingship. It is a clever twist on the narrative that takes place in this part of the zodiac. From here, we get so many stories about the Radiant Child – like those about Jesus, Krishna and Arthur – who have to be brought up with foster parents or in some way away from the family home in order to be protected from, respectively, King Herod, King Kamsa or King Uther. The myth of Saturn or Chronos eating all his children is just an older version of the theme of what comes to be known later as "the massacre of the innocents".

Anyway, Saturn gets a bad press – far worse than he deserves. Some of my deepest and most valuable lessons were received from the strict Saturn teacher and particularly each time he returns, every 29 years, into his place in the skies that he occupied at the time of my birth.

Aquarius the Water Carrier

The newborn babe is still under the firm hand of Saturn as his coracle sails into Aquarius, which is the sign of the great humanitarian. Unlike Leo, its opposite on the zodiac who craves personal recognition, Aquarius only seeks validation for his or her community and can be quite outspoken and unafraid of social disapproval when they are convinced they are acting for the good of the whole. These are all the characteristics of an excellent leader and so it's no surprise that her reborn hero acquires them here.

The sign's modern symbol of the water bearer can be traced back to the Mesopotamian god Enki, who ruled that part of the Babylonian zodiac. He is shown on cylinder seals and milestones with two rivers flowing from his head, representing the watering of the metaphorically arid wasteland, an archetypal Aquarian act.

Pisces the Fish

Third water initiation

Finally, the floating coracle reaches Pisces and here we find that the baby has grown into a sweet and sensitive child who feels such great compassion in their heart for struggling humanity that tears are sometimes shed. However, the pain felt at perceiving such a cruel world can cause the child to turn away into fantasy and make-believe. This makes people born under Pisces incredibly creative but a little on the dreamy side. Their phantasmogorical wanderings are often inspired by their guide, Jupiter, as they prepare for the day when they are old enough to go out into the world as a fierce warrior to protect the innocent and to right all wrongs.

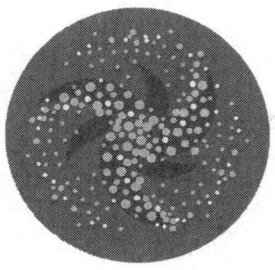

So that's the twelve signs in a nutshell – which should give you just enough information to be able to recognise their characteristics when the hero stumbles into one of them. In this way, we have much to learn from the zodiac hero and so we are going to meet two of them soon – Pinocchio and Gilgamesh - and follow their journey around the zodiac.

But it probably won't come as any surprise to hear that with an untold number of these stories being recounted mouth-to-ear over many millennia, not all zodiac heroes go through the same trials and sometimes there are not even 12 of them. Thus, for me, constructing this blueprint has been a little like trying to complete a million-word jigsaw when some of the pieces are missing. But I do have the Rosetta stone of the box lid, in the form of the primordial carpet, and there are usually a sufficient number of parts of the jigsaw in each story for us to safely assume what the missing ones would have shown.

It is a guess, sometimes, but it is a highly educated guess that is the fruit of more than 40 years of research. My aim is to provide a starting point for those who come after me with fresher archaeological discoveries providing newer and better information. The idea is that once you have "got your eye in" - in other words, learned to see the skeleton of the archetypal zodiacal journey that is poking through these two classics of their genre - you will soon be able to recognise them elsewhere, whether it's in a book, a film, the Tarot or a computer game.

It's a bit like going out to pick mushrooms at dawn. At first, you can't see any at all but once you find one, dozens suddenly appear.

So let's get started.

16. The Trials of Pinocchio

IF your only memory of the story of Pinocchio comes from watching Disney's classic animation, you might be surprised to find this naughty wooden puppet included in a book about the esoteric meanings of ancient myths. However, from the metaphors and symbols used in this old folk tale from Italy, it is clear its roots go back at least as far as the *Epic of Gilgamesh*, while even that 5,000-year-old Sumerian poem would have been a latter-day upgrade on the one told to Kroi by Tabiti in the Caucasus Mountains. In other words, it's very old indeed.

That is why I believe it's mistake to view the story of Pinocchio as a mere morality tale about the perils that befall naughty boys who refuse to listen to their elders, although it may appear that way when our Overton window offers only the narrow purview caused from wearing Christian horse blinders. I've found that most of the scrapes the young wooden puppet lands himself in were developed from the trials and tribulations of the zodiac hero and they are necessary because they exist to make him, the wooden puppet, into a "real boy".

That said, from a more modern perspective, we can clearly see Pinocchio stepping straight out of the Italian travelling marionette theatre, which developed from an older tradition that featured the likes of the battling Pulcinella and Harlequin - the earlier prototypes for Punch and Judy. This type of masked pantomime was known as the *Commedia dell'Arte*, in which a troupe of actors went from town to town in a caravan of wooden wagons and often performed from the back of them too. It had its roots in Roman and Greek "New Comedy" that in itself evolved from the Mystery Plays of the early medieval period.

However, in writing this chapter I have been presented with a quandary. The oldest version of Pinocchio dates from 1883 and it comes from Tuscany. It is titled *Le Avventure di Pinnochio (The Adventures of Pinocchio)* and was written by one Carlo Collodi. But the version most readers will be familiar with is the Disney animated one, *Pinocchio*, which was released in 1940.

So I've decided that it would be best to concentrate initially on the cinematic story to show the scaffolding of the zodiac hero underneath. In addition, the film gives us a stunningly lush visual treat that is choc-a-bloc with magical symbols for those who have the eyes to see. They fairly litter the opening sequences, from the Fibonacci-coiled candlestick holder that is mirrored in the curlicues of the table legs and the sphinxes guarding each side of the fireplace to the chessboard design on the bed coverlet of Pinocchio's creator, the carpenter and clockmaker Geppetto. The only problem is, there's a big *lacuna* between Cancer and Scorpio – and so that's where we will turn to Collodi's version. This much older Tuscan folk tale is told over 36 chapters – three chapters for each of the 12 zodiac houses. Thus it provides us with a much richer seedbed upon which to draw to give us more information – vital keys, in fact, which Walt Disney glosses over in his concertinaed, truncated version.

So I have decided to weave between the two, and in order to prevent you from getting lost, Sam Richardson has helpfully created a simplified at-a-glance graphic in **Figure 18** to show you the way.

So let's get started on our journey around Pinocchio's Wheel.

The meaning of the Italian name Pinocchio is 'pine eye' – in other words, it is a metaphor for the pine cone-shaped pineal gland also known as the Third Eye.

However, the first character we meet in the film is Pinocchio's creator-father, the carpenter clockmaker Geppetto. As we now know that one of Saturn's epithets is Old Father Time, it would appear that a clockmaker father is the perfect metaphor for the one who metes out the allotted heartbeats of a human life that, in astrological myths, begins for the Radiant Child in Capricorn, on the Winter Solstice.

The name Geppetto is a diminutive of Guiseppe, which is Italian for Joseph – in other words, here we have another carpenter father who taught woodworking to a son who was required to sacrifice his life by descending into Hell (the Underworld), as we learn from the Apostles Creed. Similarly, towards the end of the tale when he has passed through many trials, Pinocchio has to dive down into the submarinal deeps to rescue his father, Geppetto, from the belly of the gigantic whale Monstro.

The character embodying Pinocchio's inner tuition, or intuition, is named Jiminy Cricket, and he is given a much more prominent role in the film's screenplay than in Collodi's book, playing the part of Pinocchio's conscience, the still, small voice that warns us when we are about to take a wrong turn. This voice can only be perceived through finely tuned instincts and so we often, like Pinocchio, have to learn the hard way that the greater part of wisdom comes from listening to our conscience when it speaks.

Pinocchio the puppet is carved from a piece of wood that could already talk before coming into Geppetto's possession. We are not shown in the cartoon how this came about but in Collodi's story, we hear more about its origins. Geppetto gained this (pine?) wood from a master carpenter, Antonio, whom everyone called Master Cherry because, apparently, he had a large red nose. However, "Cherry" translates to *cerasus* in Latin and, along with it referring to the popular round, dark red, juicy fruit, one of its other meanings is "hymen" – the membrane or "veil" of the virgin which is broken when she first has intercourse.

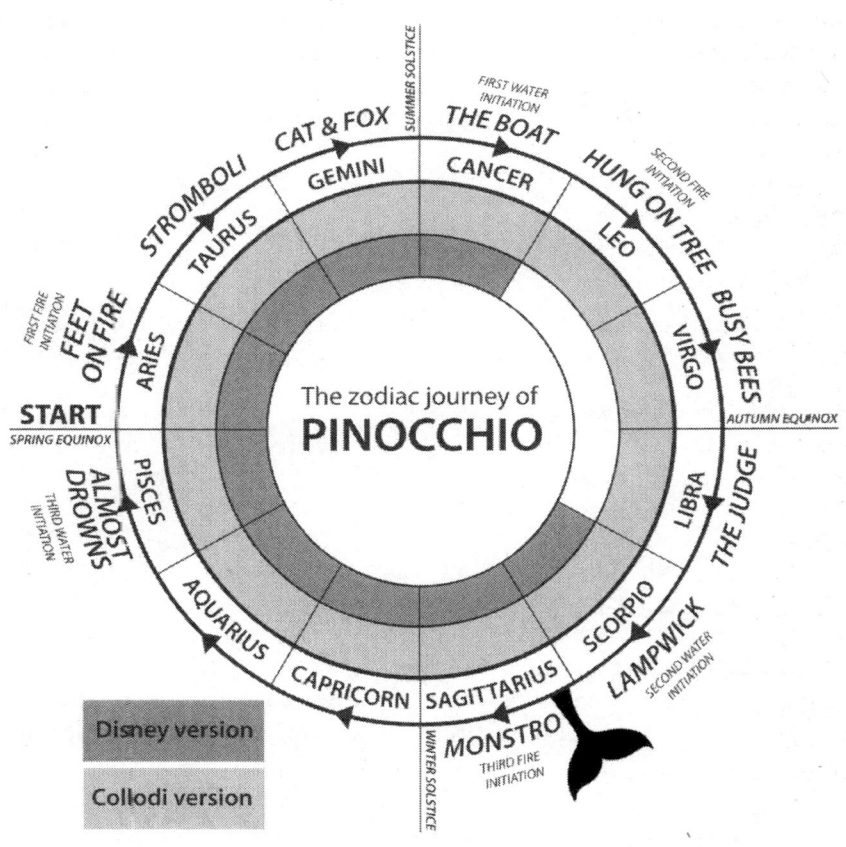

Figure 18: The Trials of Pinocchio by Sam Richardson

So with this cherry, I think this folk tale from the land of the Etruscans is giving us an alchemical clue to an act of fertility that resulted in the birth of a talking wooden puppet. This makes Pinocchio quite archetypical in that most mythological heroes come from the coupling of one human and one divine parent and like Enkidu in *The Epic of Gilgamesh* and Adam in *Genesis*, they are initially made of natural, earthy materials, like wood or clay, which symbolise the pre-initiate stage. This is a metaphor for a rough, crude substance that needs carving or moulding, refining and polishing, before it is fit for purpose.

We too are just like a young wooden puppet when we begin our journey up the Ladder of the Wise. We are almost entirely ignorant of the ways of the world and at the mercy of our impulses at Aries. It is here that Pinocchio accidentally sets his feet on fire. So like the famous cat on a hot tin roof, the Martian Fire Starter that springs up from the Earth on the Spring Equinox leaves the pilgrim wayfarer with little choice but to move, and move fast, even though he has so little intellectual growth or wisdom that he is almost entirely at the mercy of his five senses.

As Plato wrote in his *Laws 1*: 644:

Our impulses are like cords and strings, which pull us different and opposite ways, and to opposite actions; and herein lies the difference between virtue and vice.

Plato must have inspired Pinocchio's song *I've got no strings to tie me down* to illustrate the delusion at this stage. Man has free will; that much is true. But how free can we really be when the stars at our birth dictate our character and our strengths and weaknesses, which, in turn, inform the sorts of challenges we will meet? It seems to me the only freedom we have is that we get decide whether to continue climbing or just plump ourselves down on the rung we're on and sulkily refuse to budge.

Pinocchio burning his feet – the very conveyances that propel the wayfarer along the hard and winding road of life - represents the first fire initiation of the Three Cauldrons. That first step comes the next morning, when Pinocchio is sent off to school carrying textbooks Geppetto had to sell his own shirt to buy.

One of our hero's first rash decisions is to dismiss his inner guide, Jiminy Cricket. This is a typical act of the arrogant and ignorant Aries persona that delivers brusque and cavalier treatment to all that which stands in the way of their desires. But at this early stage of his development, perhaps he can be forgiven the ram-headed, stubborn ignorance that causes him to be deaf to his inner intuition.

However, Pinocchio fails to make it even as far as the schoolyard as the Fox and the Cat waylay him, persuading him to join the marionette theatre instead. Thus it seems that Disney places these two mercurial tricksters too early in the journey of the zodiac hero; they belong later on, in Gemini, where Collodi first introduces them and so that's where they are shown too in Figure 16.

In the Sicilian storyteller's tale, Pinocchio decides by himself not to go to school and join the travelling puppet show, and it is here in Taurus that he runs headfirst into his first teacher in the form of the huge, bovine theatrical impresario who was, according to Collodi:

… a large man so ugly, he evoked fear by simply being looked at. He had a beard as black as a smudge of ink and so long that it fell from his chin down to the ground: enough so that when he walked, he stepped on it. His mouth was as wide as an oven, his eyes were like two red tinted lanterns with the light turned on at the back, and with his hands, he sported a large whip made of snakes and fox tails knotted together.

The Hollywood scriptwriters called their bullish producer Stromboli, probably inspired by the name of one of the live volcanic islands arranged in an arch over northern Sicily and, in that film, one does get the sense that Stromboli is permanently on the verge of erupting. However, Collodi had given him the moniker of Mangiafuoco, meaning "Fire Eater", which is also quite apt for a character who in manifesting the grasping, materialistic side of Taurus ends up throwing Pinocchio into a padlocked cage and threatens to burn him for firewood. In other words, he was intending to steal Pinocchio's raw Martian fire, his inner creative spark lit by the initiation at Aries, which is pretty well all the little chap had going for him at that kindergarten stage.

It is here in the film that Jiminy Cricket reappears. He tries to pick the lock of the cage imprisoning our young hero but fails and then announces: "It'll take a miracle to get us out of here." This is the constant refrain of the inner voice of the zodiac hero who needs divine help at every twist and turn. And hey presto! Along comes a miracle in form of the beautiful Blue Fairy who, as Venus, rules Taurus.

"So what happened to you, dear, on your way to school?" she asks kindly

Instead of telling her the truth, Pinocchio instantly resorts to lying. He tells her he was set upon by bandits and kidnapped. Each time he repeats the tale, there seem to be more and more bandits who become fiercer and fiercer, until he suddenly notices that his nose is growing. Each time he lies, his nose increases in length until it becomes so long two birds, mistaking it for a tree branch, make a nest on it.

The Blue Fairy laughs and tells him the sprouting nose is a symbol to teach him a lesson; that the face of a liar is unmistakable to a person who listens their intuition. This is not just a moral teaching designed merely to support the customs and mores of an upright society. To me, it seems to be a rule of Nature that unless our words are as straight and true as an arrow, we will continually be misfiring in our lives and wondering why we fail to hit the mark.

In the Disney film, the Blue Fairy is missing the edginess of the double goddess of older zodiac stories. She is all saccharine sweetness and fairy dust. So after releasing Pinocchio, she just lovingly sends him on his way with a benedictory wave of her sparkling wand.

Thus, we need to repair again to Collodi's book to fully appreciate Venus's ability to inflict a reversal of fortune on the hero and teach him a lesson. Here, the bullish Fire Eater appears to take pity on the young puppet. So he releases him and gives him five golden coins, which become the cause of many subsequent adversarial challenges to come. As you will probably know, coins, stones and pentacles are interchangeable in the system of divination known as the Tarot. So the five gold coins are a symbol for the card of the Five of Pentacles, itself a metaphor for a challenge in the realm of money and finances – and this challenge pursues, sometimes literally, Pinocchio throughout the rest of the tale.

In fact, the gift of the Five of Pentacles presages a whole series of adventures that follow one after another, beginning, in Collodi's tale, as soon our hero enters the house of Gemini, where he meets the trickster side of the planetary governor Mercury in the form of the wily twins, Mr Foxy Fox and Mr Cunning Cat. Gemini is the sign of the mercurial wordsmith and, as those who forge their living by such means know only too well, it is a two-edged sword that can be employed either to enlighten the listener or to bedazzle and beguile them. As you might guess, Fox and Cat are masters in the latter as their main aim and purpose is to float through life on a magic carpet of other people's money.

So Fox and Cat persuade Pinocchio not to carry on to school but to go with them to bury the treasure of his five gold coins in the Field of Wonders where, they insist, it will grow 1,000-fold overnight. Pinocchio, as a habitual liar himself, has not yet learned that when a story seems too good to be true, it usually is. So he believes the two rogues and then they all set off for the Field of Wonders.

On the way, they stay overnight at a hostelry, the name of which tells us we are in the next sign of the zodiac. Nowadays, the house of Cancer is signified by a crab but we know from celestial globes made in the 17th and 18th century that this house used to be symbolised by another crustacean – a red lobster. And the hostelry where the three wayfarers spend the night is the Inn of the Red Lobster.

It is here that we will return to Disney's film, which diverges from Collodi, who is in no hurry for our hero to get to the Field of Wonders, having many more trials and tribulations for him before then. But for a short way, we will follow Hollywood's lead, and watch as our hero is sold to a man whose job it is to ferry naughty little boys to Pleasure Island.

We next see our hero sitting on the front seat of a speeding horse-drawn chariot next to his newfound friend, Lampwick. Pinocchio shows Lampwick a "ticket" Fox gave him to, ostensibly, grant him entry into the amusement park of Pleasure Island, to which he is being rapidly transported. It is the Ace of Spades playing card – and we will come back to this symbol later.

Pleasure Island is one of many enchanted gardens used as a device in folktales to represent the follies of being seduced by worldly temptations. For instance, we also find the pleasure garden in Japanese studio Gibhli's film *Spirited Away*. The insatiably greedy parents of *Spirited Away's* young heroine, Chihiro, are lured into an all-you-can-eat emporium in an enchanted amusement park and transformed into pigs through their gluttony. Chihiro has to undergo many trials on their behalf before they are turned back into their human forms and allowed to leave.

There are Celtic myths about people getting trapped in the Underworld through eating apples gleaned from fairy orchards. We find a similar idea in Homer's *Odyssey* when the ship's crew are tempted to gorge on lotuses. In Book IX, Odysseus recounts to his audience how north winds blew him and his men off course as they came round the southernmost tip of the Peloponnesus:

"I was driven thence by foul winds for a space of nine days upon the sea, but on the tenth day we reached the land of the Lotus-eaters, who live on a food that comes from a kind of flower. Here we landed to take in fresh water, and our crews got their midday meal on the shore near the ships. When they had eaten and drunk I sent two of my company to see what manner of men the people of the place might be, and they had a third man under them. They started at once, and went about among the Lotus-eaters, who did them no hurt, but gave them to eat of the lotus, which was so delicious that those who ate of it left off caring about home, and did not even want to go back and say what had happened to them, but were for staying and munching lotus with the Lotus-eaters without thinking further of their return; nevertheless, though they wept bitterly I forced them back to the ships and made them fast under the benches. Then I told the rest to go on board at once, lest any of them should taste of the lotus and leave off wanting to get home, so they took their places and smote the grey sea with their oar."

Upon rejoining the odyssey of Disney's Pinocchio, we're just in time to find the chariot finally reaching a port where he and his fellow mischievous rascals are disgorged on to a steamer ferry boat.

The boat is a metaphor for the massive Argo Navis, the now obselete boat-shaped constellation that used to begin near Cancer. Argo Navis was so huge, in fact, that it was considered to be too unwieldy by 18th century astronomers and they dismantled it into three separate groupings: Carina, the Keel; Puppis, the Stern; and Vela, the Sails.

But in total, the original Argo ark covered 120 degrees of the zodiac, stretching from Cancer to Scorpio. So perhaps that is why the Disney film now more or less jumps straight from Cancer to Scorpio? Or perhaps they did not want to risk boring the viewer with all the trials and travails that Collodi goes on to employ to demonstrate how our champion learns his lessons through the challenges he meets in Leo, Virgo and Libra.

Thus for now, let us continue with the film, in which the whole human cargo are ferried on the Argo to Pleasure Island, which turns out to be a young scallywag's fantasy of Paradise – with unlimited sweets to be gobbled down, schools to be destroyed, houses to be set on fire, fights to be started and gaming halls aplenty.

We are then taken to a snooker hall shaped like a huge black billiard ball with the number eight emblazoned on it. It is in here that Jiminy Cricket finds Pinocchio smoking a cigar with the badass Lampwick, who then, terrifyingly, begins to metamorphose into a braying donkey. Then we suddenly realise the chilling purpose of this hedonistic playground, which is to turn bad boys into asses fit only for the salt mines of Siberia.

The cricket stands on a snooker ball as he begins his bid to appeal to Pinocchio's good sense and we are shown that his podium is the eightball. This number clue is shown a third time when Lampwick wields his cue to violently propel Jiminy down into one of the pockets of the pool table, where he lands on that same eightball.

So this is what saves Pinocchio from the salt mines – the symbolic number 864 – or 8:8 x 8 that we already know about from the chapter on the meaning of numbers. In other words, in getting in touch with and following his intuition in the form of his conscience, Jiminy Cricket, Pinocchio's development is quickened through the first water initiation of the Three Cauldrons in the deceptively changeable Cancer and given a firmer footing on the foundation stone of dry land.

Disney now fast-forwards his audience into what some consider to be the House of Ill Repute of the zodiac. Scorpio is the sign of disillusion; the sting of its tail swiftly dispels illusion and this can feel quite brutal and painful when we have spent our lives being told, and then repeating to ourselves, stories that are not true. Now we are no longer in the child stage of development and we need to be stung awake, which means understanding what these stories are trying to teach us. We can only start to perceive reality when the magic lantern show of our imagination fails and we are left in utter darkness. Some mystics call this stage the Dark Night of the Soul.

Pinocchio and Jiminy eventually find their way home, only to walk into the darkest Scorpio scene imaginable. The home is no longer brightly lit by the blazing fire, glowing lanterns and colourfully painted characters that peopled his father's charming carved clocks and music boxes. It is now completely empty, dark, abandoned and hung with cobwebs. They peer through the dusty windows at the abandoned scene. Then, a bluebird flys down with a message; it says that Geppetto had gone out to look for his long-lost son but ended up falling into the sea, where the gigantic whale Monstro had swallowed him whole. In other words, all illusions Pinocchio may have had about the warmth and comfort of a loving family waiting for him around the hearth are now dashed and on top of that, he is pole-axed with the stinging realisation that his own naughty behaviour led to this terrible tragedy.

Pinocchio quickly pulls himself together and decides he must go and try to rescue the old clockmaker from inside the whale, even though, his cricket tells him, all hope of achieving such a happy outcome is completely against the odds. Nevertheless, the puppet insists that he will dedicate his whole life to trying to save his father

And so, to me, this is where we are faced with a disjunct in our comprehension – although the wily Disney gives the hypnotised audience a cognitive rainbow bridge for them to follow, so they don't stop to ask how it is that the selfish, short-sighted Pinocchio has magically undergone some kind of Road to Damascus flash of enlightenment that changes him, on the spot, into a boy who would sacrifice his own life to save his father.

Collodi knew better – that it was going to take more than a brush with the salt mines to mould the character of this young lad. So we will now refer to his book and follow Pinocchio's trials.

At Leo, he falls into the hands of assassins – aka Fox and Cat in disguise – who are after his five gold coins, which he has hidden under his tongue. The leonine feline, realising this, puts his hand into Pinocchio's mouth, whereupon Pinocchio bites off his paw. In punishment, the pair abscond with him into a deep dark forest, where they hang him from a giant oak tree.

This is reminiscent of Odin hanging from the World Tree for nine days in order to receive what has been translated in the Eddas as the knowledge of the runes. To me, this is a metaphor for the secret "knowledge of the stars", or starfire enlightenment. In other words, it is the second fire initiation of the Three Cauldrons.

In the last chapter, I explained how the hero often meets an ancestor or older relative at Leo, who teaches him to find his courage and gives him the wherewithal to meet his further challenges. At first, I couldn't see any ancestors or relatives in this story – until I realised this is a puppet made of wood, possibly pine, that is hanging from a tree in a (pine?) forest.

After three days, our hero is rescued and he sets off again to go home, but instead, he takes a detour and soon finds himself on the Isle of the Busy Bees – the perfect metaphor for the meticulous Virgo. Here he begins to learn the lesson of the Five of Pentacles, in other words the value of a day's work for a day's pay. He learns that in this dimension – the Middle World of Earth – in which Saturn, the Father of Time, is the Alpha and Omega, that Time is Money and Money is Time.

He makes good progress and is rewarded by the second visitation of the Venus double goddess, the ruler of Libra, in the form of the Blue Fairy, who takes him home and tells him she will look after him, like a mother. She tends and nurses him and then, when he is better, she sends him off to school. But the five golden coins are still in his pocket and Fox and Cat soon turn up to waylay him again, persuading him to go with them to sow them in the Field of Wonders. Pinocchio has still not yet developed enough wisdom to realise when he is being conned. The upshot, as I'm sure you can guess, was that he was robbed of all his worldly wealth. And in this nonsense world he is arrested and brought before the judge where his crime of being so unwise as to have all his money stolen from him is weighed on the scales of justice and he is sent to prison.

Eventually, he is pardoned and goes free, and then what follows are many other trials including facing down a huge serpent, barely escaping becoming the Green Fisherman's supper and acting as a watchdog to guard a farmer's chicken coup. It is only during these adventures that Pinocchio learns of his father Geppetto's tragic fate in going to look for him – and it is shortly after that the rapscallion Lampwick first enters the Sicilian folk tale.

Lampwick persuades our hero to play truant from school and go with him to the Land of Toys, from which Disney drew his inspiration for Pleasure Island, and it is there that Pinocchio turns into not an ass but a donkey that is sold to a circus. He is treated harshly while undergoing training in the Big Top and his life becomes a living hell. At this Scorpio stage, he dives deep into his woes where he is unable to avoid perceiving clearly the mistakes he has made that have led him to this terrible fate. He fervently wishes he could go back in time to that fateful first day when his father sent him of to school with the books paid for with his own shirt off his back. He becomes so depressed he is unable to perform the tricks required of him in the ring. So he is sold on again, this time to a man who wants to kill him and use his skin as a drum. The man throws Pinocchio into the sea to drown him and this is where we can rejoin the Disney version as the two stories begin to converge.

In the film, we find Jiminy and Pinocchio jumping off a high cliff into the sea with the cricket shouting: "Look out below!" This is the signal that the hero is now descending into the submarinal depths of the Underworld. We know the ancients used the watery deeps as a metaphor for the Underworld or the subconscious from the Alexandrian school of astrology. But it is much older than that – it goes as far back as the deluge hero who braves the floods of the firmamental waters in order to install the new pole star of the age. We find the same metaphor in the Sumerian epic about Gilgamesh who, at this stage of his quest, has to face the challenge of sailing over the Waters of Death. In Vedic literature, the deeps are known as the Garbhodaka Ocean. In my books, it is the Ocean of Dreams.

It is also the second water initiation of the Three Cauldrons.

Anyway, Pinocchio eventually finds Monstro and he is sucked into the whale's belly, where he finds Geppetto sitting and fishing on the rotting deck of a wrecked trawler.

Now, anyone familiar with the Fisher King motif from the Arthurian mythos will easily recognise him here. The Fisher King is also known as the Wounded King because only by being redeemed or saved by his son can he be healed and brought back to life – and I think there can be nothing more wounding to the heart of a parent than a lost child.

Pinocchio is now in the Sagittarius stage of the zodiac hero's journey and it is the third and final manifestation of the secret fire of the Three Cauldrons, which first sprang forth when he set his feet on fire at Aries. It is tamed and then coaxed, through his travails of Taurus, Gemini and Cancer, into a roaring hearth-fire by the time he bites off the cat's paw at Leo, which causes him to undergo a starfire initiation while hanging in a tree. Next it is refined at the Isle of the Busy Bees in Virgo, and weighed on the balance in the court of Libra. Then the hero meets Mars again at Scorpio in the form of the sting of agonising disillusion that forges his passion into a flaming arrow of intelligence fit for the Sagittarian bowman to light up a path through the interdimensional portal into rebirth at Capricorn.

Geppetto tells his son there is no chance of escape because the monstrous whale only opens its mouth to allow food in and nothing can go out in the other direction. But if you understand the astrological and alchemical blueprint of the Wheel thus far, as Collodi patently did, then what happens next makes more sense. Pinocchio has now become such a genius, outside-the-box planner and strategist that he manages to come up with a brilliant method of escape from the belly of the whale.

Pinocchio finds his Sagittarian flaming arrow, which is literally a bonfire that he builds and ignites on the deck of the wrecked fishing vessel in order to produce enough smoke to make Monstro sneeze. Then they all repair to a raft. It works. The whale sneezes the raft out of his mouth. They think they are free – but then what follows is one of the most terrifying life-and-death chases in cinematic history as the furious monster comes tearing across the waves after them and smashes their raft to smithereens.

They are eventually washed up on shore. Jiminy Cricket and Geppetto are still alive but Pinocchio does not appear to have managed to survive this third water initiation of the Three Cauldrons, which in the Alexandrian system appears at the fishes of Pisces.

However, a miracle occurs. The Blue Fairy suddenly arrives on beach and she waves her wish-fulfilling wand to grant him not only resurrection but also the status of a real boy.

If Disney were to have his way, this would be the end of the story about a naughty rapscallion who inexplicably and magically became good. But in turning to Collodi for so better wisdom, we are disappointed. He is not much help with his Christian charity interpretation of a further twist in a tale, which to me, would have originally been told to demonstrate that our hero had learned the lessons of the Five of Pentacles and the Ace of Spades.

However, you may not agree with me. So let us work our way through this addendum to the tale and I'll explain what I mean.

We join Collodi's story after they have escaped the whale and with Pinocchio still in his wooden puppet form, they are walking along the road, on the way home. Just around a corner, they bump into his old antagonists Fox and Cat. Fox had become old and thin and almost hairless, and without a tail as he had been forced to sell it for food. The Cat, after pretending to be blind for many years, had now actually lost the sight in both eyes.

"Oh, Pinocchio," Fox cried in a tearful voice. "Give us some alms, we beg of you! We are old, tired, and sick."

"Sick!" repeated the Cat.

"Addio, false friends!" answered Pinocchio. "You cheated me once, but you will never catch me again."

"Believe us! Today we are truly poor and starving."

"Starving!" repeated the Cat.

"If you are poor, you deserve it!" responds Pinocchio. "Remember the old proverb which says: 'Stolen money never bears fruit.' Addio, false friends."

Pinocchio then carries on along the road and soon encounters a number of incidents that Collodi has added in which seem designed to develop in him the principles of mercy and charity. And it is only after demonstrating that he had learned these lessons that he receives the blessings of the Blue Fairy in a dream, which transform him from a puppet into a real boy.

However, I don't think this would have been in the original story that was told to Kroy-Khasis. For one thing, the female goddess or fairy is out of place here; she only appears in the older zodiac stories around Taurus and Libra, which are the signs governed by Venus. In addition and just as importantly, in my experience learning to recognise "false friends" is the mark of a true initiate whose life lessons have forced him to forge a sword of truth sharp enough to cut through the miasmic seductions and enchantments of the likes of Fox and Cat that seek to ensnare him and then sell him off, as a donkey.

The Disney film makes much of the Ace of Spades playing card, which is in Pinocchio's hand just before he boards the boat to Pleasure Island. Spade is Latin for sword. Therefore, the Ace of Spades represents the forging of a new sword of intellect.

The sword and the pentacle are just two of four ancient symbols that we can trace back to Kroy and his people, in whose stories we find the origin of the Tarot system of divination. The myths of the Ossettians are inherited from those who peopled the Caucasus mountain region many thousands of years ago and they feature magical swords, spears, stones and cups. These symbolic objects eventually evolved into the Minor Arcana of the Tarot's swords, wands, pentacles and cups, and these four suits in turn developed, by medieval times, into the swords, clubs, diamonds and hearts of the common deck of playing cards.

The following table gives the metaphorical meanings of these four suits.

Tarot card suit	Playing card suit	Element	Meaning
Swords	Spade	Air	Intellect
Wands	Clubs	Fire	Creative power
Cups	Hearts	Water	Emotion
Pentacles/Coins	Diamonds	Earth	Material success

Figure 19: The Evolution of the Tarot

In ancient myths, the sword is the symbol of Sovereignty that can only be wielded by a true queen or king because it represents a finely honed intellect that recognises and honours the truth. That is why Arthur has to pull his sword, Excalibur, from the stone. Only by following our own Jiminy Cricket, or the inner tuition that perceives and respects the truth, can we develop our wisdom. In the case of the sovereign in more ancient times, he was not considered fit to govern until he had developed enough wisdom to rule the land, and this was achieved through shamanic fire and water initiations.

This Excalibur is forged from our own Scorpio dark side, through a fire initiation we can only reach by going through the Vale of Tears in the dark, watery depths of the Underworld. Then, like the Lady of the Lake, we can wield our sword up through the water. This is the mythological meaning of illustrations depicting the sword in the chalice.

In the plots of my last two books, which are in themselves zodiac myths, I use the magical sword from the older Celtic *Mabinogion*, which is called Fragarach. Fragarach is the sword of the faery sea pilot Manawydan, which is created by the faery smith Gofannon on the anvil of his forge in the Underworld deeps. According to these myths, Fragarach was reputed to be able to cut through lies like a knife through butter and it was said that when it was poised at an enemy's throat, he could neither move nor lie, even to himself - unlike the younger Pinocchio.

Fragarach was able to put the winds at the command of whoever wielded it and deliver a piercing wound from which no man could recover. This, in my experience, represents how the shaman works with the element of air. I have found that once you ask Air to decapitate an illusion, it can never get its head back on again, so to speak.

In the parts of Collodi's tale that Disney skips over, the Fox and Cat continually pester, cajole and bully our champion to the point of trying to murder him at every twist and turn of his journey, in order to steal his five golden coins or pentacles. He is unable to shake them off until they cause him to be falsely accused in the courts of justice at Libra, after which he is turned into a donkey and sold to a circus in Scorpio, where he has plenty of time to examine the mistakes of his life.

In my experience, the gods or spirits will continually use circumstances to try to fool us until we finally develop our own inner Fragarach sword, which not only tells us when we are being lied to but also holds liars at bay, by the throat. We may not realise it until we reach the disillusion of the "dark night of the soul". However, this stinging agony of realisation may be what it takes for us to finally see clearly enough to identify our illusory shadow side, which, until then, continually produces false phantoms, gargoyles and hobgoblins to try to delude us into being easy prey for this type of fairground conman.

These wisdom teachings are barely discernible in Disney's version of the tale, which is rushed through in a technicolour blur of a mere 84 minutes. So we cannot understand, from that rendition, the necessary occult forces and astrologically determined alchemical catalysts that are at play and essential to forge us into real human beings.

The original myth would have been told to Kroy-khasis over many nights dreaming beside the campfire after a long day's trek. There would have been no other distractions and the only fluorescent flickering would have come not from an LED-backlit screen but from the silver stars in the dark blue vault above reflecting down on the white snow-packed mountains.

The story of the hero is one about how wisdom and virtue is earned and learned through the many twists and turns of a long human life, with the help of the spirits or planetary gods, and how fortune and misfortune can both be viewed as having equal value along a path that culminates in us "redeeming our father" or our ancestors, and thus keeping our Rivers of Blood running pure and clear.

Just like Pinocchio, we all begin our climb up the Ladder of the Wise by playing truant from the lessons life wishes to teach us. It is partly through ignorance but also sometimes because we'd rather amuse ourselves in the playground of Pleasure Island than diligently apply ourselves in Saturn's classroom.

Most people don't get to the grips with appreciating the benefits of Saturn until they have passed their mid-life crisis and for women, the menopause. In late middle age, we begin to leaf through the inner photo album of our lives and, no matter how much fun we managed to pack in, we wonder what it was all for. It can seem as if we are standing in a Hall of Mirrors that are shattered and smashed into jagged shards and we find a grotesque reflection staring back at us that, for women, can look surprisingly like the mother that they'd hoped that they'd never turn into; for men, it's their fathers.

This is the point when Saturn returns to our lives for the third time – and it is a timely return. Now that many of our illusions and delusions have fallen away, we can buckle down and pay attention. But first of all, we need to leave the Hall of Mirrors. It is time to put down our candyfloss and huge stuffed panda and concentrate on looking for the big green neon sign flashing "EXIT".

17. The Epic of Gilgamesh

I WAS in two minds about whether to include this chapter in *Stories of the Stars*. It amounts to my contribution to what has been a scholarly debate going on for at least a century among a relatively few researchers, and I wondered if it would be of interest to the general reader.

Another reason for my reticence was that I don't have the full story – in fact, nobody does. A further layer of difficulty is added by the fact that the epic is spread over 12 clay tablets in five different languages – Sumerian, Hittite, Hurrian, Babylonian and Akkadian – and the Sumerian translators don't speak Hittite and the Hurrian translators don't know Babylonian, and so on. As if all that isn't enough to put us off, the cuneiform engraved text has eroded over the years, causing gaping *lacunas* in the story while there remains lots of recently excavated tablets recounting a version of this story that are still waiting to be translated.

Several prominent Akkadian scholars and translators have identified that the drama contains astronomical metaphors but, as I write, few realise they are also astrological and alchemical in that Gilgamesh meets his spirit teachers in the order of the planets found in the Alexandrian system of the zodiac along the Ladder of the Wise. And while I'm not certain that there are yet the three fire initations of the Cauldron in the *Epic of Gilgamesh*, I have identified three water initiations.

So this chapter is my small contribution to a debate that, I'm sure, will continue to develop long after we have all passed through the Veil, as more and more tablets are discovered and translated by those higher up the ladder, who have more advanced "knowledge of the stars".

So let us begin.

I must confess that is is difficult for any writer to do justice to this great, ancient drama because it is vast and far-reaching not just in its length but also in its breadth and depth. On top of that, its multi-dimensional messages spark off the mirrored memories in our Rivers of Blood and so to read it is to experience it.

As Robert Temple writes in what I believe is the best translation, in his *He Who Saw Everything*:

The Epic of Gilgamesh is alive and wriggling. You might as well try to catch hold of an eel in the water as imagine you can get hold of the Epic. Over the years I have often kidded myself that I could guess what the missing fragments contain. But as the archaeologists discover more fragments in their excavations, what they find is always a surprise. You can never second-guess the Epic. Its images are astonishing and unexpected. It will always leap at you in the dark and put a bag over your head just when you thought you could sit down and have a nice cup of tea and relax.

However, I think that I can – and anyway, we need to try to - get to grips with this "wriggling eel" because it appears to be the precursor to so many zodiac myths, particularly the *Twelve Labours of Hercules* although those trials are not in the right order. The storytellers that came after Plato, not realising the ancients' stories contained astrological as well as astronomical information, had a habit of recounting the labours in various pick 'n' mix sequences, according to whatever mood they were in that day. So by going back to the original seedbed, *The Epic of Gilgamesh*, we can find the correct arrangement.

This great, rambling saga also has added value in that it contains the oldest known deluge myth, composed at least 1,500 years before the Hebrews compiled theirs about Noah's ark. "Ark" is actually an Egyptian word, not a Judaic one, and the different dimensions of the ark in this original Sumerian myth are much more helpful in terms of making connections with sacred geometrical alignments across Time and Space, through the Rivers of Blood.

What do I mean by that?

Well, you will know by now that our instinct, intuition or "gut feelings" – which, in the last chapter, are personified by the character Jiminy Cricket - could be considered a form of memory and this has come down to us from our ancestors in the stories carried in our Rivers of Blood. During certain parts of lunar cycles, these memories take the form of kaleidoscopic, mosaic images that reflect back to us, like mirrors of the past, and sing to us in our dreams.

You're also aware that these profoundly deep sagas go right back to the time of the storyteller Tabiti, who lived at the end of the last major Ice Age, and almost certainly way further back than that. They were transmitted orally from grandmother to granddaughter and thus nothing was ever written down. This oral aspect is important: a story heard by our ears goes into a different part of our consciousness than a story seen through our eyes in glyphs or words. Thus, the earliest *Vedas* corpus of myths – the four *Samhitas* - are titled *"sruti"*, meaning "those that are heard".

And so, when we come to examine the most ancient of these myths available to us, *The Epic of Gilgamesh*, we are looking at a multi-layered, oral narrative that would have originally been based upon the heroics of the champion of the deluge in installing the new pole star for each precessional age. However, at the time it was staged as a popular dramatic performance across the land of Mesopotamia, for which we have written records, the agricultural revolution was in full swing and so laid on top of the stellar symbols, we also find the zodiac hero.

The *Epic of Gilgamesh* traces the path of an unlikely champion, a young and arrogant king with the self-serving aim of finding immortality for himself and his alter-ego or twin soul, Enkidu. Instead, though, through climbing the Ladder of the Wise around the Wheel and passing through three initiations, he finds that his quest ultimately leads him to his oldest ancestor and the cleansing and redemption of his family line. This is what the storytellers of old meant by "eternal life", millennia before genetic research. They were not as concerned as we have become, in an increasingly me-centred age, about finding the "elixir of youth" for the individual. They didn't have cellphones but if they had done, they would have been called usPhones not iPhones. In other words, they were more focused on the health and thus continuance of the group, the extended family or tribe, into the far and distant future – which at its most basic is Sovereignty.

So what we learn in their myths is that this kind of immortality can only be achieved through the wisdom and virtue the hero develops during his journey around the cosmological Wheel which has the effect of cleansing the ancestral Rivers of Blood.

It is my understanding from shamanic experience that when the Rivers of Blood are allowed to remain clogged up with the unresolved debris from the actions of past generations, the family experiences stillbirths, impotency and infertility among its members. People from these sorts of hereditary lines will find it difficult to hear the inner songs and thus the wisdom of those who went before them through the detritus of ages, and so they will be more in danger of going off course, largely through not understanding that hardship is built into the course of human life to provide the adversarial conditions to help us evolve and thus for our descendants to thrive. A life dedicated to the avoidance of suffering is a life frittered away on a fool's errand.

Anyway, I won't be publishing the whole poem here because it's far too long. Instead, I'm going to summarise it, with numbered notes showing my interpretations of the astrological and alchemical metaphors that you may find helpful although, by now, you're probably getting quite adept at spotting many of them yourself. These won't be the usual academic footnotes that merely contain "nice-to-have" but extraneous information and references; I'll be using them in such a way that you can read the understory concurrently with the surface tale.

All of this preamble is really just to say that if you feel that the examination of the deeper meanings of this gargantuan "wriggling eel" is a step too far for you, that's absolutely fine and please do feel free to skip to the next chapter.

For those still with me, I will try to simplify it as much as possible.

"Mesh" was the Sumerian word for "hero" and so in *The Epic of Gilgamesh*, we are reading the monumental, larger-than-life saga of Gilga the Hero. It is subtitled *He Who Saw Everything* because in traversing the whole of the Wheel, and meeting his challenges along it, he witnessed all that there was to see in the Three Worlds. In order for you to see everything too, as we follow Gilga around the Wheel, I recommend that you keep half-an-eye on Figure 20, which you have will seen earlier, but a reminder of it will, I hope, give both sides of your brain all the information it needs.

In **Figure 20**, the Spring and Autumn Equinoxes are shown where they would have been at the time the epic was popular – at the beginning of Taurus and the second part of Scorpio respectively. There was no house of Libra until the Greeks invented it by taking the claws of the scorpion and turning them into the scales of justice.

The epic was compiled from Mesopotamian literature going back to about 2100 BCE although there are some slightly older tablets. This means it was popular at a time when the Sun had overtaken the importance of the pole stars in these stories.

Thus, the deluge hero of the pole stars had morphed into the solar hero at the centre of a celestial circle of "Sun signs" or astrological houses which each have certain characteristics that are denoted symbolically by the zoomorphic creatures in attendance; these were probably derived from the Power Animals of the shaman - the half-animal, half-human spirits he meets for guidance in the Lower World or Underworld – and the spirits of the Upper World.

As explained previously, "zodiac" is Greek for "circle of animals" but long before Alexander the Great's vandals broke the conquered Babylonians' sky calendar in half, these zoomorphs were accompanied by Upper World gods or goddesses. Nowadays those more celestial guides are retained in modern astrology as planetary governors.

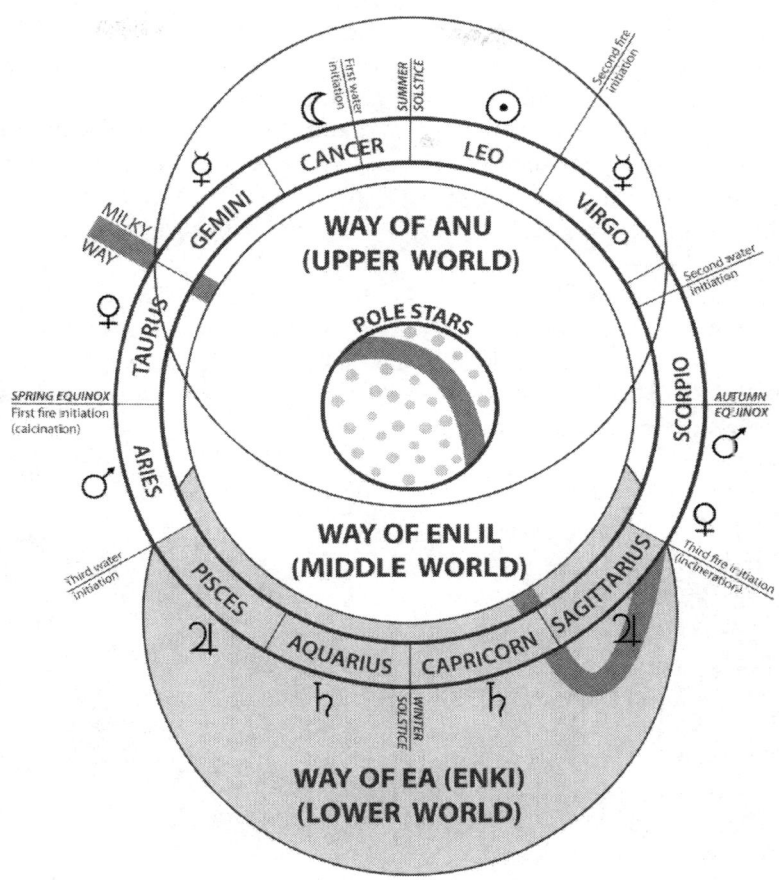

Figure 20: Babylonian cosmology found in the Epic of Gilgamesh

The storyline in the Epic of Gilgamesh is in two distinct halves and there are different schools of thought about what the first part represents. Some believe that the first few tablets contain a metaphorical account about the change of the precessional age from Taurus, which lasted roughly between 4000 and 2000 BCE, to Aries. As you will remember, astrological precession, which precipitates a change in the ages roughly every 2,000 years, runs retrograde. In other words, we are currently in Pisces and the next age will be the one 'behind', Aquarius.

Others believe the first part of the epic is an allegory for Mercury Retrograde, which is an illusion caused, from time to time, when the planet Mercury appears to going backwards.

I am more inclined to the view that the first part of the saga is about the change of the age from Taurus to Aries, as I think there is more evidence for it in the poem, and this is why, in Figure 18, , I show the Spring Equinox at Taurus. There is also an important Mercury-like helper god that appears later on in the story – but more about him later. We do know, however, that the movements of the planet Mercury were important to the Babylonians because they recorded in their star charts that the planet had 2,673 heliacal risings every 848 years. In addition, the influence of Mercury was, and still is, a vital catalyst in all alchemical operations.

Our hero, Gilgamesh, as the royal ruler of Uruk is the son of an Earthly king, Lugulbanda, and Rimat-Ninsun the Heavenly Cow (or Milky Way).

So first, let's read through Robert Temple's excellent translation of the Prologue from his book, *He Who Saw Everything*, to give us a sense of a style and tone that we're rarely exposed to today:

Prologue
He who saw everything in the broad-boned Earth
And knew what there was to be known,
Who had experienced what there was
And had become familiar with all things –
He to whom wisdom clung like a cloak
And who dwelt together with Existence in harmony,
He knew of the secret things and laid them bare
And told of those times before the Flood.
In his city, Uruk, he made the walls
Which formed a rampart stretching on
And the temple called Eanna
Which was the house of Anu, God of the Firmament,
And also Ishtar, Goddess of Love's, house.
Look at it even now,
Where cornice runs on outer wall
Shining brilliant copper – see,
There is an inner wall;
It has no equal.
Touch the threshold – ancient.
Approach the place called Eanna.
There lives Ishtar, Goddess of Love.
No king since has accomplished such deed,
Climb that wall,
Go in Uruk,
Walk there,

I say, walk there.
See the foundation terrace,
Touch, then, the masonry –
Is this not of burnt brick
And good? I say:
The seven sages laid its foundations.[1]
One third is city,[2]
One third is orchards,
One third is clay pits –
Unbuilt on land of the Ishtar Temple.
Search these three parts,
Search also the margin land:
Find the copper tablet-box;
Open it. Open its secret fastening,
Take out the lapis-lazuli tablet,
Read aloud from it.
Read how Gilgamesh fared through many hardships,
Surpassing all kings,
Great in respect,
A lord in his form.
He is the hero.
He is of Uruk,
He, the butting bull.
He leads the way –
He, the Foremost.
He also marches at the rear,
A helper to his brothers.
He is the Great Net,
Protector of his men,
He is the furious flood wave,
Who destroys even stone walls,
The offspring of Lugulbanda,
Gilgamesh is perfect in strength.
The son of the revered Cow,
Or the woman Rimat-Ninsun[3],

---

[1] The Seven Sages are the Annunaki, the half-fish, half-men founder gods that sleep in the Sumerian Underworld, the watery firmament of the Apzu, with the governing god of that third, Ea (later known as Enki), in a cube-shaped building that has the same dimensions as the original Sumerian ark. Lewis Carroll's footmen in *Alice Through the Looking Glass* are half- men, half-fish. And it gives new meaning to Jesus's 'I will make you fishers of men" - not to mention the expression "sleeping with the fishes".

[2] Uruk is divided into thirds just as the Sumerian cosmos is divided into three sections with Anu ruling the upper third, Enlil the middle third and Ea or Enki ruling the lower third.

Gilgamesh inspires perfect awe,
He opened the mountain passes,
He dug the wells
On the mountain's flank.
He crossed to the far shore,
Traversed the vast sea to the rising Sun.
He explored the rim,[4]
Sought life after death,
By his strength, he reached Ziusudra[5] the Faraway,
He who restored living things to their places –
Those which the Flood had destroyed.
Amidst the teeming peoples,
Who is there to compare with him in kingship?
Who like Gilgamesh can say:
"I am king indeed"?
His name was called Gilgamesh
From the very day of his birth.
He was two thirds god, one third man.
The Great Goddess Aruru designed him,
Planned his body,
Prepared his form.
A perfect body the gods gave
For the creation of Gilgamesh;
Shamash the Sun gave beauty,
Adad the Storm gave courage,
And so he surpassed all others.
He was two-thirds god, one-third man.
The form of his body no one can match.
Eleven cubits high he is, nine spans his chest,
As he turns to see the lands all around him.
But he comes to the city of Uruk.

Long was his journey.
Weary, worn down by his labours,
He inscribed upon a stone when he returned,
This story.

---

[3] Rimat Ninsun sounds like her name may have been derived from the Egyptian multi-breasted, serpent-headed Remenet, or vice-versa, found in the ancient Egyptian deeps of the Milky Way. Certainly both are associated with the Milky Way and we know that there was much diplomatic and commercial to-ing and fro-ing between the two cultures.

[4] The rim of the Wheel.

[5] Zisudra is the Sumerian Noah.

The story of the play that then unfolds is about how Gilgamesh became such a hero that he was able, as a result, to become an illustrious ruler of his people of Uruk. However, just like many archetypal heroes ever since, including Phil in the film *Groundhog Day*, there is not a particularly illustrious start.

When we first meet Gilgamesh, in the Middle World (or the Way of Enlil), he is a tyrannical and rampaging young buck of a king on a permanent stag night. No woman is safe from Gilgamesh's advances. He regards her virtue as his by right, even when she is somebody else's wife.[6] So the men of Uruk eventually grow tired of Gilgamesh stealing their women and they go to the temple of Ishtar to petition her to intercede.

Ishtar agrees and creates a man from clay, named Enkidu, with a personality much more like that of an animal of the Steppes than that of a refined man and physically small, Saturnine and stocky, with his feet standing square on the Earth.

The very strength of Ninurta[7]
Matted hair was all over his body,
Like the skins of cattle.
Yes, like the body of that god
Who is of the cattle, he, Samugan,
This Enkidu was innocent of mankind.

Enkidu remains in this state of pastoral innocence for many years, roaming and sleeping with the wild beasts with whom he felt more at home than with humans. Eventually, though, Ishtar appears to him as a sacred prostitute and initiates him through sacred shamanic sex rites into becoming a man. He copulates with her for six days and seven nights.[8] At the ceremonial feast to

---

[6] Gilgamesh is displaying all the characteristics of the young, self-centred Martian type at Aries, riding roughshod with a cavalier attitude over any man or woman that has the temerity to try to get in the way of the fulfillment of his fiery passions. As we know, the first operation that makes up the alchemical Great Work is the burning of the old, known as calcination, and the alchemists always began calcination at the time of the Spring Equinox when the secret fire in the waters of the Earth causes the plants to spring up.

[7] Akkadian scholars are divided on the identity of Ninurta. Some believe him to represent Mercury but I agree with those who believe that Ninurta is Saturn, for the following reasons. Certainly Gilgamesh was of an age for his first Saturn Return, a challenging time we talked about in Part 2. Upon the birth of Enkidu, Gilgamesh dreams of a star falling from the sky and his mother, the Heavenly Cow, tells him that it signifies the birth of one just like him, who he would come to love. The birth of Enkidu, therefore, appears to be the catalyctic precursor for Gilgamesh's journey around the Wheel. Later on, I show how the epic, despite its great length, only covers the first rung of the Ladder of the Wise, the calcination, which culminates in the ultimate death-and-rebirth at the end, leading into Capricorn which is governed by the Alpha and Omega of Saturn.

[8] This is the first of three uses in the Epic of the formula "six days and seven nights" and surely must pertain to the oldest of the deluge myths, where the hero battles the flood in which six of the poles drown, one after the other, leaving the seventh to be installed on the mount as the pole star of the new Age. I

celebrate his initiation, the hierodule offers him bread and beer and he drinks seven jugs of it.[9]

Soon afterwards, Enkidu arrives in Uruk, where the people marvel at how alike he is to their king. When they tell him of the likeness, Enkidu asks who Gilgamesh is, and this prompts his put-upon citizens to complain about their king's excesses. Enkidu becomes angry and is determined to call Gilgamesh to account. The two eventually meet in the street and Enkidu bars his way. They start to fight...

Then they grappled their belts and wrestled like champions -
Rushing wind meets rushing wind[10]
Heart to heart against –
Holding fast like bulls.

The fight moves along the street until they find themselves in a gateway and, as a result of such vigorous exertions, they end up shattering the door post. Gilgamesh eventually wins the wrestling match. Then, the two start to talk and once they begin to get to know each other, they warm to one another. Realising they are both equals in strength and power, each is filled with admiration for the other and it doesn't take long for them to become so close that they feel like blood brothers or twin souls [11].

So now, the two new friends want to seal their bond with an adventure. They eventually decide they should go to the Cedar Forest to slay its guardian, the evil monster Humbaba.

In Uruk, they gather together an army of 50 companions[12] and then Gilgamesh makes an official pronouncement to the people of Uruk at the New Year festival[13] of his and Enkidu's intention to "travel the wheel rim" in the

---

think it is also why the first verses of the Old Testament's *Genesis* recount how God made different parts of his creation over six days and then on the seventh day he rested.

[9] Most specialists in Sumerian mythology agree that beer is a metaphor for a hallucinogenic drink that was taken during sacred sex rites to help the initiate reach the shamanic state of consciousness. In my experience, this has the effect of firing up the lower bowl in the practice of The Three Cauldrons. Archaeologists have found engravings from the Sumerian taverns that show what they term the *coitus a tergo* drinking scenes, in which there is apparently a conflation of three ideas - of sex, beer and apparent seizure. Inanna, the precursor fertility goddess to Ishtar, is often shown drinking beer while her lover Dumuzi is standing erect while having sex with her.

There is a much fuller explanation of this practice in my book about sacred sex rites, *Reclaiming Sovereignty*, and some practical guidance on how to achieve this shamanic state of ecstasy.

[10] Air is the element of Aries.

[11] The symbol for Gemini is the twins and so the doorway is probably the gateway from the astrological house of Taurus to the house of Gemini.

[12] Fifty is the same number of crew that Jason took with him on the Argo. It may represent 7 x 7 (pole stars) + 1 (the hero), in which case, this is the same number that the Celtic Arthur took on his voyage as recounted in Taliesin's *Preiddeu Annwn*. There were also 50 men in the Greek tale of *The Odyssey*. After leaving the island of Circe, Odysseus divides his men into two boats carrying 22 each, plus if you add the six that were lost on previous raid against the Cicones, it makes 50.

[13] The Sumerian New Year festival was on the Spring Equinox, which, roughly 4,000 years ago, would have been in Taurus.

quest:

> "Listen to me, men of Uruk,
> The men of Uruk, who know ...
> There would I be strong,
> I travel the wheel-rim[14] ..."

Another clue that the pair are travelling along a zodiacal path is that it takes them three days to reach the Cedar Wood in which, so the text tells us, they traverse the distance of one month and 15 days.[15]

Then, through a long and wearying battle, with the help of Shamash the Sun god, they finally manage to defeat the monster. Afterwards, Enkidu builds a raft from the cedar wood to transport Humbaba's head back to Uruk.

Upon their return to the capital, the two are ecstatic and they are soon flush from wine and their victory. So not really in their right minds, they then decide to go off on another quest, to slay the Bull of Heaven, who is Ishtar's brother-in-law.[16]

This quest takes them into the Upper World or Way of Anu, where the Bull of Heaven turns out to be a much tougher customer. But the tenacious twins finally prevail and slaughter the beast. Then they look up to see that Ishtar has appeared on the city walls. She is full of admiration for Gilgamesh, the strong warrior. She propositions him with marriage, to which he replies with a long litany of complaints based on older myths which neatly demonstrate the double-edged sword of falling in love with the double goddess. Gilgamesh recites a long list of examples of her legendary faithlessness and capacity for betrayal to make his case for why he could never be her husband. The reality is, it is all just astrological metaphor. After the double goddess meets and conjoins with the hero the second time, at around Libra/Scorpio, she has to eventually let him, or even encourage him, to leave her and continue on his journey down into the Underworld, or he will never evolve and thus suffer eternally from arrested development.

Anyway, upon hearing this litany of complaints about Ishtar's seeming hard heartedness, Enkidu, in fury, tears a thigh from the Heavenly Bull's carcass and

---

[14] You probably don't need any help from me by now with this one ...

[15] In other words, it took them three days (in Time) to traverse a month-and-a-half (in Space or distance) along the rim of the Wheel from the Spring Equinox in Taurus to halfway through Gemini.

[16] The Mesopotamian Bull of Heaven was the Bull of Adad (Iškur in Sumerian) who wore a bull-horned headdress. He is associated with the Moon god, Sin (the planetary governor of Cancer), whose daughter is Ishtar. She performs the role of the Double Goddess in the epic and we meet her again after Gilgamesh traverses Scorpio... but more of that anon. I cannot think of better metaphor for the ending of the age of Taurus than the killing of a bull. This event was celebrated for millennia afterwards by the bull rites that were so popular with the Egyptians and the Minoans, not to mention the later Roman tauroctonies showing the Persian god Mithras killing a bull.

flings it at her. [17]

In other words, the pair end up roundly insulting the Lady of Fortune far worse than Pinocchio did when he lied to the Blue Fairy. Thus, as yet unbeknown to them, the pair are bound to suffer an irreversible reversal of fortune as a result.

So next the epic transports us into the highest reaches of the Upper World (the Way of Anu) to discover that the whole sorry business has sparked off a quarrel among three important gods: Anu, the lord of the Upper World; Enlil the lord of the Middle World and Shamash the sun god. Amid the row, it quickly becomes clear that Enlil had commanded the deaths of Humbaba and the Bull of Heaven[18]. Even so, these gods finally decide upon their judgement that Enkidu should be given the death penalty for throwing the Bull of Heaven's thigh at Ishtar. So Shamash the Sun god strikes Gilgamesh's bosom friend down with a fatal illness.

Gilgamesh is now beside himself with grief. Wracked with agonising pain and introspection, he sobs unceasingly over the body of his friend for six days and seven nights[19] under the watery, reflective Moon of Cancer. [20]

Despite Gilgamesh's pleas to the Moon in Cancer and the Sun in Leo to bring his dear friend back to life, he is ignored.

And so...

"**Gilgamesh roams the steppe,**
And weeps bitter tears
For Enkidu, his friend:
"Shall I not die like Enkidu?
Woe gnaws at my entrails,
I fear death.
So I roam the Steppe.
I must go to see Ziusudra,

---

[17] The Thigh was another name for the Plough or the Great Bear of Ursa Major. According to Robert Temple: "In the course of every 24 hours, the Thigh makes a complete spin around the Pole Star in a motion resembling 'being flung'. The Thigh is clearly depicted in numerous places, particularly in the various zodiacs carved in stone at Denderah in Egypt."

[18] Thus indicating even further that the whole drama is about the changing of the ages, whether by pole star or astrological house, and decreed by the gods.

[19] If you've forgotten the meaning of "six days and seven nights" you can remind yourself by going back to note 8.

[20] Enkidu dies in a doorway made of cedar wood that he constructed himself. We already know that he had carpentry skills because he built the raft of cedar wood to transport the head of Humbaba back to Uruk. The Sumerian name for the sign of Cancer was the Carpenter. And so Enkidu dies at the gate to the House of Cancer. We have already discussed how it is the watery sign of Cancer - governed by the Moon, in this case the father of Ishtar, Sin - that first challenges the hero to get in touch with his deeper emotions, which causes him to develop his instinct and intuition. Lewis Carroll's nonsense rhyme of the weeping Walrus and the Carpenter, which is set on the moonlit shores of a sea, appears in the Cancer part of his zodiac story, *Alice Through the Looking Glass*. For all those reasons, I think this must be Gilgamesh's first water initiation, which it would be in the Alexandrian system.

The Survivor of the Flood –
He, the son of Ubara-Tutu.
Immediately I shall travel the wheel-rim to him..."

Perhaps in his unaccustomed grief we can forgive our hero his hubris. But he decides that he will not return to Uruk until he finds the secret of eternal life, with which he will revive his dear Enkidu.

Next we come what translators calls a *lacuna* – it just means that a part of the chiselled text on the clay tablet has worn away and so there's a gap in the narrative. I'd be willing to wager, though, that when this part finally turns up intact, on an as yet untranslated tablet, it will show that Gilgamesh has gone through some sort of an initiatory[21] rite of passage in which he found his courage at Leo; when he appears again, he has obviously fought and overcome at least one lion because he is wearing lion skins.

We meet Gilgamesh again as he arrives at the Mashu Mountain.[22] There he meets the Scorpion people and tells them he has come "in search of life" and to find Ziusudra, "my forefather – he who survived the Flood. I wish to ask him about life and death".

A Scorpion man tells Gilgamesh that to find his ancestor, he will have to cross the "mountain" via a long dark tunnel – a journey no man has ever survived. But Gilgamesh now has the courage to proceed anyway.

It takes him "12 double hours" to go through the mountain. He eventually comes out into a jewelled garden with bushes bearing carnelian fruits, lapis lazuli leaves, rare stones and agate and pearls from the sea [23].

Unfortunately, there is another *lacuna* here. Fifty lines are missing. This takes us to Tablet X, but many lines are lost on that too. However, by comparing various different translations it appears that it is here that Gilgamesh meets Ishtar the Double Goddess for the second time. He finds her in a tavern on the shore of the ocean as Siduri, the Watermaiden.[24]

---

[21] The second fire initiation comes, in the system of The Three Cauldrons, at the fire sign of Leo, and so I leave this a marker for those who come after me armed with better and further information.

[22] Mount Mashu must be the Milky Way, as it is described as a Heavenly Cow stretching from "the zenith of heaven and whose udders reach the depths of the Underworld". Encountered on this stage of the Wheel, it also ties in with the Alexandrian system in which the Milky Way stretches from the cusp of Taurus/Gemini in the Upper World to the cusp of Scorpio/Sagittarius in the Underworld. The Scorpion people Gilgamesh meets there, indicating that we are in Scorpio, refer to Mount Masha as the "celestial sea". So all this to me indicates the second water initiation.

[23] Obviously an earlier precursor to the Garden of the Hesperides which was visited by Hercules.

[24] Siduri is a typical example of the mythological maidens that bring "the living waters", like the mead bearers in Old Norse myths and the Celtic well maidens. As such, they are the initiators of the sex rites that ignite the secret fire in the waters, which produces the quickening. As we read in Hamlet's Mill: 'Here is a perfectly divine barmaid by the edge of the sea, called by many names in many languages. Her bar should be as long as the famed one in Shanghai, for she has along her shelves not only wine and beer, but more outlandish and antiquated drinks from many cultures, drinks such as honeymead, soma, sura (a

At first, Siduri comes to him veiled. After a further *lacuna*, perhaps one deliberately engineered to spare the Victorians' blushes, she appears outside her tavern unveiled.[25]

Gilgamesh then explains to Siduri his quest – to find his forefather, Ziusudra, he who survived the Flood and ask him for the key to immortality.

Ishtar tries to tempt him into staying with her to enjoy "the 10 figs of marriage"[26], insisting that eternal life is not possible for him. She warns him no man has ever survived the dangerous crossing of the Waters of Death that he would have to make to find Ziusudra.

Gilgamesh, however, is undeterred. He has to continue his quest. So Siduri advises him to try to find Urshanabi the boatman, who, she claims, is the only person that can take him to Ziusudra.

After another *lacuna*, we find Gilgamesh talking to Urshanabi. Our hero explains to him, at length, his mission. Urshanabi gives him the same advice as Siduri but upon being pressed by Gilgamesh, he eventually gives in and agrees to take him.[27]

Then Urshanabi instructs Gilgamesh to go to the forest and cut down…

**"…twice sixty punting poles,
each of sixty cubits."[28]**

---

kind of brandy), kawa, pulque, peyote-cocktail, decoctions of ginseng. In short, from everywhere, she has the ritual intoxicating beverages…".

[25] Inscribed on the temple of Isis in Sais, Egypt, are the following words: "I, Isis, am all that has been, that is or shall be; no mortal man hath ever me unveiled." The symbolic meaning of the veil is part of the mythos around sacred sex rites. In order to see a goddess unveiled, the man must become a god. He can only experience his higher self god form through initiation, which is an Upper World experience of sexual ecstasy with the goddess that forms him into a real man in this world. In other words, the lack of the veil and that she has come out of the tavern is an indication, to me, that Siduri/Ishtar the Watermaiden has taken our hero through some kind of initiation.

[26] We find engravings of the Huluppa or fig tree on Sumerian cylinder seals and there are myths in which Inanna, Ishtar's precursor, planted it. This fig tree signified the World Tree, which was, and still is, a shamanic metaphor for the *axis mundi* of the Creation. The shaman, in trance, visits the Upper, Middle and Lower Worlds by climbing up and down the World Tree. This Huluppa tree was the Babylonian equivalent of the Old Norse World Tree, Yggdrasil, in that it was surmounted by an eagle and had a serpent at its base. It is likely that Tabiti would have told Kroy-Khasis stories featuring a World Tree. In Russia, a Tree of Life design has been found woven into a Scythian rug that dates to 500 BC.

[27] Nabu was the Sumerian Mercury and so we find that suffix in the name of Urshanabi, which translates to "the Priest of Two-Thirds". As shown in Figure 16, the Sumerians divided their zodiacs into thirds, with Anu ruling the Upper World, Enlil the Middle World and Ea/Enki the Underworld. Urshanabi becomes Gilgamesh's guide or "pyschopomp" into the Underworld and then eventually out again. Thus Urshanabi covers two-thirds of the zodiac, as does the planet Mercury in its orbits. Mercury also often appears as a pyschopomp and this is the role of Urshanabi as he ferries Gilgamesh down to the watery deeps of the Underworld. We can also see a similarity in the name of the Egyptian psychocomp, Anubis.

[28] To my thinking, three lots of 60s can only indicate Time and Space, especially as two are together, with the third one on the next line. For instance, the "twice sixty" gives us the 60 seconds of a minute, and the 60 minutes that make up an hour, thus producing the Time of 120 minutes or two hours. Providing a further 60 x 2 for the third, as cubits, in the next line, indicates measurements (Space) and not elapsed Time, thus 60 x 2 =120 x 3 makes 360, and 360 degrees is the exact dimensions of the zodiac. We must also include Ziusudra's ark in our thinking which, unlike Noah's boat-shaped vessel, is an exact cube of 120 cubits on each side. The word "ark" in Hebrew is *tebu*, meaning "box or chest", which is related to the Egyptian word *teben*, meaning to "revolve in a circle", and *teb*, which translates to a "a cycle of time".

In the following lines, we come upon the Time and Space formula again:

Gilgamesh and Urshanabi then boarded the boat,
They launched the boat on the waves
And they sailed away.
By the third day they had gone as far
As a normal voyage of a month and 15 days. [29]

Gilgamesh is instructed to use the poles to punt them across the Waters of Death. Each time he uses one, it breaks and goes under, just like the pole stars of the deluge hero. In the end, he has used them all up and so he takes off his cloth and uses that as a sail.[30]

Another *lacuna* ... and then suddenly, Gilgamesh is in conversation with Ziusudra. He is describing to his immortal ancestor the tragedy of his friend Enkidu's untimely death, which caused him to journey the Wheel, to find the secret of life everlasting which he knows Ziusudra is experiencing because it was granted to him for saving humanity from the Flood.

Ziusudra replies:

"Mankind, which like a reed stands fragile,
A fine young man, a fine young woman ...
These too must die ...
Once they have reached the end of life,
Are all gathered in as one,
By the Anunnaki, the Great Gods,
And she, Mammentum,
She of Fate –
She decrees the destinies.
Together they determine death,
Determine life.
As for life, its days are revealed.
But as for death,
Its day is never revealed.

Gilgamesh then asks Ziusudra to recount to him the story of how he became an immortal, which was a boon granted to him by the god Enlil for saving so many creatures from the flood.[31]

---

[29] Remembering that there was no Libra then, and thus Scorpio began further back on the Wheel, this would probably have brought them both into the cusp of Sagittarius and Capricorn.

[30] Reminiscent of Ishtar's Descent into the Underworld, where at each stage she has to shed some clothing or jewellery until she is naked before the seat of the judge, Erishkigal.

[31] There are many Ark measurements in Ziusudra's story that give us a better understanding of Sumerian sacred geometry than is found in the Hebrew story of Noah. However, I don't want us to get diverted into that, because my purpose here is to focus on Gilgamesh's journey. But if you want to look up Ziusudra's flood story, at some point, it's on Tablet XI.

After he has finished his tale, Ziusudra tells Gilgamesh that to learn the secret of eternal life, he must prove his worthiness by staying awake for six days and seven nights. Gilgamesh agrees, and then almost instantly falls asleep. So Ziusudra's wife suggests to her husband that the snoring hero should be woken and sent on his way. But Ziusudra replies to her that Gilgamesh will try to deny that he slept. So he asks her to bake some small cakes and put one beside Gilgamesh's sleeping body for each day that he remains unconscious. [32]

Finally, after the six days and seven nights, Gilgamesh awakes and instantly proves Ziusudra correct by vehemently denying he had been asleep. So Ziusudra shows him the seven cakes, which, by now, are in various stages of mouldiness and disintegration, to prove his point. Gilgamesh is instantly distraught with shame and frustration at the realisation that he has thrown away a golden opportunity to achieve the goal of his quest.

It is now time for Urshanabi to ferry Gilgamesh on, to complete the cycle, which is the return to the city of Uruk. [33] But before he leaves, Ziusudra tells him to discard his dirty animal skins and to bathe and purify himself in the waters. He then gives him new clothes and a fresh band to wear around his head. [34]

Just as Urshanabi is about to punt off, Ziusudra calls them both back. He says that he wishes to give our hero a gift in appreciation of his courage and determination in coming such a great distance. He tells him about where to find a herb that is like buckthorn and has potent rejuvenatory qualities; eating it won't give him eternal life, he says, but it has potent powers of rejuvenation that will enable Gilgamesh to live happily and healthily for much longer.

Gilgamesh instantly dives down into the sea, finds the herb and pockets it. Then he and Urshanabi begin their return journey. Along the way, they came upon a well of cool waters and as he is feeling very hot, Gilgamesh decides to dive down deep into its depths.[35] But just then a serpent comes along. It smells the herb in his pocket, goes in to grab it and swallows it whole. As it swims away, it sloughs its skin in rejuvenation.[36]

Naturally, Gilgamesh is most upset at losing such a prize.

But eventually, they arrive in Uruk and the last verse consists of Gilgamesh's

---

[32] According to Robert Temple, the small round cakes show another instance of borrowing of symbols from ancient Egypt – of course, it could be vice-versa or merely a shared design on the primordial carpet. Anyway, he has discovered that there is a non-phonetic Egyptian hieroglyph for Time that is a small round cake of bread. In addition, there is a traditional custom found in the West Country of Britain in which people offer small round cakes, hot cross buns and "corn babies" to mark the festivals of the year.

[33] According to the mythologist Joseph Campbell, the return is an equally important factor in the story of the hero as the journey itself.

[34] Clothes, particularly animal skins, symbolise the human body in its unrealised, partly bestial state. Discarding his animal skins and purifying himself in the sea, and then donning new clothes, to me signifies that Gilgamesh has reached transformation into a new body and a new life; in other words, rebirth.

[35] His third water initiation.

[36] A symbol for death and rebirth.

words as he proudly shows the Priest of Two-Thirds around the ramparts of his city.

And that's the end. Well, the end as we know it, thus far.

So my apologies if such a great epic seems unfairly squeezed into a bit of a whistlestop tour. It was just to give you the bare bones of the story. It really is worthy of much more attention that we can give here. I hope you get the chance to dive into it yourself one day, to benefit from its profound and vivid deeps. But my aim with this summary was just to get us round the Wheel followed by the oldest zodiac protagonist we have available to us in order to show my interpretation of it.

It's also interesting to me because *The Epic of Gilgamesh* is still pretty raw and so not your usual heroic fare, much of which has become infected with post-Roman Christian values. Although the protagonist shows great courage and persistence in his search for Ziusudra by crossing the perilous Waters of Death, there is no evidence in this story that Gilgamesh's trials made him a less "sinful" person. In fact, the only mention of "sin" is in the name of the Moon god. So we might wonder what actual transformation Gilgamesh experienced?

Even nearing the climax of the story, where we are given to believe that Ziusudra might be able to help him if he can pass the test of staying awake for six days and seven nights, Gilgamesh lies. So he hasn't yet learned the value of truth telling. He also covets the herb of longevity for himself and is most upset at losing it to the serpent. Therefore what is the lesson that we are meant to take away from this story? It certainly doesn't appear to be that if you are good, and do as you're told, you will go to Heaven when you die. So how is Gilgamesh a hero?

As we already know, "mesh" was the Sumerian word for "hero". From at least the eighth century BCE onwards, the word "hero" meant "man born from a god and a mortal", which we heard from the Prologue applied to Gilgamesh[37]. But it turns out it was quite common in Sumerian times for someone to have "mesh" on the end of their name. One respected scholar of Hittite, Albrecht Goetze, believed that Gilga actually meant "ancestor", making Gilgamesh the ancestral hero or hero of the ancestors. So here we are back to the theme of the purpose of the journey around the astrological Wheel of the Being that is partly god and partly mortal with the purpose of alchemically redeeming the ancestral line.

To me, this is what made Gilgamesh a hero and while I was still planning the end of this chapter in my head, a wonderful metaphor presented itself in my own

---

[37] "His name was called Gilgamesh, from the very day of his birth. He was two-thirds god, one-third man." The two-thirds of godlike DNA came from his mother, Rimat-Ninsun, the Heavenly Cow, and the remaining third from his father, the king Lugulbanda.

garden. So please let me share it with you.

I have a honeysuckle bush I planted many years ago. However, my buddleia, which I planted next to it at the same time, grew much faster and created a towering canopy. This meant the honeysuckle's roots were kept almost permanently in the dark. Thus, it was not receiving enough sunlight, moonlight and starlight to produce leaves and flowers. However, the stalks under the buddleia canopy did keep growing. And so I would wonder, from time to time, whether I should dig up the honeysuckle and move it to a brighter location. I didn't want to cut down the buddleia because the butterflies love it. Anyway, I couldn't make up my mind and while I was busy ignoring this dilemma, the honeysuckle's bare woody stalks kept growing higher and higher in the dark until this Spring, when I suddenly noticed them. I saw that they had reached the light at the top of the fence and that glossy green leaves were beginning to sprout like crazy in, what seemed to me, ecstasy at reaching the light. I am still waiting for it to flower. I am hoping it will this year – although it may be too big of an ask for a plant I've ignored for so long. But I realised it was providing the perfect metaphor for what I've gained in my spiritual teaching from *The Epic of Gilgamesh*.

It seems the ladder of my own progress is being held steady at the bottom by my ancestors, many of whom have had to remain in the dark and sacrifice their own blooming and fruiting to pour all their energies into me. It is a humbling thought and one that instantly dissolves, like detergent, the greasy residue of any kind of spiritual ego trip. In other words, there is a lesson for me, from both the honeysuckle in my outer garden and the ancestors in my inner garden. And it is teaching me the difference between individualism - through which the West has become famously creative and prosperous but which, unchecked, is now in danger of turning into an unhealthy narcissism - and individuation, the realisation of which allows us to take our part as an individual functioning optimally within the whole.

In other words, the purpose of the journey of the hero up the Ladder of the Wise is to ultimately join the perpetual choirs that are continually and joyously singing the praises of the Creation, the resonance from which, if you remember from the chapter about the holographic universe of music, is what keeps it all going. And just as a choir is made up of many individuals, they are not all self-entitled narcissists in pursuit of their own selfish aims, as both Pinocchio and Gilgamesh were when they first set out. They are individuals who have voluntarily come together to cooperate in order to create something that is sublimely beautiful and uplifting, and to do so they follow the dictates of the composer and the conductor. They adhere to the musical scores on their sheets, in which the sopranos sing the top line of the musical stave and the altos follow the line below them with the tenors under the altos and below the tenors the basses.

The members of a choir, in other words, are disciplined enough to produce four different melodies and in the most beneficial music, those melodies have been composed in such a way as to produce complete harmony. That said, within the multi-layered sound being produced, there can be up to hundreds of different individual voices and when the joyful praise being emitted is a genuine expression of unconditional love, the gods attune via their own version of unique voice recognition, through their sacred geometrical and holographic technology, and the Above comes down to the Below.

Thus, the hero is one who communicates with the Upper World planetary governing gods and, at the same time, the spirits of the ancestors who are standing in the dark of the Underworld deeps, like the roots of my honeysuckle, under the bottom rung of the Ladder of the Wise, patiently and silently inching the bare stalks ever upwards, generation after generation, until the stems finally reach the light and, at last, there is a flowering, the fruit of the loins.

One is finally born who can benefit from all that accrued *chi* or sap energy coming up from the forefathers' roots and pouring into the lower cauldron. They can gain the means to understand how to contact the ancestors and the gods and, from the tutoring of those spirits, to realise that the purpose of human life is to alchemically transform into a being whose heart is quickened with joy upon realising the extraordinary love this universe is made of, and thus redeem their family lines by joining the eternally praising choir of creation.

Plato once said that when we look into the face of our beloved, we see there the reflection of the god to whose choir we once belonged.

This is the path and destiny of the hero. And if you have read and understood this book thus far, this means you. We can be heroes... and not just for one day.

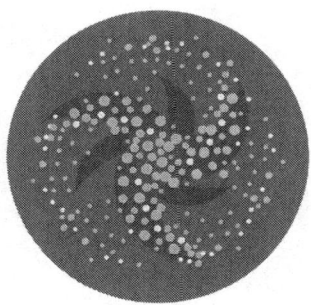

Practical exercise

To get a firm footing on the first rung of the Ladder of the Wise, we need to set up a line of communication with our ancestors.

In **2: Weather Shamans at Sea**, we met the weather shaman Sun Bear, whose powers came from the forebears with whom he attuned through unconditional love.

To focus our energies into such a nebulous emotion as unconditional love can seem a daunting task, let alone how to figure out a means of transmitting it to the ancestors, until we come across a meditation technique I call the Ecstasy of the Heart. To learn how to enjoy this simple, blissful practice, please go to **Appendix B**.

18. The Mills of the Gods

IF you wanted to choose a philosophy that would destroy the human race, you would select nihilism. The word "nihilism" comes from the Latin *nil*, meaning "null, zero, nothing" – in other words, nihilism creates the void that is at the heart of a life that is empty of meaning, morality and values. Its pointless hedonism is depicted in the Pleasure Island of *Pinocchio*, the enchanted fairground in *Spirited Away*, and Gilgamesh's untrammelled desires running rampant in Uruk before undertaking the journey around the Wheel of Fortune. We see a similar message today, too, in Postmodernism and the films which turn the heroic journey on its head; the ones that exchange a handsome hero for a heroine, or an ugly or a fat anti-hero, or a transgender disabled protagonist, all produced from the consciousness of a dystopian wasteland, an arid landscape that has been created largely by the Darwinian tenet that the process of biological evolution is driven by nothing more than the strongest fighting it out in a perpetual bloodbath for survival.

Conversely, it could be argued that the only reason the human race has survived on this planet for so long is because of those women who originally composed and sang the sagas, poems and nursery rhymes about the mythological hero, and who then passed them on orally from granddaughter to granddaughter.

The ancient mindset was about as far from nihilism as it is possible to get. Everything, to them, had sacred holographic and connectivity of meaning, which had a direct bearing on their everyday lives.

As Robert Temple writes in *He Who Saw Everything*:

"... remember that in the ancient cultures that produced The Epic of Gilgamesh there was no such thing as a purely entertaining work of literature or drama. Everything had religious connotations. Our desacralised world did

not yet exist. There were gods on every street corner. The Epic was not written just for fun or amusement. The Sumerians, Babylonians, Assyrians, Hittites, Hurrians and Elamites would all be horrified if they knew that we even thought such for a thing for an instant."

The purpose today of identifying the allegorical understories in the ancient myths about the deluge hero and the zodiac hero, and learning the magical keys and symbols, is to trigger the race memories that are flowing in our Rivers of Blood so that we can begin to view life again through the lenses of those ancestors like Kroy-Khasis, Tabiti and Maya from the Steppes, and thus stand a chance of saving our species.

When we read about how Fox and Cat continually tried to trick Pinocchio in the original Tuscan folk story, it causes us to remember instances in our own lives when we felt as if we were being gamed at every turn. We could have sworn it was as if we were at the mercy of the gods or of some evil force that just would not give us a break. Or when we hear about the courage of Arthur and his men braving the guards of the caers of the firmamental ocean to win the Cauldron, it puts steel into our own resolve when having to face the dangerous situations that occur along the path of anyone on the ladder of human life. And when we put ourselves in the shoes of Gilgamesh in his terrible, gnawing grief over the death of his twin soul, Enkidu, we go back in our own minds to the first time we were shockingly confronted with the finite reality of mortal life and the realisation that nobody gets out of here alive.

This is all part of the process of growing up into an adult who is capable of leading the generations of the future into supporting a tribe or race to thrive. Yet under the prevailing nihilistic message of our media and entertainment machine, and with the knowledge of shamanism demonised and driven underground and the Mystery teachings with its organised rites of passage for the young gasping and on its last legs, many today are in a state of retarded development. So they are looking to political leaders to rescue them from situations of their own making, unable to take control of their lives, when they should be looking to the spirits or the gods.

Perhaps in reading this book you have been reminded of Tolstoy's remark: "History would be a wonderful thing, if only it were true." However, I do have some sympathy with those social engineers tasked with organising humans that thrive on stories, in bastardising our traditional wisdom teachings to give us a viable back narrative. Perhaps it was the best they could do at the time, to satisfy our curiosity by allowing us to believe that we descend from the great heroes of the battle of Troy, a Pharaonic princess named Scota and a courageous king, Arthur, who won 12 battles, and then to reassure us that we have nothing to worry about because all our sins have been redeemed by a Saviour with 12 disciples who lived two millennia ago.

Added to that, I think it would be vastly impractical for the whole of humanity to wake up to what these metaphorical tales are trying to teach us at the same time, and that is probably why the path is ruled by the Alpha and Omega of the zodiac – Saturn, otherwise known as the Father Time, who ensures an orchestrated and manageable progression of spiritual evolution.

It takes innumerable generations of enormous effort and sacrifice for the ancestors to produce a likely candidate with enough strength and vision to clear the Rivers of Blood. On top of that, it requires great courage to face the yawning cognitive abyss of "I don't know", which is symbolised, in the Tarot, by the Fool stepping off a cliff. Yet for the handful who are ready, we must be brave enough to take that step into the unknown or we will never discover that what appears, to our limited perception, to be the brink of a terrifying cognitive chasm is actually just the space between the rungs going up the Ladder of the Wise.

There is a quote from the American historian Charles A. Beard, which I believe contains profound wisdom:

"All the lessons of history in four sentences: Whom the gods would destroy, they first make mad with power. The mills of God grind slowly, but they grind exceedingly small. The bee fertilises the flower it robs. When it is dark enough, you can see the stars."

None of us can avoid the turning of this cosmic mill and so those who try to persuade us human life should be just one long sojourn on Pleasure Island are probably lying to us, like Fox and Cat, or at least are extremely ignorant. But when we hear the whole story of the journey of the hero, as it was originally told around the campfires of our ancestors, it gives us clues as to how to make the most of what is really a huge opportunity to evolve and transform on a fundamental alchemical level.

So let me break down Beard's message according to my perception:

Whom the gods would destroy, they first make mad with power

Beard's first lesson is derived from a saying of the ancient Greeks: "Whom the gods would destroy, they first make mad." He himself added the words "with power". It could be argued that the hothead hero at Aries is mad with the newfound fiery power throbbing through his veins and sinews. However, this is not about the destruction of the individual or the soul, which is eternal and indestructible. It is about obliterating the ignorance that has been caused by forgetfulness about our true nature.

As we float in our coracle through the Pisces stage in childhood, we don't know the meaning or purpose of our life and so we dream up stories about it, or others provide them for us. These nursery tales may serve us well for a short step along the way but only enough to enable us to stay as mere wooden puppets that make for useful consumers or robots in a theatre constructed by those intent on stealing our fire of spiritual inspiration.

Being fed a continual diet of false stories about the nature of reality, we find ourselves like Don Quixote, imagining we are brave and chivalrous questing knights and mistaking conniving prostitutes for beautiful damsels in distress and the scarecrows and strawmen of the puppet theatre for terrifying adversaries. In creating such havoc and mayhem within the natural order of things, we unwittingly insult the Lady of Fortune and then the gods seem to turn against us, to "make us mad".

Gilgamesh pleads with Sin the Moon and Shamash the Sun to release Enkidu from what he considered to be the curse of death but they were unmoved. Likewise with Pinocchio, who insulted the Blue Fairy by lying to her; and so from then on, because the puppet didn't know how to find his guides in inner space, they had to manifest on the outside as a series of antagonists in the guise of highwaymen and assassins that blocked his way until he learned his lessons.

We see this theme at play most clearly in Collodi's folktale in which Fox and Cat tell Pinocchio if he buries his five gold coins in the Field of Wonders they will grow, overnight, 1,000-fold. Pinocchio ignores the advice of the bluebird and goes with the two tricksters to the Field of Wonders to bury his coins. Of course, when he returns the next morning, the coins have gone, and for the crime of having his coins stolen, he is arrested and put in prison.

It may sometimes seem to be a travesty of justice when we are penalised or have limitations put on us, which come about through our own gullibility and susceptibility to being lead by rogues rather than those who are wiser. However, we have not yet learned much wisdom ourselves at this early stage and so we are unlikely to be able to recognise it in others. We may rage at the gods at such a time, for the injustice of the situation. Yet a little Time doing "time" can also give us enough Space to reflect, as did Pinocchio as a circus donkey, and examine the errors of our ways.

The mills of the gods grind slowly, but they grind exceedingly small

There is not one millisecond of the day in which the gods are absent or not paying attention to the whole of the creation – and that means us too. One 24-hour cycle is divided into hours in which the gods rule successively, one after another. At dawn, the god of that specific named day rules for the first hour. Take Saturday, for example. On Saturday at sunrise, Saturn takes charge. He rules the first hour after dawn before handing over to the Sun for the next hour, then the Moon, then Mars, then Mercury, then Jupiter, and finally Venus who hands it back to Saturn again on the eighth hour and so on it goes, around the clock of every single day and night.

When the ancient Indians, who invented mathematics, talked about natural cycles of time, their smallest measurement was a tiny spark of a glint in the eye and their largest was a gigantic *yuga* or Age lasting trillions of years. So there are cycles within cycles within cycles *ad infinitum*.

On top of that, alchemists have to be aware which god rules the different parts of their operation. The gods even rule each of the four elements: Mercury governs air, Venus governs water, Mars governs fire and Saturn governs earth.

It may seem there is a strange paradox at play, that we have free will yet we exist within such a tightly controlled system. Yet when we zoom out into shamanic flight, we eventually begin to realise what the myths are showing us – that we are just part of a dream of the Great Alchemist, otherwise known as the Sleeper in the Land.

Lewis Carroll expressed this idea well in *Through the Looking Glass* when Alice's mercurial twin guides through Gemini to Cancer, Tweededum and Tweedledee, show her the comatose form of the sleeping Red King at the Summer Solstice:

Here she checked herself in some alarm, at hearing something that sounded to her like the puffing of a large steam-engine in the wood near them, though she feared it was more likely to be a wild beast.

'Are there any lions or tigers about here?' she asked timidly.

'It's only the Red King snoring,' said Tweedledee.

'Come and look at him!' the brothers cried, and they each took one of Alice's hands, and led her up to where the King was sleeping.

'Isn't he a lovely sight?' said Tweedledum.

Alice couldn't say honestly that he was. He had a tall red night-cap on, with a tassel, and he was lying crumpled up into a sort of untidy heap, and snoring loud— 'fit to snore his head off!' as Tweedledum remarked.

'I'm afraid he'll catch cold with lying on the damp grass,' said Alice, who was a very thoughtful little girl.

'He's dreaming now,' said Tweedledee: 'and what do you think he's dreaming about?'

Alice said 'Nobody can guess that.'

'Why, about you!' Tweedledee exclaimed, clapping his hands triumphantly. 'And if he left off dreaming about you, where do you suppose you'd be?'

'Where I am now, of course,' said Alice.

'Not you!' Tweedledee retorted contemptuously. 'You'd be nowhere. Why, you're only a sort of thing in his dream!'

'If that there King was to wake,' added Tweedledum, 'you'd go out— bang!—just like a candle!'

'I shouldn't!' Alice exclaimed indignantly. 'Besides, if I'm only a sort of thing in his dream, what are you, I should like to know?'

'Ditto,' said Tweedledum.

'Ditto, ditto!' cried Tweedledee.

He shouted this so loud that Alice couldn't help saying 'Hush! You'll be waking him, I'm afraid, if you make so much noise.'

Alice does eventually awaken the Red King, inadvertently, when she reaches the Winter Solstice and then she herself wakes from her dream about the enchanted land through the looking glass.

Carroll would have taken the idea of the sleeping Red King from an ancient Indian Vedic myth in which the whole of the universe exists only in the mind of the god Vishnu, who is fast asleep and dreaming on a shell in the Garbhodaka Ocean. It is said that when Vishnu wakes up, it will be the end of his dream and the end of the universe that he imagined into existence.

The awakening of the Red King and Vishnu are metaphors for the initiate's awakening to the fact that they are grist to the mills of the gods that grind slowly but grind exceedingly small – and that their purpose here is to clear and purify the ancestral line and become part of the perpetual choir of the Creation.

The bee fertilises the flower it robs

On Collodi's Isle of the Busy Bees, Pinocchio comes under Virgo, which is governed by Mercury, the god of the merchants and all things mercantile. Here, the puppet finally starts to understand the natural laws that govern human interactions, production and commerce. The realisation that begins to grow as the journey of the zodiac hero continues into Libra, is that Nature is constantly striving to achieve a state of equilibrium, represented by the scales of justice in that part of the zodiac, and as we are part of Nature too our actions and reactions in our dealings with one another also have to be balanced. We should only receive as much as we give. If we try to take more than is our due, we will eventually end up in the dock before the judge and we will have to pay it back, one way or the other.

When it is dark enough, you can see the stars

The hero is bitten by the serpent at Scorpio and then he tumbles down into the deeps of the Underworld, which is ruled by Jupiter, to face trials that will ensure the redemption of his ancestral line if they are passed. These trials mainly consist of unearthing lots of stinking, fetid, rotting stuff that we'd rather not look at and then, from the seeming impossibility of transforming this lead into gold, we descend into the depression of the Dark Night of the Soul. But when we finally look up, into all that unremitting blackness, we start to notice that it is glittering and we can see the stars.

If we have been taught properly – in other words, if we have the "knowledge of the stars" – then the presence of the stars remind us that we can only fulfil these tasks and obligations by petitioning the spirits or gods. We cannot do it ourselves. And so eventually, with otherworldly help, we emerge from this tunnel with the new Sun at Capricorn on the Winter Solstice and are guided as a reborn human by Saturn through Aquarius and then by Jupiter through Pisces, after which the whole cycle begins again.

Last word

If you're feeling daunted by the seeming humungous size of the task ahead or are becoming convinced it is up to you to save the human race, please don't. You can only see to your own progress and so you are not in the least responsible for the advancement up the ladder of anyone else. Just be here now and do your best. That's all any of us can do.

But in addition, this seeming Fall of the human race that appears to have taken place over the past two millennia may not necessarily be a bad thing, in and of itself. Most are not aware that it was the alchemists themselves who drove the thinking of the Age of the Enlightenment in the 17th and 18th centuries. It was because they no longer wanted a dogma to be dominant in consensual reality that was diverting more and more from its original alchemical and cosmologically-based philosophy, and interfering in their own experiments. So it was those occultists, like John Locke, William Jefferson and Sir Isaac Newton, who were employed by the ruling classes to supply the priest scribes with our mythologies, who decided to take the "ora" or oracle out of the laboratory. Could it be that they judged that the age of **calcification** – i.e. the rule of the raging and passionately jealous Jehovah god - was over and so with their new narratives which led to Darwinism, they **dissolved** its tight grip on people's thinking and then **separated** the subjective from the objective and the church from the state?

If so, and they were right in their assumptions, it could mean we are about to reach the fourth rung of **conjunction**, ruled by Venus, and the spiritual will rejoin the material, at least for a while anyway, in this rainbow dream of the Great Alchemist.

Of course, I don't know if this is true for sure, but I do find it a useful conceptual tool to work with. The beauty of this idea is that it takes us out of a feeling of oppressed victimhood and helplessness, which is anathema to progress up the ladder. It also rescues us from the nihilism and narcissism that is the ultimate destination of the current trajectory of consensual consciousness in the West.

It's a thought anyway... and quite a positive one, I think, on which to end this book.

Appendix A – Flood Myths

In this section, you will find all the deluge myths that I've been able to amass over the years. By comparing them with the Noah's Ark story, you'll see there are so many similarities in their core structures that it's obvious – well, to me anyway - that it's the same story being told over and over again.

As stated previously, these flood myths were originally cosmological teaching stories about the precessional journey around the ecliptic, which led to the changing of the pole star. When each pole star gave way to another new pole star, it is described in these sagas as the end of an age, which is signified by a flood in the Milky Way.

It's impossible to tell which is the oldest flood myth of those listed below – but officially, it's the one about Atrahasis, which is dated to the 18th century BCE. However, it is my educated guess that the Egyptian and Indian deluge myths are equally ancient, if not more so.

Sumer and Babylon

Atrahasis

It happens three times over many thousands of years that the gods become distressed by the disturbance from the humans on Earth, caused by overpopulation. They first deal with the problem by destroying humanity through a plague; the second time, they cause a great famine.

Both times, the god Enki (of the Underworld) advises men to bribe the god Enlil (of the Middle World) to try to stop him sending the tribulations. But those bribes didn't work and so the third time Enlil was annoyed by the humans, he advised the gods to wipe them all out with a great flood that would cover most of the Earth. However, Enki had the good man Atrahasis build an ark and so he escapes along with his family, his cattle, wild animals and birds.

When the storm comes, Atrahasis seals the door with bitumen and cuts the boat's rope. The storm god Adad rages, turning the daytime sky black. After the seven-day flood, the gods regret their action. Atrahasis makes an offering to them, at which the gods gathered like flies, and then Enki established that some women should be barren to avoid over-populations in the future.

Ziusudra

The council of gods decides to destroy mankind with a great flood and so Enki, the god of the Underworld, relays the words spoken at this otherworldly council to the priest-king Ziusudra (meaning "Long of Life") through a reed wall with Ziusudra listening to him on the other side. Enki advises him to build a boat of reeds and take into it the seeds of all living creatures. The vessel is not boat-shaped but more like a cube, measuring an exact 120 cubits on each side. (The word "ark" in Hebrew is *tebu* meaning "box or chest", which is related to the Egyptian word *teben*, meaning to "revolve in a circle" and *teb* which translates to a "a cycle of time".)

Anyway, soon violent winds arrive and a flood of rain comes which covers the Earth for seven days and nights. Then Ziusudra opens a window in the vessel, allowing sunlight to enter, and he prostrates himself before the sun-god Shamash. After landing, he sacrifices a sheep and an ox and he bows before Anu and Enlil. For protecting the animals and the seeds of mankind, he is granted eternal life and taken to the country of Dilmun, where the sun rises – and where Gilgamesh eventually finds him.

Utnapishtim

The gods, led by Enlil of the Middle World, agreed to cleanse the Earth of an overpopulated humanity but Utnapishtim was warned by the god Ea (Enki) in a dream. So he and others build a large boat (of one acre in area with seven decks) in just a week. Then he loads it up with his family and "the seed of all living creatures".

The waters of the abyss rise up and a storm rages for six days. Even the gods were frightened by the flood's fury and upon seeing all the people killed, they repented and wept. The waters covered everything except the top of the mountain Nisur, where the boat landed.

Seven days later, Utnapishtim released a dove but it returned upon finding nowhere else to land. Then he sent out a sparrow, which also returned, and then finally a raven, which never came back. Thus he knew the waters had receded enough for the people to emerge. Utnapishtim made a sacrifice to the gods and he and his wife were given immortality.

Berossus (*a Hellenistic-era Babylonian writer and astronomer from the beginning of the third century BCE.*)
The antediluvians were giants who became impious and depraved, except one among them that revered the gods and was wise and prudent. His name was Noa, and he dwelt in Syria with his three sons Sem, Japet and Chem and their wives Tidea, Pandora, Noela and Noegla.

From his knowledge of the stars, he foresaw destruction and so he began building an ark. Seventy-eight years later, the oceans, inland seas and rivers burst forth from beneath, attended by many days of violent rain. The waters overflowed all the mountains and the whole human race was drowned, except Noa and his family, who survived on his ship. The ship came to rest at last on the top of the mountain Gendyae.

India
Manu, the first human, found a small fish in his washwater. The fish begged the man for protection from the larger fishes, in return for which it would save Manu from a flood. Manu kept the fish safe until it grew larger and larger until eventually it became the size of a giant whale.

Meanwhile, Manu warned king Satyavarata about the dangers to humanity being caused by the depravity of the age, and he sent him a large ship. He told the king to gather himself, medicinal herbs and pairs of brute animals to go aboard it to save themselves from a great deluge.

Seven days later, the Three Worlds were flooded and darkened. Manu's great whale then appeared in the ocean, a million leagues long, and Satyavarata tied the ark to its horn.

There is also a *Rig Vedas* story about Indra, the storm god, releasing the waters of the deluge, which had been damned up by the water serpent, Vritra. The Egyptian story about Set (below) is similar but with the Apap-dragon taking the place of Vritra.

Egypt
Egyptian myths are choc-a-block with deluges that are not just confined to water. There

are deluges of milk, deluges of day, deluges of night, deluges of blood and deluges of beer, to name just a few.

The oldest Egyptian flood myth is dated to around 6,000 years old and it is so ancient that comes from a time before Set (or Sut) became the anti-hero. He and his sons are the governors of the Moon and Saturn. In this story, Set sends forth a deluge to destroy the evil Sebau, the Sami, the Apap-dragon and the Long-Armed Ones. Later on, in the solar-based mythologies, Set is superseded by Osiris as Lord of the Deluge, and by Horus and his sons, the governors of the Sun.

In a later Egyptian deluge myth, Nnu the patriarch conducts his vessel across the cosmic sea of Nun (the Milky Way) piloted by the two birds of Isis, who governs the deluge of light at daybreak, and her sister Nephthys, who governs the deluge of nightfall.

Another recounts how the lunar god Taht steered his ark across the cosmic ocean as one pole after another capsises - six in all - leaving only the seventh one on the mount upon which he finally rested.

Finally, there is the story of goddess Hathor, who comes down to Earth to destroy man with her "eye" of Ra (the Sun). She wreaks havoc and devastation with her deluge of heat and fire. Ra then takes pity on man and sends a flood of beer to put out the fires.

Greece
There are at least two floods in Greek mythology:

Xisuthrus
The god Chronos (Saturn) came in a vision to warn Xisuthrus, the 10th king of Babylon, that a great flood is coming on the 15th day of the month of Daesius. The god orders the king to write a history of man and bury it in Sippara. Then he instructs him to build and provision a vessel that is five stadia long by two stadia wide, with which he should save his friends and relations, and all kinds of animals. Xisuthrus asks where he should sail and Chronos answers: "To the gods, but first pray for all good things to men."

Xisuthrus builds the ship and loads it up as ordered. The flood comes in a raging storm. After it has abated somewhat, the king sends out birds to find trees that would indicate that there is dry land, but they all return with empty beaks. Later, he tries again and the birds return with mud on their feet. On the third trial, the birds don't come back. Then Xisuthrus sees that land is appearing above the waters and he eventually brings his ship aground in the Corcyraean mountains, in Armenia.

Xisuthrus then disembarks with his wife, daughter and a pilot, and they all sacrifice to the gods. Those four were then granted the boon of going to live with the gods. The other humans at first are grieved when they cannot find the four of them, but then they hear Xisuthrus's voice in the air above them, telling them to be pious and to seek his writings at Sippara.

In a second Greek myth, the father of the gods, Zeus, sends a flood to destroy all of humanity. But Prometheus warns his son, Deucalion, about the coming deluge and advises him to build an ark.

Scandinavia

In Norse mythology, there are two deluges:

The first occurs at the dawn of time, before the world was formed. Ymir, the first giant, is killed by the god Odin and his brothers Vili and Ve and when he falls, so much blood flows from his wounds that it drowns almost the entire race of giants, with the exception of the frost giant Bergelmir and his wife. They escape in a ship and survive to become the progenitors of a new race of giants. Ymir's body is then used to form the Earth while his blood becomes the sea.

The second flood recounts a final battle between the gods and the giants that is known as Ragnarök. During this apocalyptic event, Jormungandr, the great World Serpent that lies beneath the sea surrounding Midgard, the realm of mortals, rises up from the watery depths to join the conflict, resulting in a catastrophic flood that drowns the land. However, following Ragnarök, the Earth is reborn and a new age of humanity begins.

The Americas

The Quechua (pre-Inca Andean)

In this deluge myth, the world itself wants to come to an end and a llama, knowing this, becomes too depressed to eat. When the llama's owner complains about it rejecting all food, the llama informs him of an imminent great flood and then suggests they go to Villca Coto mountain. The deluge comes as soon as they arrive on the mountain's peak, upon which there are already many kinds of animals. Afterwards, when the waters abate, the family of man begins to multiply once more.

Mayan
The gods use a flood to destroy the wooden people, an early imperfect version of humanity.

The Shaur (Andes Mountains)
In a tobacco-induced dream, a hunter is told by the daughter of the water spirit Tsunki to return to a river. When he obeys her, he finds a woman on the river's shore, and so he follows her to her father's house and there becomes her husband. He then has to return to his home on Earth and so the woman takes the form of a snake so that she can stay with him. However, once while he was off hunting, his two Earthly wives torment her and so she returns to her father Tsunki. Tsunki flies into a rage at her maltreatment and sends a flood over the whole Earth that drowns everyone except the hunter and one of his daughters, who escape to a mountaintop. Eventually, these two repopulate the world.

The Caddo (Texas/Oklahoma)
Four monsters grow so large and powerful they are high enough to touch the sky. Then a man hears a voice telling him to plant a hollow reed. He obeys the command and finds that the reed grows very quickly. Soon he, his wife and pairs of all good animals enter the reed. The waters then rise to cover everything except the top of the reed and the heads of the monsters. A turtle destroys the monsters by digging under them and uprooting them. The waters then subside and hot winds dry the Earth.

The Hopi
The people repeatedly become distant from Sotuknang, the creator. So twice the god destroys the world; first by fire and then by cold. Eventually, he re-creates the world while the few people who still live by the laws of the creation take shelter underground with the ants.

Then it so happened that the survivors of the floods themselves became corrupt and warlike.

Sotuknang guides the ones who had retained their wisdom to Spider Woman, who cuts down giant reeds and shelters the people in the hollow stems with a little water and food. Then Sotuknang causes a great flood with rain and waves, and the people float in their reeds for a long time. Finally, they come to rest on a small piece of land and Spider Woman unseals their reeds and pulls them out by the tops of their heads and they find that they still have as much food as they started with.

The reed people send out birds to find more land but to no avail. Then they grow a tall reed and climb it to the top but still they can see only water. However, guided by their inner wisdom, which comes from Sotuknang through the door at the top of their heads, the people travel on, using the reeds as canoes.

They sail north-east and find progressively larger islands. The last of these is large and fruitful and the people want to stay there. But Spider Woman urges them on. So they sail even further north-east, paddling hard as if going uphill, until they come to the Fourth World. The shores there are rocky and there doesn't appear to be any place to land. But by opening the doors at the tops of their head, they find a current that takes them to a sandy beach.

Then Sotuknang appears to them, and tells them to look back. They do so to see the islands, the last remnants of the Third World, sinking into the ocean.

Michoacan (Mexico)
When the waters of the deluge begin to rise, a man named Tezpi enters into a great vessel, taking with him his wife and children and diverse seeds and animals. When the floods abate, the man sends out a vulture but the bird finds plenty of corpses to eat and so it doesn't come back. Other birds also fly away, never to be seen again. Finally, he sends out a hummingbird and that returns with a green bough in its beak.

Tarahumara (Northern Mexico)
The people are fighting among themselves and so Father God (Tata Dios) sends rain, drowning everyone. After the flood, God sends three men and three women to repopulate the Earth and they plant three kinds of corn, which still grow in the country.

Toltec (Mexico)
One of the Tezcatlipocas (the sons of the original dual god) transforms himself into the Sun and then he creates the first humans. He does this out of pride, to show off to his brothers. The other Tezcatlipocas gods become angry at his audacity and ask Quetzalcoatl to destroy the Sun and the Earth, which the supreme god promptly does with a great flood, and the people become fish. This ends the first age. The second, third, and fourth Suns end, respectively, with the crumbling of the heavens, a rain of fire and devastating winds.

Nahua (central Mexico)
The people of the Earth during three previous ages are destroyed by being, respectively, devoured by jaguars, swept away by the wind and turned into monkeys, and in a rain of fire are transformed into birds. The Sun of the fourth age lasts 676 years. Then one day, the heavens come down and the people are inundated and turned into fish.

In the next age, the god Titlacahuan (Tezcatlipoca) tells a man known as Nata ("Our Father") and his consort named Nene to hollow out a cypress log and enter it during the vigil of Toçoztli, when the heavens would come crashing down. He seals them in with a single ear of corn apiece to eat. When they finish eating all the kernels, they hear the waters declining.

Mixtec (northern Oaxaca, Mexico)

The Earth is well populated but then mankind commits a magical fault for which they are punished by a great deluge. The Mixtec people are the descendants from the few survivors.

Quiché (Guatemala)

The wooden people, an early version of humanity, are imperfect because there is nothing in their hearts and minds, and they don't remember Heart of Sky. So Heart of Sky destroys them in a great storm of black rain of resin. Animals come into the houses of the people and attack them; even pots and stones crush them. Then the dogs and turkeys tell them: "You caused us pain, you ate us. Now we eat you."

The people try to escape out of their houses, to go into the trees and the caves. But their houses collapse, the trees throw them off and the caves slam shut. Today's monkeys are the descendants of these people, mere manikins. This was all before the Sun dawned on the Earth.

Africa

Kwaya (Lake Victoria)

The ocean is enclosed in a pot which is kept by a man and his wife under the roof of their hut and used to fill their larger pots. The man tells his daughter-in-law never to touch it because it contains their sacred ancestors. But she grows curious and touches it. It shatters, and the resulting flood drowns everything.

Yoruba (southwest Nigeria)

A god, Ifa, is tired of living on Earth and so he goes to dwell in the firmament with Obatala, the sky god. But without Ifa's assistance, mankind cannot interpret the desires of the gods, and so one of the gods, Olokun, in a fit of rage, destroys nearly everybody in a great flood.

Far East and Asia

Vogul

After seven years of drought, the Great Woman says to the Great Man that the rains had come elsewhere: how should they save themselves? The Great Man takes counsel with the other giants and they decide to make boats from cut poplars and anchor them with ropes of willow roots that are 500 fathoms long. The boats are provisioned with seven days of food and with pots of melted butter to grease the ropes.

When the waters come, those who failed to make similar preparations are inundated and drown. After seven days, the waters sink. But all plants and animals have perished - even the fish. The survivors, on the brink of starvation, pray to the great god Numi-târom, the creator of all living things.

Yenisey-Ostyak (north central Siberia)

Floodwaters rise for seven days. Some people and animals climb on to floating logs and rafts to save themselves. A strong north wind blows for seven days and scatters the people, which is why there are now different peoples speaking different languages.

Tuvinian (Soyot) (north of Mongolia)

The giant frog (or turtle), which supports the Earth, moves and this causes the cosmic ocean to begin flooding it. An old man had had a premonition about this deluge and so he had built an iron-reinforced raft. He boards this raft with his family and they are saved. When the waters recede, the raft is beached on a high wooded mountain where, it is said, it remains today. After the flood, the god Kezer-Tshingis-Kaira-Khan creates everything that we see around us today. Among other things, he teaches people how to make strong liquor.

Tibet

Tibet is almost totally inundated until the god Gya takes compassion on the survivors and draws off the waters through the Bay of Bengal. Then he sends teachers to civilise the people who, until then, had been little better than monkeys. These newly civilised peoples repopulate the land.

Ifugaos (Philippines)

A great drought dries up all the rivers. The old men suggest digging in a riverbed to find the soul of the river. After three days of digging, a great spring gushes forth. But while the Ifugaos celebrate, a storm comes up and the river keeps rising. The elders advise the people to run for the mountains but only two make it to safety, a brother and sister, who are on separate mountains. After six months, the waters recede. The sister later finds herself with child and she runs away in shame but the god Maknongan assures her that her shame has no foundation.

Kammu (Thailand)

A brother and sister are warned of a coming flood by a mouse and so they seal themselves in a drum. After the flood recedes, the two re-emerge and although they look far and wide for others, it turns out that they are only survivors. Then a malcoha cuckoo sings to them: "Brother and sister should embrace one another." So they sleep together and after seven years, their child is born as a gourd. A little later, hearing noises from the gourd, they burn a hole in its shell and people of the different races come out: first to emerge are the Rumeet peoples, then the Kammu and the Thais, and then the Westerners and the Chinese.

Australasia

New Guinea

Lohero and his brother are angry with their neighbours, so they put a human bone into a small stream. Soon a great flood comes and the people have to retreat to the highest peaks until the sea recedes. Once the land is dry again, some of the people return to the valleys but others stay to make their homes on the ridges.

Batak (Sumatra)

Naga-Padoha, the giant snake on which the Earth rests, grows tired of its burden and shakes it off into the sea. But the god Batara-Guru causes a mountain to fall into the water to preserve his daughter and, from her, the human race descends. Later, the Earth is placed on the head of the snake Yuma-Komashtam'ho, who causes a great rain that starts to flood out the larger, dangerous animals. He is then persuaded that the people need some of the animals for food. So he evaporates the waters with a great fire, which turns the land to desert in the process.

Appendix B – The Ecstasy of the Heart

Through understanding about the system of The Three Cauldrons, we soon realise the heart is the portal to the ancestors. I've found that giving genuine and joyful thanks to the forefathers by breathing my gratitude into the heart is like throwing open the floodgates to a whole cornucopia of magical powers.

By the heart, I mean the organ of the heart and not the area of the chest that is normally referred to as the heart chakra. To be honest, I don't deal in chakras as I can find no evidence for them in the Vedas, nor much mention of them at all until certain gurus came to the West from India in the 19th century.

Anyway, this is a very simple and an amazingly blissful experience bordering on ecstasy, hence its name. I learned it from Tom Kenyon, the sound healer shaman.

Please do enjoy!

Sit or lie down – whatever feels the most relaxed for you.
Close your eyes and breathe evenly for a minute or two.
Now concentrate on your heart – the organ on the left side of your breast. Breathe into your heart and as you do so, express love and gratitude to your heart for continuing to beat – with neither praise nor payment - for the whole of your life, even while you're asleep. Your heart is ever your most faithful and stalwart servant, and now is the time to give it recognition in the form of unconditional love and gratitude.

You will probably by now be starting to experience some wonderfully blissful tingles in your energetic field. This is the auric energy starting to heal, so just enjoy it!

When you're ready, imagine a photo or a painting of your most recently deceased ancestors that is sitting in your heart. Then, as you continue to direct your feelings of unconditional love and gratitude towards your heart, the ancestors will receive it, and you will soon dissolve into bliss and ecstasy.

If you practice this meditation technique regularly, you will come to realise that the physical heart is actually a portal to other dimensions. So in thanking those who came before you, you're actually sending loving energy into the Other Worlds where they now reside, and strengthening the connection between you and them.

This channel is a bit like a hosepipe, which, after years of disuse and neglect, may have become flattened and twisted. The force that is created by sending through fresh, gushing energy, in the form of love and gratitude, untwists that hose and opens up the channel of communication again.

Bibliography

Ancient Egypt: The Light of the World by Gerald Massey
Ancient Transpacific Voyaging by Steve Wyatt
Becoming an Alchemist by Catherine MacCoun
Elen of the Ways by Elen Sentier
Hamlet's Mill by Giorgio de Santillana and Hertha von Dechend
Jesus and the Goddess: The Secret Teachings of the Original Christians by Timothy Freke and Peter Gandy:
Lost Gods of England by Kathleen Herbert
Mythology of the British Isles by Geoffrey Ashe
On the Ruin of Britain by Gildas
Pagan and Christian Creeds by Edward Carpenter
Pistis Sophia: The Gnostic Tradition of Mary Magdalene, Jesus and his Disciples by G.R.S. Mead.
Scientific Evidence for Pre-Columbian Transoceanic Voyages to and from the Americas by John L. Sorenson and Carl L. Johannessen
Secrets of a Faery Landscape by Coleston Brown
Shamanism: Archaic Techniques of Ecstasy by Mircae Eliade
Sky Dragons and Celestial Serpents by Alastair McBeath
Taliesin: The Last Celtic Shaman by John Matthews
The Archetypal Significance of Gilgamesh by Rivkah Schärf Kluger
The Book of Fairy and Folk Tales of Ireland by W.B. Yeats
The Celtic Chakras by Elen Sentier
The Complete Idiot's Guide to Alchemy by Dennis Hauck
The Elder Gods: The Otherworld of Early England by Stephen Pollington
The Faery Teachings by Orion Foxwood
The Lost God of England by Brian Branston
The Mind In the Cave: Consciousness and the Origins of Art by David Lewis Williams
The Mystery of the Cathedrals by Fulcanelli, translated by Mary Sworder
The Origins of Mythology in the Upper Palaeolithic Cultures of Eurasia by Bennett Blumenberg
The Path of Alchemy by Mark Stavish
The Shamanic Guide to Death and Dying by Kristin Madden
Vedic Cosmography and Astronomy by Richard L. Thompson
Worship of the Serpent by John Bathurst Deane

FURTHER READING

Reclaiming Sovereignty

Shamanic Earth Magic

by Annie Dieu-Le-Veut

Reclaiming Sovereignty explores in detail how shamans and high priestesses sparked Sovereignty in ancient times through sacred sexual rites. It shows how these hierodules or sacred prostitutes were in touch with the spirits of the land and thus were able to transmit their wisdom to the king or pharaoh through spiritual love during his coronation night.

These practices became known as Sovereignty rites, because they triggered an inner alchemical process that fired up the king's higher brain centres, giving him a superior intelligence and thus the ability and the right to reign. The crown that the king wears on his head is the outer symbol to indicate that the inner crown of the cranium had been illuminated.

In Part 1 of **Reclaiming Sovereignty**, you will learn about the archaeological, alchemical, anthropological and mythological evidence underpinning this occult understanding about Sovereignty. Then in Part 2, you're taken on a practical step-by-step journey designed to get you in touch with the spirit of Sovereignty through shamanic sex. Finally, in Part 3, you will receive guidance on the practice of Earth magic and discover how to work more consciously with landscape zodiacs, standing stones, sacred sites, leylines and the stars above, to be in communication with the spirits of the land.

The Grail Mysteries

The Virgo Teachings and the Peacock's Tail

by Annie Dieu-Le-Veut

In **The Grail Mysteries**, the reader benefits from the Virgo Teachings that are received by a prostitute living in post-Roman Britain, and whose late middle-age is utterly transformed when she discovers that she comes from a long line of hierodules and is thus a true queen of the Blessed Isles.

As we follow her awakening, we learn that a true queen is not necessarily one who is anointed with oil on her forehead by the Archbishop of Canterbury. It is one who carries the faery blood and who is anointed by the nectars that flow from the awakening of the Black and Gold serpents during shamanic sex magic with the divine.

She finds out that a true queen does not necessarily wear a crown on her head and that when she does, it is only to symbolise that the crown in her cranium has been fired up by the ignition sparked after the Red and White serpentine drops have fallen on to her pineal gland, or third eye, and her Inner Sun has risen within her.

In this way, a true queen holds the Sovereignty of the nation, which has been passed into her safekeeping by the spirits of the land. Only a true queen can make a king who is fit to rule.

The Grail Mysteries is a sequel to my last book, **The Bright World of the Gods**, although you don't have to read that to enjoy this one! So it charts the continuation of the love story between Arawn, the Lord of the Underworld, and Elen, the Upper World spirit, who have taken human form on Earth. We also join Myrddin (Merlin), Taliesin, Manawydan, Creiddylad, Gwyddion, Arianrhod and the eight dwarves in their quest to bury the Thirteen Treasures of Britain. All this, despite the best efforts of the Eye of Soros, Bricriu of the Poison Tongue and Vlak the Dragon Slayer, who are furiously trying to steal the Sovereignty of the Isles of the Blessed.

You will also hear Taliesin's moving rendition of an original *Mabinogion* myth about how a huge and bitter gulf came about between Ireland and Britain – a gulf that is still to be bridged properly and which led to the head of the giant king Bran being buried in the land, for protection.

The Bright World of the Gods

A true faery story from the mists of Avalon

by Annie Dieu-Le-Veut

The Bright World of the Gods was gifted into my Dreamtime by the spirits of the land that inhabit the other dimensions found, shamanically, through the mists of Avalon in Somerset, England. These spirits are known locally as the Gentle Folk, or the Fae, although you might know them better as faeries.

So this is a real faery story for enlightened adults that comes from a benevolent Elder race whose role it is to guide the steps of humanity. As such, it is perfect for curling up with by the fire when the white frost of the Sugar Plum Faery is crackling the grass underfoot, or to inspire dreaming on balmier days, under a gnarled old apple tree in an enchanted wood.

In this romantic magical mystery tour around the enchanted Glastonbury landscape, you will follow Bridie and Gwyn ap Nudd as they meet the challenges necessary for alchemical inner growth that leads to full spiritual realisation, along with other archetypal characters that have stepped out of Celtic myths such as Manawydan, Gwyddion, Creiddylad, Taliesen, Elen and Morgan the Fae.

You may just want to enjoy this epic tale on a superficial level as a beautiful love story that is full of intriguing escapades and interesting ideas – which is fine. But those looking for keys to unlock faery doorways into deeper cosmological teachings will also find them here along with the instructions on how to unlock them.

Either way, just relax and wander through the wondrous hills and dales of *The Bright World of the Gods,* and let it permeate into your own Dreamtime so that it can do its magic there and give you insights into your own destiny – and the meaning of your life.

The Therapy Book

From aromatherapy to zero balancing - and everything in between

by John Board

This is the ultimate natural health reference book for your shelves, with comprehensive information on more than 200 **holistic, alternative and complementary health therapies** in an easily understandable format.

The Therapy Book is **easily searchable**, uses **plain language** and is organised into **easy-to-digest, bite-sized chunks**, so you will soon know…

- what each therapy is
- how each therapy works
- what each therapy can be used for
- whether the therapy is effective
- whether there are any known side effects

It's the perfect gift for discerning individuals who like to look after their own health and wellbeing, as well as holistic health practitioners who wish to continue their professional development.

Made in the USA
San Bernardino, CA
14 October 2018